LAW, VIOLENCE, AND THE POSSIBILITY OF JUSTICE

LAW, VIOLENCE, AND THE

POSSIBILITY OF JUSTICE

edited by Austin Sarat

PRINCETON UNIVERSITY PRESS   PRINCETON AND OXFORD

Copyright © 2001 by Princeton University Press
Published by Princeton University Press, 41 William Street,
Princeton, New Jersey 08540
In the United Kingdom: Princeton University Press, 3 Market Place, Woodstock

Library of Congress Cataloging-in-Publication Data

Law, violence, and the possibility of justice / edited by Austin Sarat
   p. cm.
Includes bibliographical references and index.

ISBN 0-691-04844-4 (cloth : alk. paper)—ISBN 0-691-04845-2 (pbk. : alk. paper)

1. Law—Philosophy. 2. Violence (Law) 3. Justice. I. Sarat, Austin.
K235.L397 2002
340′.11—dc21   2001027838

British Library Cataloguing-in-Publication Data is available

This book has been composed in Sabon

Printed on acid-free paper. ∞

www.pup.princeton.edu

Printed in the United States of America

10 9 8 7 6 5 4 3 2 1

10 9 8 7 6 5 4 3 2 1
(Pbk.)

Contents

LAW, VIOLENCE, AND THE POSSIBILITY OF JUSTICE

CHAPTER ONE

Situating Law Between the Realities of Violence and the Claims of Justice

AN INTRODUCTION

Austin Sarat

IT SURELY COMES as no surprise to say that violence of all kinds is done everyday with the explicit authorization of legal institutions and officials or with their tacit acquiescence. Law without violence is unthinkable, yet if law were to be no more than violence it would not be law at all.[1] Law depends on violence and uses it as a counterpunch to the allegedly more lethal and destructive violence situated just beyond law's boundaries. But the violence on which law depends always threatens the values for which law stands. Some of this violence is done directly by legal officials, some by citizens acting under a dispensation granted by law, and some by persons whose violent acts subsequently will be deemed acceptable. Moreover the pain that these acts produce is everywhere, in the drama of law's sporadic vengeance as well as in the ordinary lives of those subject to legal regulation.[2]

The bloodletting done, authorized, or condoned by law occurs with all the normal abnormality of bureaucratic abstraction. As a result, the violence of law is often untraceably dispersed. Indeed it is this distinctive combination of bloodletting and bureaucracy that makes law possible, insures its continuous presence in our minds and imaginations, and holds us before the law.[3]

Despite its undeniable significance, law's violence has played little role, and occupied little space, in legal theory and jurisprudence.[4] Or, when it is present, awareness of the violence done or authorized by officials is divorced from legal interpretation, as if the act of speaking or writing the words of law could be separated from the inscription of those words on the bodies of citizens. This absence and this divorce have serious consequences since the fate of law is inextricably tied up with the fate of legal theory.

By failing to confront law's lethal character and the masking of its interpretive violence, legal theory tacitly encourages officials to ignore the bloody consequences of their authoritative acts and the pain that those acts produce. Moreover, by equating the conditions of legal legitimacy with that masking, much of jurisprudence promotes righteous indifference and, as a result, allows law's violence to continue unabated. While I am neither so idealistic nor so naive as to imagine that a change in legal theory would in itself end bloodletting done, authorized, or approved by legal institutions, this book seeks to move violence to the center of theorizing about law and to connect it to the question of justice. Does law's violence stand as an impenetrable barrier to the achievement of justice in and through law? Or, alternatively, is violence necessary to the realization of justice?

These ought to be perennial questions of legal theory, but unfortunately, they are not. Perhaps this is why the work of Robert Cover was, and is, so significant as a moment in late-twentieth-century jurisprudence. Cover, who died in 1986, taught at Yale Law School and produced a limited but highly influential corpus.[5] At the heart of his work was an effort to think about law in relation to the institutional reality of its intimate engagement with violence while also attending to its normativity and its normative aspirations.

"Between the idea and reality of common meaning falls the shadow of the violence of the law, itself."[6] This one sentence reveals, with great simplicity and directness, Cover's awareness of the tragic character of law's violence and its world-altering reality, a reality so awesome that its mere "shadow" stands as a barrier between present experience and the realization of an "idea." Thus in Cover's work one finds a mournful story of violence set against utopian possibility, and an appeal to legal scholars to enter the shadows and explore law's violent underside.[7] However, one also finds an acknowledgment that the violence of law is, despite its tragic character, different from and preferable to other forms of violence—the violence of the lynch mob or the lawless state—which, in their own way, cast even more destructive shadows. Law's violence is to be preferred, albeit reluctantly, as a way of counteracting and containing that other violence, as a way of saving us from the darkest possibilities of human existence.

Cover compellingly called our attention to law's "jurisgenerative" and its "jurispathic" qualities.[8] "Law," Cover argued,

> may be viewed as a system of tension or a bridge linking a concept of reality to an imagined alternative. Thus, one constitutive element of a *nomos* is the phenomenon George Steiner has labeled "alternity": "the 'other than the case,' the counterfactual propositions, images, shapes of will and evasions with which we charge our mental being and by means of which we build the changing, largely fictive milieu for our somatic and our social existence." But the concept of a *nomos* is not exhausted by its "alternity"; it is neither utopia nor pure vision. A *nomos*, as a world of law, entails the application of human

will to an extant state of affairs as well as toward our visions of alternative futures.[9]

Cover used the word "nomos," or "normative universe," to argue that law is crucially involved in helping persons "create and maintain a world of right and wrong, of lawful and unlawful, of valid and void."[10] The nomos that law helps to create, Cover believed, always contains within it visions of possibility not yet realized, images of a better world not yet built. But, he reminds us, law is not simply, or even primarily, a gentle, hermeneutic apparatus; it always exists in a state of tension between a world of meaning in which justice is pursued, and a world of violence in which "legal interpretation takes places in a field of pain and death."[11] It is here that Cover confronted and described what was for him a fundamental tension—namely, despite its destructive, world-destroying power, the violence of law an indispensable presence in our lives.

Law, Violence, and the Possibility of Justice seeks to energize scholarly interest in the violence of law and to connect that subject to the question of justice. It brings together essays by leading interdisciplinary legal scholars, each of which uses Cover's work as a starting point and a source. As each of the essays measures the violence of law as well as violence's impact on law and on the possibilities of justice, each provides more than a celebration or critique of Cover's work. The essays consider Cover's theorization in light of the contemporary situation of law and of the work of such thinkers as Sigmund Freud, Walter Benjamin, Emmanuel Levinas, and Jacques Derrida. Thus this book is about Cover but also about the phenomenon—violence in law—to which his work so provocatively pointed.

The essays in *Law, Violence, and the Possibility of Justice* call attention to the fact that law is both constituted in response to metaphorical violence and yet is a doer of literal violence; law, which is the peaceful alternative to the chaos and fury of a fictive state of nature, inscribes itself on bodies. It "deals pain and death"[12] and calls the pain and death that it deals "peace." Once established, law is maintained through force; it is maintained as an apparatus of violence that disorders, disrupts, and repositions preexisting relations and practices all in the name of an allegedly superior order.[13] That order demonstrates its "superiority" in ferocious displays of force and in subjugating, colonizing, "civilizing" acts of violence. Violence thus may be said to be integral to law in three senses: it provides the occasion and method for founding legal orders,[14] it gives law (as a regulator of force and coercion) a reason for being, and it provides a means through which law acts.

Yet law denies the violence of its origins,[15] as well as the disorder engendered by its own ordering efforts, in that law proclaims the force it deploys to be "legitimate."[16] Legitimacy is thus the minimal answer to skeptical questions about the ways in which law's violence differs from the turmoil and disorder that law is allegedly brought into being to conquer. What this claim to legitimacy implies, in this minimal answer, is that law's violence is rational, controlled, and purposive, that law makes force the servant of the word.

To say that law's violence is legitimate is to juxtapose the alleged rationality of legal coercion and the irrationality of a violence that knows no law. It is to claim that law's violence is controlled through the legal articulation of values, norms, procedures, and purposes external to violence itself. It is to claim that the force of law serves common purposes and advances common aims in contrast to the anomic or sectarian savagery beyond law's boundaries.[17]

Yet neither this rationality nor common purpose necessarily is just. Thus, even on this account of the nature of law's violence, the question of justice is deferred. Does law's violence serve justice? Can a violent legality ever be truly just?

Justice, Drucilla Cornell argues, "is precisely what eludes our full knowledge." We cannot "grasp the Good but only follow it. The Good . . . is a star which beckons us to follow."[18] While justice, or what Cornell calls the Good, is, on her account, always present *to* law, it is never completely realized *in* law.[19] Or, as Judith Butler puts it, "[T]he law posits an ideality . . . that it can never realize, and . . . this failure is constitutive of existing law."[20] Law exists both in the "as yet" failure to realize the Good and in the commitment to its realization. In this failure and this commitment, law is two things at once: the social organization of violence through which state power is exercised in a partisan, biased, and sometimes cruel way,[21] and the arena to which citizens address themselves in the hope that law can, and will, redress the wrongs that are committed in its name.[22]

These thoughts remind us that running throughout the history of jurisprudence and legal theory is a concern about the connections between law and justice and about the ways law is implicated in injustice. Commentators from Plato[23] to Derrida[24] have called law to account in the name of justice, have asked that law provide a language of justice, and have demanded that it promote, insofar as possible, the attainment of a just society. Yet the justice described is elusive, if not illusory, and in some scholarship disconnected from the embodied practices of law, including law's violence.

In an earlier day, speaking about law and justice was not so vexing or difficult. Justice (*jus* meaning "law") was a legal term, pure and simple.[25] At the outset, then, "justice was defined and constituted by laws which were 'given' and held to be unchanging and unchangeable."[26] This ineluctable link between justice and law, as put forth by Hobbes, had the virtue of making the boundaries of justice more or less clear; but it had the considerable vice of labeling even heinous, iniquitous laws just. Justice could do no critical/reconstructive work because it was impossible to think of justice as external to law.

Apart from Hobbes,[27] most natural-law thinkers have resisted this result by insisting that unjust laws are not law,[28] though doing so meant the end of any easy identification of positive or human law with "real" or binding law. The alternative, embraced by perhaps a majority of those who continue to be at ease in this idiom, is to cut justice and law free from one another, to insist that justice is more than mere conformity to law,[29] and to acknowledge that even unjust laws might nonetheless be law.[30] Most recently, the distance between law and justice has been recognized in postmodern theorizing about ethics.[31] Thus, as Douzinas and Warrington argue,

> [J]ustice has the characteristic of a promissory statement. A promise states now something to be performed in the future. Being just always lies in the future, it is a promise made to the future, a pledge to look into the event and the uniqueness of each situation. . . . This promise, like all promises, does not have a present time, a time when you can say: "there it is, justice is this or that." Suspended between the law and the good . . . , justice is always still to come or always already performed.[32]

Severance of the definitional tie between justice and law has left both notions free (if also bound) to acquire new identities.[33] In both cases, former boundaries have been enlarged. Thus, matters other than those directly regulated by law (for example, the distribution of wealth) are viewed as falling under the purview of justice, and patently unjust legal arrangements (for example, apartheid in South Africa) are accepted as lawful despite their moral repugnance.[34] But as Clarence Morris notes, "Though there can be law without justice, justice is realized only through good law."[35] In fact, law and legal theory continue to be shaped by concerns about justice and injustice, just as understandings of these latter notions are shaped by an awareness of law and the concerns of legal theory.[36]

If there is so close a link between law and justice there must, in turn, be a link between law's violence and its capacity to attain, or aspire, to justice. "A just and responsible decision," Douzinas and Warrington contend,

> must both conserve and destroy, or suspend, the law enough to reinvent it and rejustify it in each case. Each case requires a unique interpretation which no rule can guarantee absolutely. But, at the same time, there is no just decision if the judge does not refer to law or rule. . . . This is the reason that we cannot say

that a judgment is just. A decision . . . cannot be declared just because justice is the dislocation of the said of law by the-unrepresentable-saying of ethics.[37]

It seems reasonable to suggest, that justice is both present to and absent from law, present as an aspiration even as a constant reminder of the impossibility of bringing the Good into sight and translating it into legal judgment.[38] As Derrida says, "From this point of view, justice would be the experience that we are not able to experience."[39]

These observations call to mind a variety of uncertainties and ambivalences regarding the relationship of law and justice, but they fall far short of embracing the extreme position that justice should be jettisoned from legal discourse. Rather, they remind us of the vastness of our subject, of the difficulty of constructing a single account capable of holding together its many strands, and of the space that exists to theorize anew about violence, justice, and law.

In all legal orders, law's violence threatens to undo law, to destabilize it by forcing choices between its normative aspirations and the need to maintain social order through force.[40] But unfortunately, except in the utopian imagination, there is no symmetry in the relations among violence, justice, and law. Violence is never similarly endangered by the claims of justice or the operation of law. Law sits poised between the present reality of violence and the promises of a justice not yet realized. Yet this positioning of law is generally neglected in current theorizations.

Some scholars, emphasize the meaning-making, community-building character of law, and de-emphasize its coercive aspects. They liken law to literature as a resource in building what they see as humane societies.[41] Others take violence as a subject of inquiry, but its connection to the nature of law remains unelaborated.[42] A third trend in legal scholarship appears, at first glance, to respond to these defects by speaking about many different types of violence and theorizing about their connections to law. Under the force of critical theory and deconstruction, the use of the word "violence" proliferates; we are reminded that law is violent in many ways—in the ways it uses languages and in its representational practices,[43] in the silencing of perspectives and the denial of experience,[44] and in its objectifying epistemology.[45] Where once it seemed quite obvious that when one talked about law's violence one would be referring to the infliction of physical force, today critical theory and deconstruction have left violence with a confusion of meaning.

The expanding idea of violence threatens to undo the subject itself. If everything is violent, then the word and the idea lose their meaning and their normative and critical bite. If the critique of violence must take on all cognitive, linguistic, and cultural practices, then it will be overwhelmed and undone. Thus the first act in the effort to explore the relations of violence, justice, and law must be a "violent" act of repositioning our language; we must treat law's violence first and foremost in its embodiment and effects on embodied subjects.

Our efforts in that direction are nourished by Cover's insistence that the meaning-making, community-building, literary quality of law should not distract us from the fact that, as he put it, "Legal interpretation takes place in a field of pain and death"[46] and that "the violence [of law] is utterly real . . . a naive but immediate reality . . . unlike the psychoanalytic violence of literature or the metaphorical characterization of literary critics and philosophers."[47] With these admonitions Cover invites us to imagine and construct a jurisprudence of violence and to theorize about the impact of violence on the possibility of attaining justice in law.

Law, Violence, and the Possibility of Justice takes up that invitation by critically engaging with Cover's own efforts and theories. In so doing, it considers such questions as: What does it mean to talk about the violence of law? Do high rates of incarceration, as well as increased reliance on capital punishment, indicate that law in the United States is turning more violent at a time when violence is being restrained and disciplined in legal regimes elsewhere? Does a focus on law's violence artificially separate meaning and materiality, leading us to focus on the most visible, though some would argue least important, aspect of law's apparatus of social control? Does violence express, or distort, the "essence" of law?

The first essay, Jonathan Simon's "The Vicissitudes of Law's Violence" resists talk of the "essence" of law, taking Cover to task for treating violence as "an ontological feature of law." Simon insists that a jurisprudence of violence must be attentive to the contingent and variable relationship of law and violence and to the historical contingencies that contribute to making law more or less violent. He suggests that Cover's "Violence and the Word" was written at a crucial moment in the transformation of American law. By Simon's account, Cover correctly described the movement from ideology to violence as a major modality of legal life at the end of the twentieth century. Yet while acknowledging that contribution, Simon faults Cover for producing not only a reified, but, in addition, a simplified vision of law's violence.

The analytic bite of Cover's work derives, Simon contends, from its almost exclusive focus on the dyadic relationship between judges and prisoners, those whose words authorize law's violence and those who experience it. Yet Cover leaves out juries, corrections officers, police, and others without whom law could not, and would not be, an apparatus of violence. Simon argues that a jurisprudence of violence needs to attend to the interests that sustain law's violence and that promote greater or lesser reliance on violence as a tool for ordering society. In addition, he suggests that scholars need to examine the specificity of the various technologies of violence that law deploys.

Here Simon suggests that Cover is not helpful in treating imprisonment as if it were the same as torture and in ignoring the impact that penological ideas have in shaping social and legal life. Prisons, he says, are richer and more complex, and perhaps more horrible, than one would understand from reading Cover. Most importantly, Simon argues that Cover is guilty of a kind of fatalism about law's violence, overestimating at once its centrality as well as the capacity of judges to control and discipline it. Simon shares Cover's concern for the intensification of violence in law, but calls our attention to the forces that might be brought to bear in enlisting it on the side of justice.

Just as law's violence may be a historically contingent phenomenon, the conditions necessary to sustain that violence may alter or limit the possibilities of law itself. This is the argument that Austin Sarat and Thomas Kearns develop in "Making Peace with Violence: Robert Cover on Law and Legal Theory." Like Simon, they praise Cover's insistence that jurisprudence take violence seriously and, like him, they also worry that Cover was too sanguine about the ability of law to control its own violence.

Sarat and Kearns note that Cover was both a critic of, and an apologist for, law's violence. In his critical mode, he saw the fury of state law as a barrier to the achievement of a normatively rich, legally plural community, and he urged judges to tolerate and respect the normative claims of communities whose visions of the good did not comport with the commands and requirements of state law. He argued that unless judges could articulate normative arguments more compelling than those presented by such communities, a just legal order would respect and accommodate the latter rather than violently impose itself.

Yet Sarat and Kearns contend that Cover recognized the need for law's violent impositions, and that he attended carefully to the prerequisites for law's successful use of violence. For law to achieve such success, in Cover's view, its social organization would have to find resources both to overcome and, at the same time, regulate cultural and moral inhibitions against the use of physical force. To overcome those inhibitions, strong justifications would have to be provided.

As Sarat and Kearns read the corpus of Cover's work, they find a two-fold message: "Wherever possible, withhold violence; let new normative worlds flourish. But, for the sake of justice, do not forget that law's violence is sometimes necessary and that its availability is not automatic but must be carefully provided for." To do its job, then, law must be violent, but its violence must be used sparingly. It is to this injunction that Simon's essay calls attention, suggesting that law's violence is today not used sparingly. For Sarat and Kearns, like Simon, Cover seems too optimistic that this twofold admonition can be realized in fact. As they see it, the conditions necessary for the effective deployment of force—in particular the generation of strong justifications—promote excess not restraint, universalism not toleration. Attention to Cover's work, they contend, demonstrates how the imperatives of doing violence radically limit the possibilities of attaining justice through law.

It is with these possibilities that the next two essays are most concerned. Marianne Constable reads Cover's "Violence and the Word" as symptomatic of a conception of law that, in her view, precludes the aspirations to justice that, in his other essays, Cover says are necessary to law. Cover falls into this trap by equating law with positive law, the law of command. Moreover, his understanding of the relations between violence and the word reiterates distinctions between performance and speech, body and mind, which complicate efforts to attain justice in and through law.

While Cover regrets the loss of self and community, which he says is necessarily part of the project of a violent legality, Cover's "sociological account" of law, Constable argues, precludes the recovery of both. Cover seems resigned to what is lost. Unlike either Freud, who through therapy, or Foucault, who through resistance, identifies ways to carry on the struggle for justice, Cover, at least in "Violence and the Word," seems resigned to a world in which violence separates law from justice.

Constable insists that a jurisprudence of violence should not be so resigned. Cover's account of law as violence is not, she insists, shocking to modern readers. That fact marks our comfort with a conception of law that equates it with its opposite—violence and the destruction of a shared world. Unlike Sarat and Kearns, who by Constable's account, give Cover too much credit for exploring the possibility of justice in law, Constable suggests that if law is violent then we should rethink its claim to be law. Law, she argues, is the word for the establishment of a common world dedicated to pursuing justice.

The next essay, by Shaun McVeigh, Peter Rush, and Alison Young, takes up Constable's project of loosening the grip of violence on our understanding of law by situating Cover's work in relationship to the postmodern ethics of Emmanuel Levinas and Jacques Derrida. Unlike Levinas and Derrida, who think about law in relation to the "ethics of alterity," namely respect for the vocation of Other as Other, Cover, they contend, tries to connect thinking about justice to the institutional practices of law. This theorizing, what they call the " 'middle' ground of legal reason," is not simply the positivism that Constable identifies. Cover's work, in their view, tries to combine elements of positivism with natural-law thinking.

Despite this effort, Cover, they argue, does not understand adequately the role of either violence or justice in legal life. Law can neither be simply violent nor simply just. Law's violence is different from brute force precisely because force and justice are *together* the "impossible conditions of law's possibility." The justice of law is a movement in response to the Other. Law's violence provides an opportunity for that movement.

McVeigh, Rush, and Young point to Cover's interest in messianism as highlighting the conditions for a lawful justice. Messianism is one way that keeps law open to the promise of the "yet to come." Taking this idea as their cue, they call for a jurisprudence of violence that refigures legal judgment as an ethical, as well as institutional, practice. Such a conception would hold judgment responsible to the claims of justice and not solely, or primarily, to the need to provide the conditions for the effective deployment of violence.

The last essay, by Peter Fitzpatrick, picks up McVeigh, Rush, and Young's interest in the constitutive connections of violence, justice, and law. Fitzpatrick begins by insisting on the accuracy of Cover's famous opening sentence in "Violence and the Word": "Legal interpretation takes place in a field of pain and death." For Cover, the word necessarily operates in a field of violence, but it is not itself violent. Again and again, Fitzpatrick argues, Cover draws this distinction: "There is a radical dichotomy between the social organization of law as power [as violence] and the organization of law as meaning," and he would "insist" that law as the word becomes violent only "in the context of the organized social practice of violence."[48] Cover wants to prevent law from being suffused in its violent context. Why is this his aspiration? Fitzpatrick asks.

Fitzpatrick's essay suggests that an answer can be extracted obliquely from "Violence and the Word," and, somewhat more directly, from Cover's "*Nomos* and Narrative." Fitzpatrick, like Constable, reads Cover as saying not just that law is violent, but that there is *nothing* in law that is apart from violence. If law as legal interpretation routinely can be transformed into violence, how or where is law not violent? Cover is obsessed with this question, and it is one that must be central to any consideration of the complex relations of violence, law, and justice. What is crucial for Cover is how or where interpretation becomes operatively joined to action. But this search is, according to Fitzpatrick, completely frustrated. Cover finds nothing. Pure interpretation, as Cover has it, is indeterminate. And there must be the violence of active "real-world" determination for it to have existence.

Legal interpretation, then, becomes violent in its specificity. It does not, however, prove possible for Cover to produce an idea of interpretation that is simply transformable, something that would cross from the form of interpretation to the form of violent action. Law as nonviolent interpretation remains exasperatingly unconnected to the violence of active application. That lack of connection would fit neatly with Cover's being unable to find a place where the transformation from interpretation to action takes place. His efforts at this constantly locate a void. So, if we combine interpretation and action in law, are we left, Fitzpatrick asks, with law as nothingness—with law as void?

As Fitzpatrick sees it, far from being vacuous, the void to which Cover's work points is peopled with a bustling repleteness. Cover sees legal interpretation as "central" in "integrating" every "role, deed and word" within or impinging on law. To do this, law as interpretation must be responsive, adaptive, acceptant, giving of itself. Law then, Fitzpatrick argues, must be nonviolent. Law must encompass and yet be "in between" the violent, finite particularity of action and the nonviolent infinite responsiveness of interpretation (of the word) to all circumstance, to all possibility, and to justice itself. Law, Fitzpatrick suggests—contra Constable and in common with McVeigh, Rush, and Young—is the name we give to this necessary but impossible union of violence and nonviolence. It is always violent but never only violent; always oriented toward justice but never fully just.

Taken together, the essays collected in *Law, Violence, and the Possibility of Justice* suggest that law sits, albeit sometimes unrecognizably, between the call of justice and the imperatives of a violent ordering of the societies in which we live. Law traffics in violence, as Simon contends, sometimes more and sometimes less. Yet, as Sarat and Kearns note, the conditions that enable it to do so, tend to excess, threatening the claims of justice. Are those claims fully constitutive of law, as Constable contends, or partially and complexly so, as McVeigh, Rush, and Young argue? In either instance, contemporary jurisprudence should take up the challenge of conceptualizing and mapping the ways that, as Fitzpatrick suggests, law, at one and the same moment, can be both violent and nonviolent, unjust and just. The work presented in this book, precisely through its extended engagement with and critique of Cover, takes one important step in that direction.

NOTES

1. This duality is highlighted in Austin Sarat and Thomas R. Kearns, eds. *Law's Violence* (Ann Arbor: University of Michigan Press, 1992).

2. For a discussion of this kind of pain see Austin Sarat, ed., *Pain, Death, and the Law* (Ann Arbor: University of Michigan Press, 2001).

3. See Jacques Derrida, "Force of Law: The 'Mystical Foundation of Authority,'" trans. Mary Quaintance, *Cardozo Law Review* 11 (1990): 919.

4. This fact is discussed in Austin Sarat and Thomas R. Kearns, "A Journey Through Forgetting: Towards a Jurisprudence of Violence," in *The Fate of Law*, ed. Austin Sarat and Thomas R. Kearns (Ann Arbor: University of Michigan Press, 1991).

5. Much of Cover's work is collected in Martha Minow, Michael Ryan, and Austin Sarat, eds., *Narrative, Violence, and the Law: The Essays of Robert Cover* (Ann Arbor: University of Michigan Press, 1992).

6. Robert Cover, "Violence and the Word," *Yale Law Journal* (1986): 95, 1601, 1629.

7. This is an invitation that others are taking up. See, for example, Derrida, "Force of Law."

8. "The Supreme Court, 1982 Term—Foreword: *Nomos* and Narrative," *Harvard Law Review* 97 (1983): 4. All subsequent notes will refer to this work by its shortened title, "*Nomos* and Narrative."

9. Ibid., 9.

10. Ibid., 4.

11. Cover, "Violence and the Word," 1601.

12. Ibid., 1609.

13. See Walter Benjamin, "Critique of Violence," in *Reflections*, trans. Edmund Jepchott (New York: Harcourt Brace, 1978), 287. See also Karl Olivecrona, *Law as Fact* (Copenhagen: E. Munksgaard, 1939), chapter 4.

14. See Derrida, "Force of Law."

15. Ibid., 983–84.

16. See Robert Paul Wolff, "Violence and the Law," in *The Rule of Law* ed. Robert Paul Wolff (New York; Simon and Schuster, 1971). Also, Bernhard Waldenfels, "The Limits of Legitimation and the Question of Violence," in *Justice, Law, and Violence*, ed. James Brady and Newton Garver (Philadelphia: Temple University Press, 1991).

17. See Susan Jacoby, *Wild Justice: The Evolution of Revenge* (New York: Harper and Row, 1983).

18. Drucilla Cornell, "From the Lighthouse: The Promise of Redemption and the Possibility of Legal Interpretation," *Cardozo Law Review* 11 (1990): 1697.

19. See Drucilla Cornell, "Post-Structuralism, the Ethical Relation, and the Law," *Cardozo Law Review* 9 (1988): 1587.

20. Judith Butler, "Deconstruction and the Possibility of Justice: Comments on Bernasconi, Cornell, Miller, Weber," *Cardozo Law Review* 11 (1990): 1716. Butler argues that "this horizon of temporality is always to be projected and never fully achieved; this constitutes the double gesture as a persistent promise and withdrawal. . . . Cornell argues that it is necessary to repeat this gesture endlessly and thereby to constitute the posture of vigilance that establishes the openness of a future in which the thought of radical alterity is never completed."

21. See Alison Young and Austin Sarat, "Introduction to 'Beyond Criticism: Law, Power and Ethics,'" *Social and Legal Studies: An International Journal*, 3 (1994): 328: "[L]aw is simultaneously a denial of the ethical in the name of the political and a denial of the political in the name of the ethical."

22. See Sally Merry, *Getting Justice and Getting Even: Legal Consciousness Among Working Class Americans* (Chicago: University of Chicago Press, 1990).

Also, Austin Sarat, "'. . . The Law Is All Over': Power, Resistance and the Legal Consciousness of the Welfare Poor," *Yale Journal of Law & the Humanities* 2 (1990): 343.

23. See, for example, Plato's *Republic*, trans. G.M.A. Grube, rev. C.D.C. Reeve (Indianapolis: Hackett, 1992), books I and IV, especially.

24. See Derrida, "Force of Law."

25. See Frank H. Knight, "On the Meaning of Justice," in *Justice*, ed. Carl J. Friedrich and John W. Chapman (New York: Atherton Press, 1963), 1.

26. For the proposition that law defines justice, see Thomas Hobbes, *Leviathan* (Indianapolis: Bobbs-Merrill, 1958).

27. Ibid., 119–20.

28. See Thomas Aquinas, *Summa Theologica*, eds. William Baumgarth and Richard Kegan (Indianapolis: Hackett, 1988). For a more recent formulation of this position see Robert P. George, *Natural Law Theory: Contemporary Essays* (Oxford: Clarendon Press, 1993). See also, John Finnis, *Natural Law and Natural Rights* (Oxford: Clarendon Press, 1980), and Russell Hittinger, *A Critique of the New Natural Law Theory* (South Bend, Ind.: University of Notre Dame Press, 1987).

29. Plainly, the Greeks did precisely this by arguing that justice should be understood first and foremost as a property of persons, not of institutions or laws; it is clear, too, that the link between law and justice is ruptured also by those many who would insist that the concept of justice applies directly to the affairs of the family without, necessarily, any reference to law.

30. See H.L.A. Hart, *The Concept of Law* (Oxford: Clarendon Press, 1961), chapter 9. Compare with Lon Fuller, *The Morality of Law*, rev. ed. (New Haven: Yale University Press, 1964), chapters 2 and 3.

31. See, for example, Drucilla Cornell, "Post-Structuralism, the Ethical Relation, and the Law," *Cardozo Law Review* 9 (1988): 1587. Also, her book *The Philosophy of the Limit* (New York: Routledge, 1992).

32. Costas Douzinas and Ronnie Warrington, "The Face of Justice: A Jurisprudence of Alterity," *Social and Legal Studies: An International Journal* 3 (1994): 23. As Thomas Keenan asks, "Doesn't the appeal to a universal justice of the future, with which to counter the evident violence of today and tonight, threaten precisely this erasure of the alterity of the future (which is to say its futurity) which the thought and promise first opens?" See Keenan's "Deconstruction and the Impossibility of Justice," *Cardozo Law Review* 11 (1990): 1680.

33. See Jack Balkin, "Being Just with Deconstruction," *Social and Legal Studies: An International Journal* 3 (1994): 393.

34. On the moral repugnance of apartheid, see Geoffrey Bindman, *South Africa: Human Rights and the Rule of Law* (London: Pinter Publishers, 1988).

35. Clarence Morris, "Law, Justice, and the Public's Aspirations," in *Justice*, 170. In another essay in the same volume, Iredell Jenkens suggests that "justice is the form of order that man seeks to create through law." See Jenkens, "Justice as Ideal and Ideology," 217.

36. See, for example, Ronald Dworkin's seminal paper on law and the model of rules in his *Taking Rights Seriously* (Cambridge: Harvard University Press,

1977), particularly the second chapter titled "The Model of Rules I." Here it is plain that Dworkin seeks an account of law that will meet certain minimal elements of his understanding of the demands of justice. Conversely, J. R. Lucas is intent on explaining how laws can be unjust though nonetheless valid and obligatory. See Lucas's *On Justice* (Oxford: Clarendon Press, 1980). Theories of law and theories of justice often, though not always, work in tandem or in constructive tension.

37. Douzinas and Warrington, "The Face of Justice," 23. See also Derrida, "Force of Law," "To be just," Derrida claims, "the decision of a judge . . . must not only follow a rule of law or general law, but must also assume it, approve it, confirm its value, by a reinstituting act of interpretation, as if ultimately nothing previously existed of the law in every case" (p. 961).

38. See Balkin, "Being Just with Deconstruction," 16. "Laws," Balkin argues, "apportion responsibility, create rights and duties, and provide rules for conduct and social ordering. Law is always, to some extent and to some degree, unjust. At the same time, our notion of justice can only be articulated and enforced through human laws and conventions. We may have a notion of justice that always escapes law and convention, but the only tools we have to express and enforce our idea are human laws and human conventions. Our conception of the just relies for its articulation and enforcement on the imperfect laws, conventions, and cultural norms from which it must always be distinguished."

39. Derrida, "Force of Law," 947.

40. See Dominic LaCapra, "Violence, Justice, and the Force of Law," *Cardozo Law Review* 11 (1990): 1065.

41. See James Boyd White, *Justice as Translation* (Chicago: University of Chicago Press, 1990).

42. See, for example, David Garland, *Punishment and Modern Society* (Chicago: University of Chicago Press, 1990).

43. See Catherine MacKinnon, *Feminism Unmodified* (Cambridge: Harvard University Press, 1987).

44. See Martha Minow, *Making All the Difference: Inclusion, Exclusion, and American Law* (Ithaca: Cornell University Press, 1990).

45. See Robin West, "Disciplines, Subjectivity, and Law," in *The Fate of Law*, ed. Austin Sarat and Thomas R. Kearns (Ann Arbor: University of Michigan Press, 1991).

46. Cover, "Violence and the Word," 1601.

47. Robert Cover, "The Bonds of Constitutional Interpretation: Of the Word, the Deed, and the Role," *Georgia Law Review* 20 (1986), 818–19.

48. Cover, "Violence and the Word," 1602, note 2.

CHAPTER TWO

The Vicissitudes of Law's Violence

Jonathan Simon

Rᴏʙᴇʀᴛ Cᴏᴠᴇʀ's ᴇssᴀʏ "Violence and the Word," published in 1986, slipped into town in the midst of what might be called "the discursive turn" in American academic life. Social sciences, long dominated by traditional concerns with the harder structures of interests, organizations, and public opinion, began to open up to studies of the softer connective tissues of the social order located in language, narrative form, and rhetoric. Literary scholars expanded their jurisdiction well beyond the canons of literature to explore texts belonging to the terrain of politics and science. Academic law, traditionally focused on a dialogue with courts began to engage with work in economics, sociology, history, and philosophy. And "theory," mainly European in vintage, flowed freely for the first time in graduate seminars all over campus.

For many, it was the best of times as the disciplinary boundaries that had long segmented scholarship in universities began to falter. It was possible to propound radical ideas at even the most established and prestigious institutions in the country. Even the political triumph of the New Right, evident in Reagan's landslide 1984 election victory, did not dampen spirits in this nominally left-of-center academic culture. In Reagan, an actor after all, it seemed that even reaction had become just another kind of performance, a signifier chasing the absent signified of an imaginary past ("Morning in America").

Something else was stirring in America in the mid-1980s that was not only ignored in the academic celebration of discourse, but was also less visible precisely because of the focus on discourse. The United States was in the first decade of an escalation in punishment that has seen the restoration of the death penalty and a quadrupling of the prison population. Rising from a forty-year low in the early 1970s, incarceration rates in the United States had surpassed South Africa and the Soviet Union by the late 1980s.[1] At present, more than a million adults are in prison in the United States (up from 328,000 in 1980), while nearly three percent of the entire population is under some form of correctional custody.[2] This penal expansion has been particularly harsh on minorities. By the early 1990s, nearly a third of the country's young black men were in some form of criminal justice custody on any given day.[3]

Thus, academics were discovering how important newspapers, novels, and poetry were to political authority, while violence, domination, and repression were returning as important components in the maintenance of the late modern social order.[4] It is against this contradictory background that Cover's essay should be reread. "Violence and the Word" pointed to this growing resurgence of violence at the center of American political power. I will argue that we should recognize Cover's as a prophetic voice, warning his academic readers in particular that the power of cultural forms, including law, must not be permitted to cover over the relationships of those forms, especially law, to mechanisms of organized violence. At the same time, however, we must recover the historical dimension that Cover elided in his discussion of criminal punishment.

Cover was not a criminologist, or even a criminal law professor. Indeed he explicitly notes that criminal punishment is only the most "direct" example of law's violence.[5] In his effort to describe his increasingly dark vision of American law and politics, he falls back on a largely untheorized understanding of the power to punish. As a consequence, Cover unreflectively accepted features of contemporary penality[6] as inevitable aspects of law's violence, at least in the United States.[7] This chapter seeks to relocate his major insights into a more theorized view of punishment in modern society by placing "Violence and the Word" into the context of the important transformations in penality that have taken place over the past twenty years and that continue.

From the Village of Ideological Control to the Chain Gang of Repression

For a brief season in the late 1960s, a television show called *The Prisoner* captured the imagination of many viewers and has remained something of a cult show ever since. The show featured actor Patrick McGoohan as a man who finds himself held captive in a special settlement known as "the village" after attempting to resign his position presumably somewhere high in the intelligence service of what appears to be Great Britain. This pretty campus-like settlement is apparently a political prison, but McGoohan's character, referred to by the masters of the village as "number six," is never able to determine just which government is operating the village, or for what reasons. Is he a captive of his own government? Or has he been captured by the other side? Each episode of *The Prisoner* portrayed McGoohan's efforts to resist the constant efforts of the village masters to learn the reasons for his resignation and to force him to accept the largely passive stance of the other village residents/inmates.

The masters of the village are shown as ruthless manipulators of minds who artfully create illusion after illusion. But beyond its then trendy critical perspective, *The Prisoner* offered a picture of power that is now rather curious, although it shared this with far less critical shows like *Mission Impossible*. In this picture, power is exercised mainly through ideology. With apparent endless resources at its disposal, power aims at producing fantastic deceptions to fool its enemies into cooperating. In this picture, the enemy of the state cannot simply be physically dominated or killed, the enemy must be won over by complicated manipulations of ideology and belief.

In every episode McGoohan eludes the forms of mind control and seduction thrown at him and in most he ends up making a direct physical effort to escape. At such moments a particularly strange member of the village control-apparatus emerges. This character, referred to as "number three," is a large spherical entity (presumably a robot of some sort) that rises from the sea just off shore of the village, and chases McGoohan. Inevitably our hero is overtaken by this spherical nemesis, which is often shown covering him over like a large beanbag or a giant bubble. It is easy now to dismiss "number three" as an over-the-top attempt at psychedelic special effects, or perhaps a campy bit of ironic self parody of the sort found in the *Batman* television show of the same period. But when *The Prisoner* is read as a text about modern political power it suggests something more interesting. While the state is represented as ruthless, it is not sanguinary. Power operates through deception, through technologies of "brain washing," through drugs and therapies, even through psycho-surgery, but the one strategy that this all powerful and wealthy state apparatus cannot deploy is violence against its citizens, even when they are in revolt.[8]

Consider a different kind of prisoner in the 1990s. Petr Taborsky was an undergraduate at the University of South Florida in 1987, when he worked as a laboratory assistant on a corporate-sponsored research project looking into sewage treatment methods. Taborsky discovered a method for making a clay-like substance used in cat litter into a powerful waste treatment medium by heating it to super high temperatures. Taborsky fell into a dispute with the professor in charge of the project, and with the University, over who had a right to patent the discovery. Taborsky claimed to have made the discovery after the sponsored research for which he was paid had been completed. The dispute moved from civil to criminal when the University accused Taborsky of theft for taking two lab notebooks with him when he left the University. He claimed they were his notes. The University claimed that all notes associated with the project belonged to them. In 1990 Taborsky was convicted of grand theft and sentenced to one year of house arrest and fifteen years of probation. He was also ordered not to use the disputed notebooks.

The battle continued in the patent office, and in 1992 Taborsky successfully obtained three patent rights associated with the discovery. Lawyers for the University complained to prosecutors that Taborsky had violated his probation. When Taborsky refused to comply with a judge's order to assign the patents to the University, he was sentenced to three and a half years in prison and the court assigned one of his patents to the University as restitution. Frank Borkowski, then president of the University of South Florida, petitioned the judge in a hand-delivered letter urging "that Mr. Taborsky should be incarcerated for his crime"[9] He was transferred from jail to a maximum-security prison where he eventually found himself detailed to the recently revived "chain gang."[10] After embarrassing press coverage, the University itself petitioned to have him released[11] and the governor ordered Taborsky moved to a halfway house. Taborsky was released from confinement in April of 1997 after more than three years of incarceration during which his marriage dissolved.[12]

It is surely problematic to treat these two stories as examples of law's violence. The Prisoner was, after all, only a television show (and not a particularly successful one in capturing market share). Moreover, if it was a story about anything, it was about lawless power in the state's security apparatus. The story of Petr Taborsky received considerable press coverage precisely because it was atypical to see a middle-class university student,[13] with technical training and entrepreneurial zeal, put on a chain gang for what amounted to recalcitrance in resolving a civil dispute with an academic institution. But these stories remind us how different the picture of power is in the late 1990s from what it was in the late 1960s. It is true that the liberal state in the 1960s had not ceased to rely on violence. The Vietnam War, and the repression of antiwar protesters and other domestic opponents, like the Black Panthers, evidenced plenty of violence. Yet the idea that power operated largely through ideology and the seduction of consumer opportunity captured something important about the social order in the 1960s.

The great social theorist of that era, Herbert Marcuse, described this new face of power as "repressive desublimation."[14] According to Marcuse, modernizing societies coercively demanded the repression of pleasure in the name of the "reality principle" of productivity (a process Freud described as "sublimation"). In contrast, affluent postwar society, bolstered by technological rationality, was able to abandon the coercive task of discipline and instead rule by encouraging people to indulge their drive for pleasure (thus the term "desublimation"). For Marcuse, this transformation threatened to undermine the traditional sources of the progressive critique of social domination in the artistic celebration of pleasure. The contradiction between culture and reality was being washed out, leaving the "one dimensional man" of the book's famous title.

In the 1970s, Michel Foucault offered another analysis of power in contemporary societies that paralleled Marcuse's in some respects. Foucault argued that since the seventeenth century, the mechanisms of power (in the state and elsewhere) had moved away from the traditional power of the state to kill and tax (deductive power) and had come to rely on techniques of administering life. Rather than being seen solely in terms of its capacity to repress and dominate, this new power, which Foucault called "bio-power,"[15] was enabling, investing its subjects with identities and capacities.[16] It is true, Foucault pointed out, that modern war and its atrocities far exceed the violence of traditional conflict. But this power of death in modern society is increasingly rationalized in terms of its relationship to the administration of life, that is, to fostering the health and well-being of the population:

> This formidable power of death—and this is perhaps what accounts for part of its force and the cynicism with which it has so greatly expanded its limits—now presents itself as the counterpart of a power that exerts a positive influence on life, that endeavors to administer, optimize, and multiply it, subjecting it to precise controls and comprehensive regulations.[17]

Whatever their failings as political theory, Marcuse's picture of a powerful society capable of governing through pleasure rather than repression, and Foucault's account of an enabling and pastoral power invested in the creation of internalized controls in its subjects, captured the zeitgeist of the 1960s. It was precisely the picture against which events like the police riot at the 1968 Democratic convention in Chicago, the execution-style killing of Black Panther leader Fred Hampton in 1970 by state law officers in the same city, and the 1971 national guard killings of protesting students at Kent State University in Ohio and Jackson State University in Mississippi, stood out as shocking. This was not how a modern liberal state behaved toward even its dissident citizens. Even for "ordinary criminals," law's violence seemed to diminish in the 1960s. In 1972, the United States prison population was a smaller portion of the total population than at any time since 1927, and the death penalty, still a significant part of legal punishment in the early 1960s, trickled to a stop by 1969.[18]

The past two decades have seen a fundamental alteration in the exercise of law's violence in the United States. The incarceration rate had already doubled by the time of Cover's article from 103 per hundred thousand residents in 1974, to 216 in 1986. Since then, it has doubled again to 476 in 1999.[19] If present trends continue, an estimated 1 out of every 20 persons will be imprisoned at some time during his or her life.[20] The death penalty, in the meantime, has moved from a symbolic debate to a small but regular feature of American penality. When Cover's article was published, 68 prisoners had been executed in the decade since executions resumed in 1977. In the succeeding decade and a half, more than 350 prisoners were executed.[21] Once the subject of newspaper headlines, executions have become a routine act of state power.

The implicit message of *The Prisoner*, that power needs to win over even its most recalcitrant dissidents, that it operates through psychological methods and will go to tremendous lengths to avoid physical violence, has been reversed. With hundreds of thousands of people in prison for offenses that might have been treated as a mental health problem over two decades ago, no one can doubt the willingness of the contemporary state (and other institutions like universities and private employers) to use violence against those who refuse to obey its norms. Cases like Petr Taborsky's remind us that such violence is available even against those who can hardly be described as posing a danger of violence to others.

VIOLENCE AND THE WORD

Cover's "Violence and the Word" still haunts us over a decade later in part because it sounded such a dissonant note in the intellectual trends of its time (including that established by his own influential work). In the 1970s and 1980s, mainstream American academics were in many respects just catching up with European social theory of the 1960s. The concept of ideology had moved from its periphery fringe to the center of analysis in the humanities and the social sciences. Structuralist and poststructuralist theorists from Europe, widely translated in the 1970s, were rapidly absorbed into American academic work. These new approaches seemed to suggest that hard realities like the state, science, and the capitalist economy were themselves artifacts of discursive formations that could be "read" by discerning cultural critics. In these works, the picture of power was moving away from a focus on specific agents to the role of discursive structures and symbolic systems in structuring choices.[22]

These trends began to infiltrate legal scholarship as well. Several years before "Violence and the Word," Cover published his celebrated "*Nomos* and Narrative,"[23] which drew on a broad array of theorists to suggest that law was at least as much about forging a normative order of meaning as it was about social control. This piece was just part of a large stream of work by legal scholars who looked to literature and religious texts as the proper context for legal texts. On the left, the critical legal studies movement argued that law operated to replace the need for violence by constructing power relationships as inevitable and natural.[24] Constitutional law scholars moved away from their focus on the relationship of judicial interpretation to the coercive power of the legislative and executive branches[25] toward a concern with the methodology of interpretation.[26] Sociologists, historians, political scientists, and anthropologists interested in law and society, who had traditionally looked at the conflict between idealized rules and the reality of power, began to prioritize the way legal rules themselves constituted and reshaped power relations.[27]

Against these trends, or at least their most enthusiastic expressions, "Violence and the Word" insisted that law must be analyzed in terms of its inevitable relationship to violence. Cover did not deny that law might operate as language, symbol, and ideology, but argued that these aspects were inevitably altered by its institutional links to the mechanisms of effective violence. According to Cover, the methodology of legal interpretation must always recur to the sociological conditions under which violence is effectively organized and exercised. To those who dreamed of law achieving the coherence and beauty of great literature, Cover insisted that real judges could never allow such considerations to outweigh the practical necessity of assuring institutional cooperation in the exercise of violence.

> Legal interpretation . . . can never be "free"; it can never be the function of an understanding of the text or word alone. Nor can it be a simple function of what the interpreter conceives to be merely a reading of the "social text," a reading of all relevant social data. Legal interpretation must be capable of transforming itself into action; it must be capable of overcoming inhibitions against violence, in order to generate its requisite deeds; *it must be capable of massing a sufficient degree of violence to deter reprisal and revenge.*[28]

To those who would dismantle law in the name of liberation, Cover warned that the potential for violence to resume its role in the polity without the mediation of law was an ever-present threat.

> As long as death and pain are part of our political world, it is essential that they be at the center of the law. The alternative is truly unacceptable—that they be within our polity but outside the discipline of the collective decision rules and the individual efforts to achieve outcomes through those rules.[29]

The great value of "Violence and the Word" is precisely in its alarming insistence that law's violence be acknowledged, not just at the extremities of the legal order, but at the center of the process in judicial interpretation. If "legal interpretation takes place in a field of pain and death,"[30] than those who treat it as poetry or ideology risk not only missing the true significance of its gestures, but also being complicit in masking the inevitable brutalities of legal institutions. But Cover's powerful call of conscience was strangely combined with a countermove of normalizing of law's violence. This countermove, which Sarat and Kearns aptly phrase "making peace with violence," introduced fundamental distortions into his argument, limiting the very critical attention his prophetic voice had mobilized.[31]

In the remainder of this essay, I want to take up two fundamental distortions in Cover's "Violence and the Word" that led him to normalize unduly the conditions of law's violence in the 1980s (and since). First, Cover treated law's violence as a story primarily about dyadic relationship between judge and prisoner in the arms of the law. In Cover's analysis of law's violence, juries, lawyers, correctional officers, and communities are present only in the most formalistic ways. Second, Cover treated violence as an ontological feature of law. He ignored historical vicissitudes in the forms, purposes, and quantity of punishment.

Both of these distortions have their most important consequence in shaping our attitude toward reconciling law's violence with the aspiration that law achieve "a common and coherent meaning."[32] In Cover's view, such an aspiration is futile and distracting. Because law is ultimately about dealing in violence, "there is a tragic limit to the common meaning that can be achieved."[33] Cover maintains that this utterly distinguishes the judicial act of interpretation from all other ways that the social meaning of law's violence might be debated or deployed.

> For as the judge interprets, using the concept of punishment, she also acts—through others—to restrain, hurt, render helpless, even kill the prisoner. Thus, any commonality of interpretation that may or may not be achieved is one that has its common meaning destroyed by the divergent experiences that constitute it.[34]

This view should be contested in two respects. First it ignores the experience of law's violence on those outside the judge/prisoner dyad. What of the lawyer, whom Justice Brennan imagined in his dissent to *McCleskey v. Kemp*, who must tell her client that his chances of being executed are determined in part by his race and the race of his victim?[35] What of the African-American jurors asked to authorize punishment on yet another young black man charged with selling drugs? Even if these experiences are different than that of the judge ordering, or the person receiving punishment (and they surely are), why should they be relegated to the realm of ideology, literature, or political debate? They belong to the realities of law's violence. Cover seems to acknowledge this:

> Legal interpretation may be the act of judges or citizens, legislators or presidents, draft resistors or right-to-life protestors. Each kind of interpreter speaks

from a distinct institutional location. Each has a different perspective on factual and moral implications of any given understanding of the Constitution. . . . But considerations of word, deed, and role will always be present in some degree.[36]

But in choosing to highlight the judicial position as definitive of law's violence, Cover exaggerates the essential polarity between the punisher and the punished. Citizens, especially as jurors but in their other capacities as well (for example, past or future subject of punishment, parent, neighbor, teacher), may have far greater ambivalence about the procedural and sociological context of punishment than Cover's judge-centered model allows. This goes for prisoners as well. There is substantial psychological evidence suggesting that procedural fairness does matter, even to those who lose in legal conflict.[37] Even if this literature discounts the differences between experimental consciousness and that constituted by litigation (and especially criminal litigation), we should not assume that the fairness of proceedings are utterly irrelevant to prisoners.

Second, Cover errs in assuming that prisoners' experience of law's violence is so totalizing as to shut out any of its procedural or sociological dimensions. He draws his conclusions on the effects of violence from Elaine Scarry's influential discussion of torture.[38] But it is a mistake to assume that all punishment is the same as torture. We should not ignore that imprisonment is a form of violence, but we need not assume that it must be a world-destroying violence (more on the form of punishment shortly).

THE PUBLICS OF LAW'S VIOLENCE

One consequence of Cover focusing on the judge/prisoner dyad is to leave out any serious questioning of the broader public in whose name law's violence is exercised. This allows Cover to speak for the general interest in confessing his own general satisfaction with the asymmetry of power between punishers and punished. "If I have exhibited some sense of sympathy for the victims of this violence, it is misleading. Very often the balance of terror in this regard is just as I would want it."[39] This helps him to sidestep the question of whose interests the criminal law is written to reflect, whose conduct it constrains, or how justice is carried out. It appears not to matter what crime the offender is punished for, whether it is armed robbery or possession of marijuana. It appears not to matter what the features of the justice system are that bring the prisoner to the point of sentencing. It is irrelevant whether counsel represented the prisoner, whether he could command the presence of witnesses on his behalf, or whether the jury that convicted him was drawn from a representative pool of his community. Distanced from these disturbing features by his ontological gaze, Cover found it possible to make a grim pact with law's violence to protect him and us from them.

This is especially problematic because along with the resurgence of penal violence in the 1980s there was an increase in racial disparity. Death sentences continue to be disproportionately handed down in cases involving white victims.[40] There continues to be strong evidence of racial discrimination in the exercise of police arrest powers, in the decisions of prosecutors to charge, and in the sentences prisoners receive. Equally as disturbing, the rapidly growing prison population is increasingly composed of racial minorities.[41] Even if not discriminated against on their way through the process, the concentration of minorities in prisons has profound consequences for the meaning of law's violence.[42]

The overrepresentation of racial minorities, especially African Americans in the prisons of the United States is not altogether surprising. In virtually every society, disadvantaged and discriminated-against groups find themselves figuring disproportionately among the punished. In the United States, African Americans have been imprisoned at a far higher rate than whites from at least the end of the Civil War. In the early decades of the twentieth century, African Americans made up over a fifth of the confined population (in jails and prisons) while constituting only about 11 percent of the population.[43] By the 1990s, however, African Americans made up over half of the prison population, although their overall percentage of the population had changed only slightly (12 or 13 percent).[44] This despite the fact that the focus on driving out discrimination in criminal justice has continued to be promoted by the courts long after many aspects of the civil rights movement stalled legally.

To some extent this continues to reflect deeply embedded forms of discrimination in the way police and prosecution are targeted at crime. But the escalation of this disproportion, during a period in which concerted efforts have been made to reduce official discrimination, is especially destabilizing to American democracy. As African Americans have achieved a far greater measure of citizenship in the wider community, their increasing share of the "unfree" population has come to constitute an independent source of alienation from government.

Recent scholarship has begun to explore the complex attitudes of the larger African American community toward lawbreakers and toward the criminal justice system.[45] There is no simple rejection of the law, but neither is there acceptance of every use of law's violence. General social surveys continue to show higher levels of fear of the police among African-Americans than among whites. African Americans, especially those who live in areas of urban poverty, experience high levels of victimization and fear of crime. Many support aggressive use of techniques like curfews and community policing aimed at disrupting criminal activities.

There is particular concern about the heavy use of imprisonment because of its devastating effects on the presence of adult males in the minority households, and the attendant results on the socialization of the next generation. This is especially true of the harsh sentences enacted in recent years against those who participate in illegal market transactions, like drug sales. To the extent that these markets have become one of the few sources of economic activity especially for young males, and of support for inner-city households, severe punishment for participating in them may seem a fundamental injustice. Some may respond by nullifying the law in order to reject its violence.

A more complicated and nuanced view of law's violence is also true of prisoners (who now make up a non-trivial portion of the adult male African-American population). As anyone who has ever talked with prisoners knows, they are intensely conscious of what they perceive as injustices in their legal treatment. This is not limited to their own cases. In 1996 when Congress rejected the proposal of the U.S. Sentencing Commission to modify the significant differences in sentences for trafficking in crack and powder cocaine, riots broke out in federal prisons all over the country.[46] Prisoners were apparently appalled at Congress's endorsement of the documented racial effects of the crack differential, even though the proposal would have had *no* retroactive effect. Likewise, even non-death-row prisoners routinely protest executions.

Once we bring in even a preliminary look at differences in the ways in which different publics are situated in terms of crime and punishment, the terms of Cover's effort to make peace with law's violence become especially suspect. For Cover, who was a rather economically privileged white academic, the primary dilemma may have been between the repugnance of law's violence and the social need for peace among its varied normative orders. But for others, law's violence is perceived as a threat to their very capacity as a community to sustain a normative order.

PENALTY AND LAW'S VIOLENCE

For a long time, the declining severity of law's violence has been constitutive of the very sense of modernity in Western societies.[47] The outlines of that optimistic history are still familiar. More or less parallel with the rise of enlightenment thought and republican political institutions in Europe and North America, the tradition of punishment through painful rituals on a public scaffold came under intense criticism. The prison became the most successful of a number of efforts to produce alternative punishments.[48] From this perspective, the public torture of bodies had been a practice well suited to symbolizing the awesome nature of monarchical power. Modern societies were better served by punishments that valorized its distinctive social relations like freedom, private life, and the pursuit of economic welfare. From the start, many had to acknowledge the failures of this vision. Enlightenment ideals of control established purely through surveillance and moral discipline were always tempered with heavy reliance on the whip and punitive confinement in "the hole." But reformers could always offer improvements, and the direction of progress was clear.

This view was subjected to a permanent and devastating revision by a wave of historical and sociological scholarship on the prison, beginning with Erving Goffman's *Asylums* (1961), continuing with David Rothman's *Discovery of the Asylum* (1971), and Michel Foucault's *Discipline and Punish* (1977).[49] This scholarship raised many complex and nuanced points about the history of the prison, but virtually all shared a sense that the traditional view of the prison as a trajectory away from violence understated the coercive aspects of the penitentiary, not just in its failures but also in its very design. Rothman argued that the vision of the prison enthusiastically pursued by Americans in the early Republic had more to do with recapturing the virtues of the colonial past than those of its capitalist future. Foucault saw the prison as a schema for modernity; but far from a lesson in freedom and limitations on power, it marked for him a broad change in the very economy of power in Western societies. If the painful spectacles of the scaffold had been abandoned, it was for a new set of technologies of power that promised to deliver a far more efficient form of control. From this perspective, our continuing reliance on the prison suggested a "disciplinary society" committed to ever more minute interventions in the lives of people through implementation of disciplinary practices mandated by the imperative to be normal. By the time of Cover's essay, this view was reaching the peak of its influence among students of penality.[50]

Cover's treatment, of punishment is, at first glance, quite bizarre when seen against this discussion of penal history. In eliding the distinction between imprisonment and torture, Cover appears to be denying both the optimistic story and its revisionist critiques. The prison, in Cover's view, is neither a humane renunciation of torture nor a pragmatic alternative form of coercion. It simply is the same as torture as far as law's violence is concerned:

> Just as the torturer and victim achieve a "shared" world only by virtue of their diametrically opposed experiences, so the judge and prisoner understand "punishment" through their diametrically opposed experiences of the punishing act. It is ultimately irrelevant whether the torturer and his victim share a common

theoretical view on the justifications for torture—outside the torture room. They still have come to the confession through destroying in the one case and through having been destroyed in the other. Similarly, whether or not the judge and prisoner share the same philosophy of punishment, they arrive at the particular act of punishment having dominated and having been dominated with violence, respectively.[51]

But in associating punishment with torture, Cover ignored important sociological features of modern punishment intimately tied up with the prison. First, Cover ignored the specificity of the prison as a particular organizational technology of exercising the power to punish. The revisionists may be right that the prison is not the palladium of humanity that its proponents often claimed, but sociological observers have found that it provides all kinds of possibilities for inmates to resist and modify the exercise of power there.[52] Second, Cover ignored the importance that penological ideas, especially rehabilitation, have had in shaping modern penality. Claims to rehabilitate through punishment, which dominated official penology for most of the twentieth century, were always frought with contradictions. At the same time, they imposed enduring constraints on the severity of violence, and for a while altered the very conditions of exercising power within the prison. In the end, I want to argue that we should both correct Cover's oversight of the specificities of penal practice and ideology and see in his dogged focus on the violence of punishment an insight, albeit misrecognized, into contemporary changes in penality.

The Prison: Machine or Community?

Torture, as discussed by Elaine Scarry, ultimately destroys the victim's normative world. In that sense, it excludes both shared meanings with the torturers and the capacity for shared meanings (at least of any deep sort). To accomplish this, torturers must establish complete and unconditional control of the victim's body. The early designers of the prison also dreamed of near total control (although to avoid pain!). The penitentiary movement in early nineteenth century, for example, emphasized isolation of inmates in single cells and permitted congregation, if at all, only under disciplined labor, military drilling, or other conditions that promised to establish multiple controls on the bodies of prisoners.

Cover seems to treat this level of control as a realistic condition of punishment. He treats the prison organization as an extension of the judge's will, even as he recognizes in it a permanent constraint on the interpretive work of judges.

When judges interpret the law in an official context, we expect a close relationship to be revealed or established between their words and the acts that they mandate. That is, we expect judges' words to serve as virtual triggers for action. We would not, for example, expect contemplations or deliberations on the part of jailers or wardens to interfere with the action authorized by judicial words. But such a routinization of violent behavior requires a form of organization that operates simultaneously in the domains of action and interpretation.[53]

Later in the essay, Cover analogizes the relationship of prisons to the judicial act to a machine-like system.

> The judge in imposing a sentence normally takes for granted the role structure which might be analogized to the "transmission" of the engine of justice. The judge's interpretive authorization of the "proper" sentence can be carried out as a deed only because of these others; a bond between word and deed obtains only because a system of social cooperation exists. That system guarantees the judge massive amounts of force—the conditions of effective domination—if necessary. It guarantees—or is supposed to—a relatively faithful adherence to the word of the judge in the deeds carried out against the prisoner.[54]

'But this story is accurate only at the most superficial level. A judge's order that a particular convicted offender serve a certain term of years in the state prison is more than likely to be fulfilled, except as altered by other legal structures like parole or good time credits. Escapes are rare, and while prison bureaucracy sometimes breaks down, it almost never happens that a warden decides to keep someone in prison longer than the sentence called for by their legal superiors. But as sociologists have long revealed, the experience of imprisonment is a different matter. There the image of the prisoner as a passive body in the grasp of an efficient and bureaucratically organized machine breaks down rather completely.

Donald Clemmer's classic study of life in a maximum security prison, *The Prison Community*,[55] revealed that the dominant influence on the norms and mores of prison life was not law, or even the administration of prison, but the inmate community and its culture. Clemmer coined the term "prisonization" to describe the process of normative change that prisoners underwent during their confinement. Far from reflecting the power of the prison to impose its will on the prisoners, prisonization norms were defined by opposition to the staff and its mandates.[56] The prison value-system celebrated those prisoners capable of manipulating and deceiving staff and reserved its most severe sanctions for those who actively cooperated with staff against other prisoners.

Clemmer was concerned about the implications that prisonization had for the official penological goal of rehabilitation (more on that later), but prisonization also had clear implications for the administration of prisons, and especially for the idea of the prison as machine-like instrument of law's violence. Clemmer suggested that inmates were not primarily passive receivers of imprisonment. Their own norms and hierarchies necessarily became a problem for prison administration. In the absence of a willingness to carry out a violent repression of the prison community, the governance of the prison would have to move through the prison community.

Gresham Sykes's observations of another maximum-security prison over twenty years later revealed an inmate culture just as robust and oppositional as what Clemmer had observed.[57] Sykes argued that prison authority, is in fact, constituted through a complex set of accommodations with inmate culture in terms that refute Cover's machine-like image of the prison.

> The ability of the officials to physically coerce their captives into the paths of compliance is something of an illusion as far as the day-to-day activities of the prison are concerned and may be of doubtful value in moments of crisis. Intrinsically inefficient as a method of making men carry out a complex task, diminished in effectiveness by the realities of the guard-inmate ratio, and always accompanied by the danger of further violence, the use of physical force by the custodians has many limitations as a basis on which to found the routine operation of the prison. . . . Unable to count on a sense of duty to motivate their captives to obey and unable to depend on the direct and immediate use of violence to insure a step-by-step submission to the rules, the custodians must fall back on a system of rewards and punishments.
>
> Now if men are to be controlled by the use of rewards and punishments—by promises and threats—at least one point is patent: The rewards and punishments dangled in front of the individual must indeed be rewards and punishments from the point of view of the individual who is to be controlled.[58]

The 1960s and 1970s would see profound changes to the prison community, but not in a way that stripped inmate culture of its power to shape the practice of imprisonment. First, starting in the 1950s, an intensification of the commitment of correctional regimes to a rehabilitative focus introduced a variety of new normative forces into prison society. The old inmate values of autonomy and noncooperation had to be compromised in order to win parole board endorsement. Informing remained a harshly sanctioned activity, but at least a sardonic willingness to participate in academic and psychological programming became a feature of life for ordinary prisoners. Second, starting in the 1960s, African-American and Latino inmates became the largest component of the prison population. At virtually the same time, inmates, and especially African-American and Latino inmates, began to be influenced by the growth of racial identity politics in the larger society during the late 1960s. This has profoundly altered the prison community that Clemmer and Sykes studied. Prison sociologists have observed the organizing force of racial identity since the

1970s.[59] The old values of individual inmate autonomy and collective solidarity against the staff has been reconfigured around racial gangs. But as before, prison administration combines efforts to combat the gangs with strategies of governance that presuppose them. In short, the prison of 1990s is no more a transmission of the engine of justice than it was in the 1930s.

Cover might claim that his interest was only in the fact of being in prison as a sentence and not on the organization of prison life. But the pain of imprisonment is only partially constituted by the separation and isolation accomplished by placing the subject in prison. It is also compounded by the culture of violent abuse among inmates, and between correctional officers and inmates. When an inmate is raped and turned into a sex slave for the rest of his or her sentence, it is a hollow view of law's violence that would treat that pain as irrelevant.[60] When an inmate is murdered by other inmates who consider his crime a capital one, this is the real sentence even if not handed down by a judge.

Interestingly, in the late 1980s and early 1990s, a new model of prison has begun to develop in the United States that promises (in a limited domain) to establish the kind of machine Cover envisioned. Most of the states and the federal government now operate what are called "supermax" or "maxi-max" prisons to hold inmates with serious disciplinary violations or who are suspected of being gang members. These new prisons use special procedures and technologies in an effort to eliminate inmate community as a factor in prison life. Prisoners in these establishments are isolated to their cells (either alone or with another inmate) twenty-three hours a day. All forms of work or correctional programming are eliminated to avoid having any contact among inmates or even between inmates and staff. Even constitutionally protected activities like showering, access to the law library, and to religious counseling, are conducted either in-cell, or in special isolation rooms.

In addition to eliminating the opportunity for prisoners to form a culture, the supermax also aims at tightly regulating staff interaction with inmates to prevent the kind of accommodation that Sykes described. Even routine monitoring of inmates is mediated by closed circuit television. Most of these new prisons have replaced the classic open barred cell with a solid steel door in which food and observation holes have been made. To further protect the staff, a plastic shield is installed over some doors to prevent bodily fluids or any other projectiles from being thrown by inmates. When more direct contact is required by inmate disobedience, specially trained teams of correctional officers, modeled on police SWAT teams, typically carry out the response. Often this involves removing the inmate from the cell, a process known in the administrative language of these prisons as a "cell extraction." The cell extraction team members are dressed in special protective clothing and full headgear. Their entry is preceded by firing tear gas canisters into the cell often followed by Taser darts, which deliver an immobilizing electric shock. In some prisons this procedure is carried through once initiated even if the inmate desists from resistance and submits to restraint.

In the supermax prison, perhaps for the first time in the history of the prison, Cover's image of a punishment apparatus with a machine-like capacity to operate on formal rules and without modification by inmate culture promises to be realized in-depth. But the emerging evidence on these new prisons suggests that the result has not been the containment of law's violence but in some cases its unraveling. Violence suggestive of the rituals of the scaffold or the nineteenth century prisons has been reported by inmates and outside observers at a number of supermax prisons. One of the most detailed pictures comes from California's state-of-the-art Pelican Bay supermax prison in a remarkable opinion by Judge Thelton Henderson of the United States District Court for Northern California.[61] Inmates of the supermax prison brought a class-action lawsuit alleging cruel and unusual punishment for a variety of features of the regime ranging from the psychological effects of its near total isolation, to the grossly inadequate provision of mental and medical health care, to excessive use of force by the staff. While declining to find the isolation strategy unconstitutional in its very conception, Judge Henderson did find for the plaintiffs on a number of their specific complaints. Judge Henderson noted the contrast with the typical prison condition lawsuit:

> This . . . is not a case about inadequate or deteriorating physical conditions. There are no rat-infested cells, antiquated buildings, or unsanitary supplies. Rather, plaintiffs contend that behind the newly minted walls and shiny equipment lies a prison that is coldly indifferent to the limited, but basic and elemental rights that incarcerated persons—"including the worst of the worst"— retain under the First, Eighth, and Fourteenth amendments of our United States Constitution.[62]

The opinion provides a catalog of violence reminiscent of the earliest days of confinement. One severely mentally ill inmate who had antagonized the staff by smearing himself and his cell with his own feces, was placed in a scalding bath by a team of guards who scrubbed him aggressively with a bristle brush. The resulting second and third degree burns were so severe that the inmates skin began to fall off his legs after he was removed from the bath. While the officers denied that they were aware of the potential for harm, witnesses testified that they joked that they were turning the prisoner, an African-American, into a "white boy" and invited other staff to join in.[63] In another practice condemned by the court, inmates, sometimes injured by violent cell extractions, were left in large outdoor cells during winter weather.[64] Naked and sometimes bleeding, these inmates were exposed to the full view of the prison staff (including large numbers of secretaries and other noncustodial staff).

Perhaps the most extreme example of the violence generated at supermax prisons comes from Corcoran State Prison, a second supermax facility in California. There the death of an inmate revealed what was apparently a longstanding practice of "gladiator fights" between inmates from rival gangs, set up by the staff for their own amusement. The staff arranged for two members from a Latino gang to be brought together with two members of an African-American gang without warning. The inmates were told to fight one on one and threatened with being shot if they interfered with the other fight. One of the African American inmates was shot in the head by staff after ignoring orders to desist. Several of the correctional officers were ultimately indicted in federal court for conspiracy to violate the civil rights of the inmates.[65]

These new prisons oddly move closer to Cover's machine-like picture of the prison and to his association of imprisonment with torture. But Cover ignored the very different cultures of the prison that have developed and continue to exist in most American jurisdictions. More important, by treating the prison as an instrument of an unchanging need for violence in law, Cover avoided confronting the historical developments that are promoting a massive regression in human rights for prisoners in the United States.

From Normalizing to Waste Management

In addition to ignoring the historical and political specificities of the prison as an instrument of punishment, Cover's analysis of law's violence also ignores issues of historical change in the quantity and rationality of criminal punishment. Having associated punishment with torture, Cover strongly implied that the mode or purpose of punishment is irrelevant. But it is not so clear that punishment of any sort and for any purpose is a generic act of violence with little important distinction. Official justifications of punishment are notoriously slippery. When Congress enacted a new sentencing system in 1984, it endorsed all the major purposes of punishment.[66] Yet beneath the surface of statutory language, there are more significant changes in the discourse and practices of punishment. These discourses and practices send important signals to the bureaucracies, that administer punishments about how to relate to their charges. Since one of Cover's most important arguments is that the interpretation of law always takes into account the burden of effectively guiding just such bureaucracies, changes in the discourses and practices of punishment mediate law's violence and meaning in important ways that courts should recognize.[67]

From the end of the nineteenth century until the 1970s, the official purpose of imprisonment in the United States was rehabilitation. New institutions created early in the twentieth century, like parole, probation, and the juvenile court, were products of rehabilitative thinking. They aimed to provide a foundation for individualizing justice to meet the correctional needs of the offender, but for the most part these were coopted by the organizational needs of the traditional prison system.[68] With a few innovative exceptions, this official penology had relatively little influence on the operation of the prison until after World War II. Then, state governments, their revenues high from full employment and their ambitions raised by the New Deal, looked on corrections as a natural site for investment in social order and long-term economic health. As a result, between the 1950s and the 1970s, rehabilitation began to have a more profound organizational influence on prison life.

The historical record of rehabilitative penology in its brief activist phase has yet to be truly written. Since the mid-1970s the dominant view has been that it was a failure because programs capable of proving themselves effective in reducing recidivism by social-science standards were few. It is true that many of those who promoted rehabilitation as a penal goal founds its practice wanting, especially in prison settings. Many called for the abandonment of imprisonment in favor of community-based correctional strategies. But by the late 1960s, rehabilitation was also being attacked on political as well as technical grounds. From the left, the focus of correctional specialists on the individual problems of offenders was attacked both on the grounds that it obscured the real basis of crime in inequality, and that it led to totalitarian encroachments on the liberty and dignity of prisoners. From the right, rehabilitation was castigated as part of the decline in individual responsibility and moral standards. The reliance on parole boards to individualize sentences based on rehabilitation was viewed as undermining confidence in the law and deterrence against crime. This view was surely bolstered by the historic surge in violent crime that took place in the United States from the mid-1960s until the mid-1970s.

Both sides of this critique may have influenced Cover's thinking about punishment. Indeed, many of these criticisms anticipated Cover's concern for the adequate functioning of institutions of collective violence. But both the left and right ignored important features of rehabilitation when seen as a program for organizing prisons and rationalizing state crime-control measures. First, whatever its clinical successes, rehabilitation was having a profound organizational influence on both staff and prisoners.[69] Because these changes were soon swamped by the politicization of crime and punishment, it is hard to know how enduring or profound these changes might have been, or what their implications might have been for law's violence. Secondly, as a political and legal rather than scientific matter, rehabilitation expressed the logic of liberal governance as that was being redefined in the mid-twentieth century around the imperatives of social welfare and human rights.[70]

Suffice it to say that the case for rehabilitative penology as a social policy remains largely untested. Likewise, we cannot dismiss the potential for a system that pursues rehabilitation with integrity, if not necessarily instrumental effectiveness, to achieve greater levels of common understanding between punishers and punished. By the time Cover wrote "Violence and the Word," the rehabilitative ideal had been largely eclipsed. Many advocates of dismantling rehabilitation believed that a punishment based solely on moral desert and limited by principles of proportionality would have the best chance of respecting the humanity of prisoners and establishing a common ground of meaning.[71] Told honestly that they were being punished for their conduct, and set free from the psychological manipulations involved in rehabilitative regimes, prisoners, retributionists believed, could experience punishment while maintaining their dignity as citizens and their capacity to rejoin the political community that was punishing them. Some states adopted new sentencing codes influenced in part by this movement. California, most famously, stated in its sentencing statute that the "purpose of imprisonment for crime" was punishment.[72] The new codes provided narrow ranges for judges to use in sentencing offenders to prison. The idea was to treat all crimes the same, and to prevent the attempts at individualization promoted by rehabilitation. The codes also eliminated administrative mechanisms for shortening or lengthening these sentences so that prisoners would recognize their punishment as governed by law and not by the prison personnel.

In many respects, the just deserts approach (as it was called by some), with its focus on the importance of making punishment law-like and tied to courts, parallels much of Cover's critique although not his more pessimistic perspective. Whether just deserts, if consistently applied, would have created a new understanding of punishment among prisoners and prison bureaucracies, one based on respect for the moral purposes of punishment and the legal rights of prisoners, is impossible to know, for this approach was quickly abandoned. Within several years of adoption, most of the new codes were dramatically changed as political concern with crime drove legislatures to lengthen sentences and limit the power of judges to determine the sentence in favor of prosecutorial discretion. The focus on retribution was subordinated by the goals of deterring potential offenders and incapacitating those already in the arms of the law.

By the mid-1980s, concerns for justice, fairness, and equality had become subordinated to the goals of incapacitation and deterrence. As guiding visions for organizing imprisonment, these rationales dramatically

change the relationship of law to the offender. Under deterrence principles, the length of imprisonment is determined by the need to discourage
others from committing future offenses.[73] Under incapacitation principles, the goal is to prevent crime by keeping prisoners in a place where
they cannot commit crimes. Lengthy sentences are justified on speculative
calculations regarding the numbers of crimes that criminals may be expected to commit if they were released. Thus the actual sentence no longer
needs reflect either the individual moral desert of the offender or unique
treatment needs. Indeed, extraordinarily long sentences may be justified
based on factors totally unrelated to the status of either the crime or the
criminal, such as the relative attractions of different kinds of crime and
the difficulties of catching and convicting offenders. The prison becomes
little more than a warehouse of which the purpose is to contain the prisoner. There is no institutional interest in the moral desert of the offender
let alone the background conditions that may have helped determine his
or her criminal career.

Rehabilitative penology and its retributivist critics of the 1970s imagined that reconciliation, or at least shared understanding, could be
achieved between those who wield law's violence and those on whom it
is wielded (albeit each in different and flawed ways). The currently dominant goals of general deterrence and incapacitation represent a conscious
abandonment of any effort to reach coherent or common meanings in
law's violence. The logic of punishment in the emerging new penology
represents law's violence emptied of any interpretive relationship with the
prisoner at all.[74] Under those circumstances, punishment is stripped of its
redemptive promise and directed solely at producing value to society as
either vengeance or public safety.

The resurgence and retrenchment of the American death penalty is
even a stronger move in this direction. Having defined punishment as a
kind of torture, Cover, it was not surprising, found the death penalty an
acceptable manifestation of law's violence. Indeed, in his writings, Cover
comes close to endorsing the death penalty as the most honest form of
law's violence, and when appropriately carried out, the greatest achievement of judicial interpretation:

> The fact that capital punishment constitutes that most plain, the most deliber-
> ate, and the most thoughtful manifestation of legal interpretation as violence
> makes the imposition of the sentence an especially powerful test of the faith and
> commitment of the interpreters.[75]

Compared to a history of frequent recourse to lynching and vigilan-
tism, Cover suggested that the contemporary death penalty revealed the
depth of America's commitment to legality. But here again, there is a
tendency in Cover to treat these acts of punishment as having a history

only in the thinnest sense. There is no exploration here of what it means that the death penalty almost died out in the United States during the 1960s as large numbers of Americans ceased to recognize it as an appropriate punishment. Nor is the effect of a renewed death penalty on the meaning of punishment in the rest of the criminal justice system raised. But a punishment so unambiguously and deliberately intended to exterminate the criminal must cut off any attempt at dialogue or even recognition of the offender's humanity, and not simply in capital crimes. Around this increasingly eliminationist version of utilitarian public policy, a new culture of vengeance and populist punitiveness is growing with even more disturbing implications for the maintenance of common understandings and human rights.[76]

In short, Cover in "Violence and the Word" assumed that punishment is inevitably as empty of the possibility of meaningful dialogue with the punished as the incapacitative prison warehouse or the death penalty. In one sense, he prophetically articulated a hardening of the punitive impulse that was going on in the 1980s. But lacking a historical and sociological analysis of changing mechanisms and purposes of punishment, Cover cut himself off from consideration of whether law's violence could be mediated in any important way. Ironically, this led both to the fatalism and optimism suggested by the conclusion of his essay.

Mission Impossible: Domesticating Law's Violence in an Era of Escalating Punishment

Cover's essay ends with the image of law engaged in a never complete but nonetheless realistic effort to discipline and domesticate violence. This effort requires a set of secondary rules capable of organizing the many actors who must cooperate to "do that violence safely and effectively."[77] Judges and others who produce legal interpretation must discipline their own efforts to the needs of this collective process, foregoing appeals to more coherent and satisfying notions of justice. Such appeals will be frustrated anyway, according to Cover, by the pain that inevitably drives apart the subjects and objects of punishment.

In the sections above, I have argued that Cover's narrow focus on the judge/prisoner dyad, and his unhistorical treatment of penality, may have lead him to both exaggerate and understate the chasm between society and the punished. In this sense, Cover accurately described the emerging penality of the 1980s with its abandonment of any enduring moral links to those subject to punishment. At the same time, he reified this thinking into an ontological theory of punishment. In this section, I challenge the other side of this tradeoff. Abandoning a deeper commitment to common justice might indeed be acceptable if it achieved a successful domestication of law's violence. But in the decade since Cover's essay (and his own untimely death), it has become clear that historical change in penality is driving an intensification of law's violence that threatens to escape from the earnest efforts of judges and penal administrations.

The year after Cover's article appeared, a new federal sentencing system came into effect. The United States Sentencing Guidelines, approved in 1984,[78] represented at the federal level the shift to a penality of incapacitation and general deterrence. Ironically, the new sentencing system, and its analogues in many states, has dramatically undermined the capacity of judges to domesticate violence, a capacity that Cover celebrated. Under the guidelines, judges are severely restrained in their ability to choose a sentence for federal offenders. Prison sentences are established by a complicated formula that takes into account the offender's past record, the specific penal section violated, and a variety of offense-specific characteristics of the crime (e.g., used a gun, injured a victim, possessed a certain weight of drugs, etc.). These factors are worked into a sentencing matrix that generally allows the judge a sentencing range no greater than a quarter of the maximum sentence.[79] Certain individual variations, like a downward departure for substantial cooperation with the government, are worked into the guidelines themselves. Judges may depart from the applicable guideline range only "if the court finds that there exists an aggravating or mitigating circumstance of a kind, or to a degree, not adequately taken into consideration by the Sentencing Commission in formulating the guidelines that should result in a sentence different from that described."[80] For certain crimes, like drug trafficking and illegal gun possession, Congress has even further restricted courts by setting minimum mandatory terms that circumscribe the bottom of the guideline range if applicable.

The net effect of these sentencing reforms (paralleled in many state systems) has been to reduce dramatically the ability of judges to craft sentences.[81] Instead, a great deal of discretion is provided to prosecutors, who can decide which factors to charge and which defendants will be permitted departures for cooperating with the government.[82] The results have struck many on and off the bench as perverse. Low-level players in large drug operations often face extremely lengthy sentences because they can be charged with the entire weight of drugs associated with the illegal trafficking and because low-level players typically have little information that the government can use. In several highly publicized instances, federal judges have resigned rather than continue to sentence prisoners under such a severe and intractable code. Other sitting judges have complained bitterly about the law, with more than half indicating that they would rescind the guidelines.[83]

The escalating prison population is also threatening a profound regression in the living conditions for prisoners. In 1994, the federal system was operating at 125 percent of capacity. At least seven states were operating in excess of 150 percent of capacity. One state with the nation's largest prison population, California, was at 200 percent of capacity.[84] These conditions, which have grown worse during the 1990s despite an unprecedented prison construction effort, have led to an escalation of violence within prisons. Some now speak of a "culture of rape" in which inmates not protected by a gang are subject to sexual slavery and lethal assaults.[85]

These changes are often the result of deliberate decisions by law makers to make prison more punitive. Legislatures across the country have acted to strip prisons of any signs of comfort for inmates including televisions, air conditioners, and recreation equipment. It was the intervention of judges in the 1970s and 1980s that compelled prisons to limit crowding, address uncontrolled violence, and provide basic forms of legal accountability over their staff.[86] Today, the ability of judges to redress these conditions is being directly checked by Congress. The Prison Reform Litigation Act of 1995[87] limits the jurisdiction of federal judges to consider prospective relief in prison-conditions suits and invites state prisons unilaterally to abrogate consent decrees entered into, in the face of civil lawsuits challenging prison conditions.

There are also increasing limits on the ability of courts to intervene to assure the constitutionality of death sentences. The Anti-Terrorism and Effective Death Penalty Act of 1996 strips the ability of courts to hear successive habeas corpus claims by death-row inmates. In a remarkable case, the Supreme Court itself specifically forbid the 9th Circuit Court of Appeals from issuing any further stays of execution in the case of Robert Alton Harris, who was then executed despite the readiness of that court to hear a further appeal.[88]

Beneath the level of the life-tenured federal judiciary, the capacity of judges to hold law's violence accountable is under even greater attack. Several state supreme court justices have been removed by popular ballot in response to perceived willingness to prevent executions.[89] The increasingly ugly public mood about punishment is blurring the lines between legal and extra-legal violence. In Florida, for example, observers were horrified when foot-high flames erupted from the head of condemned inmate during electrocution. Attorney General Bob Butterworth dismissed outcry over the botched execution, stating, "People who wish to commit murder, they better not do it in the State of Florida, because we may have a problem with our electric chair."[90]

In "Violence and the Word," Cover argued passionately that judges should put aside their more utopian aspirations for justice in the name of effectively disciplining law's violence. He suggested that judges must always consider the institutional context in which their orders will be carried out. Cover illustrated this point with a discussion of a remarkable episode involving the trial of a Polish hijacker in a special United States court set up in Berlin specifically to hear the case. In 1979, Herbert Stern was appointed as an Article II judge for the United States Court for Berlin. Stern oversaw the jury trial that convicted the hijacker. When faced with the interpretive task of sentencing him, however, the judge confronted the peculiar political structure in which this punitive act of law would be embedded. In the absence of assurances from the Justice Department, or any other guarantee that his jurisdiction would continue, Stern found that he could not assume "that constitutional violence is always performed within institutionally sanctioned limits and subject to the institutionally role-bound action of others."[91] In a terse opinion, Stern castigated his own government for refusing to create conditions necessary for constitutional punishment, and responded by sentencing the convicted hijackers to time served. In Cover's words,

> Herbert Stern's remarkable sentence is not simply an effective, moving plea for judicial independence, a plea against subservience which Stern's government tried to impose. It is a dissection of the anatomy of criminal punishment in a constitutional system. As such, it reveals the interior role of the judicial word in sentencing. It reveals the necessity of a latent role structure to render the judicial utterance morally intelligible. And it proclaims the moral intelligibility of routine judicial utterance when the structure is no longer there. Almost all judicial utterance becomes deed through the acts of others—acts embedded in roles. The judge must see, as Stern did, that the meaning of her words may change when the roles of these others change. We tend overwhelmingly to assume that constitutional violence is always performed within institutionally sanctioned limits and subject to the institutionally circumscribed, role-bound action of others. Stern uncovered the unreliability of that assumption in the Berlin context and "reinterpreted" his sentence accordingly.[92]

The escalating scale of punishment, and the rapid coarsening of attitudes about punishment in America, is fundamentally changing the conditions under which judges and others perform the acts of interpretation that Cover viewed as essential to contain law's violence. Cover died before the full implications of America's increasing commitment to governing itself through crime were clear. It is futile to speculate how a thinker as brilliant and mercurial as Robert Cover would react to the intensification of penal violence in the past decade and a half. Still the tremendous expansion of the penal violence coupled with concerted efforts to limit the power of judges could not have failed to affect his apparent equanimity about law's violence in 1986. One might start by asking whether in light of Judge Stern's example, federal judges facing the array of changes discussed above can ethically continue to hand down prison sentences.

Conclusion

Robert Cover's plea that academics not ignore the institutional mechanisms that link interpretation and violence in the production of law is more important than ever. At the same time, it is crucial to explore the historical and sociological conditions under which law's violence is exercised. Cover sensed a danger that the flourishing interest in the role of interpretation and meaning in law could produce a false sense of the utopian possibilities of law, and elide the rigor necessary to prevent violence from escaping the grasp of law. Today, however, that very real danger is now more than matched by the danger that we may accept as natural or inevitable a level of violence that is, in fact, a dramatic historical regression. For that reason we should not follow Cover's premature effort to "make peace with violence." There may be a "tragic limit to the common meaning that can be achieved" in the law of even a democratic society.[93] But in the past two decades we have experienced a significant retreat from the effort to reach those limits. While it is essential to recognize the forms of violence that guarantee the effective operation of law, and assure their institutional support, it is a mistake to reify the current descent of punishment into vengeance and waste management as the inevitable face of law's violence.

Notes

1. See Marc Mauer, *Americans Behind Bars: The International Use of Incarceration, 1992–3* (Washington D.C.: The Sentencing Project, 1994).

2. See Stan C. Proband, "Jail and Prison Populations Continued to Grow in 1996," *Over Crowded Times*, 8 (1997): 5–6.

3. See Marc Mauer and Tracy Huling, *Young Black Men and the Criminal Justice System: Five Years Later* (Washington D.C.: The Sentencing Project, 1995).

4. In recent work, I have begun to explore a complex of trends, not only the growing prison population but also the role of criminal violence, fear of crime, and the valorization of the experience of victimization, which seem to be transforming the way Americans govern themselves. I call this "governing through

crime." See Jonathan Simon, "Governing through Crime," in *The Crime Conundrum: Essays on Criminal Justice*, ed. Lawrence M. Friedman and George Fisher (Boulder: Westview Press, 1997).

5. Robert Cover, "Violence and the Word," *Yale Law Journal* 95 (1986): 1601, 1607.

6. The term "penality," which is not a misspelling of "penalty," references the ensemble of practices, discourses, and institutions through which penalties in a particular time and place are articulated and imposed. See David Garland, *Punishment and Modern Society* (Chicago: University of Chicago Press, 1990), 20–21.

7. Cover did recognize that law's violence could not be treated as generic and his argument is directed explicitly to the peculiarities of the United States and its political culture ("Violence and the Word," 1607–8).

8. The final episode reveals that Maghoohan is himself Number One. On some level this explains why the system is reluctant to undertake violent action against him, at the same time it invokes the truism that in democratic societies the people are sovereign.

9. "University Does a U-Turn on Jailed Ex-Student's Fate," *Roanoke Times & World News*, 22 June 1996, sec. A4. The University of South Florida did not take a consistently punitive attitude toward student crime. When a star basketball player at the school was accused of rape by another student, the University tried to keep the story from the police and media, and permitted the accused to play while ignoring their own disciplinary procedures. When the issue finally came to light, Borkowski was quoted describing the alleged assault as a "lover's quarrel." In the view of one editorial columnist, the University's action in the Taborsky case was premised not on retributive outrage but a desire to assure future corporate sponsors of their full loyalty. See Martin Dyckman, "A Justice System Gone Awry," *St. Petersburg Times*, 11 June 1996, sec. 9A.

10. Mireya Navarro, "Dispute Turns a Researcher Into an Inmate," *New York Times*, national edition, 9 June 1996, sec. A22.

11. Martin Dyckman, "A Justice System Gone Awry," *St. Petersburg Times*, 11 June 1996, sec. 9A.

12. In September of 1997, a Florida court formally terminated his probation removing the threat of reconfinement on his theft conviction. See, "Ex-Researcher Wins Challenge, Chemist's Probation Ends, But He Vows to Fight Patent Issue," *Florida Today*, 29 October 1997. Taborsky continues to struggle to have his conviction nullified.

13. Taborsky, ironically, was a refugee from the former Czechoslovakia who came to the United States with his parents in 1968 after the Soviet invasion of that country. His family, far from rejecting him after his conviction, saw his resistance to the university as a continuation of their own legacy. According to his father, Jiri Taborsky, "In some five hundred years of the recorded history of my family, you will not find anyone who abdicated his rights or liberties, may it have been under the king, the emperor, the republic, the Nazi occupation or the communist regime." See Monica Davey, "Researcher's Long Battle with USF Rooted in Family," *St. Petersburg Times*, 29 July 1996, sec. 1A.

14. Herbert Marcuse, *One Dimensional Man: Studies in the Ideology of Advanced Industrial Society* (Boston: Beacon Press, 1964), 59.

15. Michel Foucault, *The History of Sexuality, Volume. 1: An Introduction*, trans. Robert Hurley (New York: Random House, 1978), 143.

16. Ibid., 136–7.

17. Ibid., 137.

18. Bureau of Justice Statistics, *Sourcebook of Criminal Justice Statistics, 1994* (Washington, D.C.: National Institute of Justice, 1996), 615.

19. Allen J. Beck, "Prisoners in 1999," *Bureau of Justice Statistics Bulletin* August 2000, NCJ 183476 (Washington, D.C.: U.S. Department of Justice).

20. Bureau of Justice Statistics, *Correctional Populations, 1995* (Washington, D.C.: National Institute of Justice, 1997), 1.

21. Sourcebook of Criminal Justice Statistics Online, http://www.albany.edu/sourcebook/1995/pdf/t687.pdf.

22. See Louis Althusser, *Lenin and Philosophy, and Other Essays*, trans. Ron Brewer (New York: Monthly Review Press, 1971); Michel Foucault, *Discipline and Punish: The Birth of the Prison*, trans. Alan Sheridan (New York: Pantheon, 1977); Steven Lukes, *Power: A Radical View* (New York: MacMillan, 1974).

23. Robert Cover published this article as "The Supreme Court, 1982 Term—Foreword: *Nomos* and Narrative" in *Harvard Law Review* 97 no. 4 (1983). All subsequent notes will refer to this work by its shortened title, "*Nomos* and Narrative."

24. See David Kairys, ed., *The Politics of Law: A Progressive Critique* (New York: Pantheon, 1982).

25. See Alexander M. Bickel, ed., *The Least Dangerous Branch: The Supreme Court at the Bar of Politics* (Indianapolis: Bobbs-Merrill, 1962); John Hart Ely, *Democracy and Distrust* (New York: Norton, 1980).

26. See Ronald M. Dworkin, *Law's Empire* (Cambridge, Mass.: Belknap Press, 1986); Philip C. Bobbitt, *Constitutional Fate: Theory of the Constitution* (New York: Oxford University Press, 1982).

27. See E. P. Thompson, *Whigs and Hunters: The Origin of the Black Act* (New York: Pantheon, 1975); "Symposium: Law and Ideology" *Law & Society Review* 22, no. 4 (1988).

28. Cover, "Violence and the Word," 1601, 1617.

29. Ibid., 1628.

30. Ibid., 1601.

31. Austin Sarat and Thomas R. Kearns, "Making Peace with Violence: Robert Cover on Law and Legal Theory," in *Law's Violence*, ed. Austin Sarat and Thomas R. Kearns (Ann Arbor: University of Michigan Press, 1992).

32. Cover, "Violence and the Word," 1601, 1628.

33. Ibid., 1629.

34. Ibid., 1609.

35. "At some point in this case, Warren McCleskey doubtless asked his lawyer whether a jury was likely to sentence him to die. A candid reply to this question would have been disturbing. First, counsel would have to tell McCleskey that few

of the details of the crime or of McCleskey's past criminal conduct were more important than the fact that his victim was white" (*McCleskey v. Kemp*, 481 U.S. 279, 320, [1987], Justice Brennan, dissenting).

36. Cover, "Violence and the Word," 1618.

37. See Tom Tyler, *Why People Obey the Law* (New Haven: Yale University Press, 1990).

38. Elaine Scarry, *The Body in Pain: The Making and Unmaking of the World* (New York: Oxford University Press, 1985), cited in Robert Cover, "Violence and the Word," 1601–2.

39. Cover, "Violence and the Word," 1607.

40. The Supreme Court accepted this as true in *McCleskey v. Kemp*, even while declining to find the death penalty unconstitutional under such conditions.

41. Black and Hispanic inmates accounted for 61.9 percent of the prisoners held in U.S. state and federal prisons as of year end 1999. See Beck, "Prisoners in 1999," *Bureau of Justice Statistics Bulletin*, 9.

42. See Michael Tonry, *Malign Neglect—Race, Crime, and Punishment in America* (New York: Oxford University Press, 1995).

43. Jerome G. Miller, *Search and Destroy: African American Males in the Criminal Justice System* (New York: Cambridge University Press, 1996), 52.

44. Ibid., 54.

45. Regina Austin, " 'The Black Community,' Its Lawbreakers, and a Politics of Indentification," *Southern California Law Review* 65 (1992): 1769; Paul Butler, "Racially Based Jury Nullification: Black Power in the Criminal Justice System," *Yale Law Journal* 105 (1995): 677; Tracey L. Meares, "Charting Race and Class Differences in Attitudes Toward Drug Legalization and Law Enforcement: Lessons for Federal Criminal Law," *Buffalo Criminal Law Review* 1 (1997): 137.

46. "Federal Prison Lockdown Ordered Nationwide as Inmates Set Fires, Riot," *Corrections Digest* 26, no. 43 (1995): 1.

47. See Emile Durkheim, *The Division of Labor in Society* (New York: Free Press, 1933).

48. Others included chain-gang-like penal work-crews and transportation for forced labor far from home.

49. Erving Goffman, *Asylums: Studies of Total Institutions* (New York: John Wiley & Sons, 1961); David J. Rothman, *The Discovery of the Asylum* (Boston: Little Brown, 1971); Michel Foucault, *Discipline and Punish*. See also, Michael Ignatieff, *A Just Measure of Pain: The Penitentiary in the Industrial Revolution* (London: Penguin Books, 1978) and Dario Melossi and Massimo Pavarini, *The Prison and the Factory: Origins of the Penitentiary System* (Totowa, N.J.: MacMillan Press, 1981).

50. Cover himself cited Foucault ("Violence and the Word," 1601, 1609, note 20).

51. Ibid., 1609.

52. See Gresham Sykes, *The Society of Captives: A Study of a Maximum Security Prison* (Princeton: Princeton University Press, 1958); James B. Jacobs, *Stateville: The Penitentiary in Mass Society* (Chicago: University of Chicago Press, 1977).

53. Cover, "Violence and the Word," 1613–14.

54. Ibid., 1619.

55. Donald Clemmer, *The Prison Community* (New York: Holt, Rinehart & Winston, 1940).

56. Clemmer's observations were based on one prison, but his claims about prisonization have been supported in other empirical tests. For one such body of research and one of the best discussions of the prison culture issue generally, see Stanton Wheeler, "Socialization in Correctional Institutions," in *Socialization in Correctional Institutions*, ed. David Goslin (New York: Rand McNally, 1969).

57. Gresham Sykes, *The Society of Captives*.

58. Ibid., 49–50.

59. See John Irwin, *Prisons in Turmoil* (New York: John Wiley & Sons, 1980).

60. Charles M. Sennott, "Prison's Hidden Horror," *Boston Globe*, 1 May 1994. (Westlaw, 1994 WL 5969383)

61. *Madrid v. Gomez*, 889 F. Supp. (1995) 1146.

62. Ibid., 1155–56.

63. Ibid., 1167.

64. Ibid., 1171.

65. See Marx Arax and Mark Gladstone, "Grand Jury Indicts Eight for Abuses Inside State Prison Corrections: Federal Officials allege guards set up fights at Corcoran, using one as a pretext to kill an inmate," *Los Angeles Times*, 27 February 1998, sec. A1.

66. 18 U.S.C.A. s. 3553 provides that federal sentences should serve the following purposes: "To reflect the seriousness of the offense, to promote respect for the law, and to provide just punishment for the offense; . . . to afford adequate deterrence to criminal conduct; . . . to protect the public from further crimes of the defendant; and . . . to provide the defendant with needed educational or vocational training, medical care, or other correctional treatment in the most effective manner."

67. For example, in *Morrissey v. Brewer* 408 U.S. 471, 484 (1972), Chief Justice Burger discussed the rehabilitative orientation of parole and probation as one reason to provide less due-process protection in parole and probation revocation procedures.

68. David J. Rothman, *Conscience and Convenience: The Asylum and Its Alternatives in Progressive America* (Boston: Little Brown, 1980).

69. See, generally, Jacobs, *Stateville: The Penitentiary in Mass Society*.

70. The enormous influence of the Holocaust and the responsive rise of human rights rhetoric on the promotion of rehabilitative penology by organizations like the United Nations is too rarely noted.

71. American Friends Service Committee, *Struggle for Justice: A Report on Crime and Punishment in America* (New York: Hill and Wang, 1972); Andrew von Hirsch, *Doing Justice: The Choice of Punishments* (New York: Basic Books, 1976).

72. California Penal Code, s. 1170(a)(1)(West 1996).

73. The focus here is on what is often called "general deterrence." A somewhat different logic is introduced if the goal is to deter the specific offender from future offenses once released from prison, a strategy known as "special deterrence."

74. Malcolm Feeley and Jonathan Simon, "The New Penology: Notes on the Emerging Strategy of Corrections and Its Implications," *Criminology* 30 (1992): 449.

75. Cover, "Violence and the Word," 1601, 1609.

76. See Jonathan Simon and Malcolm Feeley "True Crime: The New Penology and Public Discourse on Crime," in *Punishment and Social Control: Essays in Honor of Sheldon Messinger*, ed. Thomas G. Blomberg and Stanley Cohen (New York: Aldine De Gruyter, 1995), 147–80.

77. Cover, "Violence and the Word," 1601, 1628.

78. 18 U.S.C. s. 3551 et seq.

79. 28 U.S.C. s. 994(b)(2).

80. 18 U.S.C. s. 3551(b).

81. A recent Supreme Court decision suggests that judges may have somewhat more discretion in departing than many have previously believed. In *Koon v. United States*, 116 S.Ct. 2035, 2053 (1996), the Supreme Court held that Congress did not intend to eliminate judicial discretion to individualize sentences in regard to factors not considered by the guidelines. Ironically, the Court acted in the case of the white Los Angeles police officers who were convicted of violating the federal rights of Rodney King by delivering a severe beating recorded in a now-famous camcorder tape. The district court reduced the sentence of Koon and the other officers on four grounds. The Supreme Court upheld two of them, including the fact that victim misconduct played a substantial role in the crime and the fact that the defendants were susceptible to abuse in prison.

82. In 1995, 68 percent of all downward departures from the guidelines were from cooperation with the government. See Joan Biskupic and Mary Pat Flaherty, "Justice By the Numbers: Loss of Discretion Fuels Fustration on Federal Bench," *Washington Post*, 8 October 1996, sec. A1.

83. Ibid.

84. Bureau of Justice Statistics, *Sourcebook of Criminal Justice Statistics, 1994*, 13–14. Capacity is an imprecise notion. The Bureau of Justice Statistics asks states for several different measures of capacity and then compares their current populations. The numbers above are based on the highest possible measure of capacity. If a lower one is used, twice as many prisons are at 150 percent capacity or above.

85. Ibid.

86. It is another sign of his lack of historical vision that Cover says nothing about this concerted judicial effort to control law's violence in prisons. See, James B. Jacobs, *Stateville: The Penitentiary in Mass Society*; Malcolm M. Feeley and Edward L. Rubin, *Judicial Policy Making and the Modern State: How the Courts Reformed America's Prisons* (New York: Cambridge University Press, 1998).

87. 18 U.S.C.A s. 3626 (1997).

88. *Vasquez v. Harris*, 503 U.S. 1000 (1992).

89. Stephen Bright, "Political Attacks on the Judiciary: Can Justice Be Done Amidst Efforts to Intimidate and Remove Justices from Office for Unpopular Decisions?" *New York University Law Review* 72 (1997): 308.

90. Ron Word, "Flames Erupt from Inmate's Head, A.G. Says It's a Deterrent," Associated Press, 25 March 1997.

91. Cover, "Violence and the Word," 1601–2.

92. Ibid., 1621.

93. Ibid., 1624.

CHAPTER THREE

Making Peace with Violence

ROBERT COVER ON LAW AND LEGAL THEORY

Austin Sarat and Thomas R. Kearns

V IOLENCE," Walter Benjamin argues, "violence crowned by fate, is the origin of law."[1] Violence is a perverse utopia of action without form and instinct without deliberation[2] from which all law—natural or positive—is the fall.[3] Absent the threat, prospect, or possibility of disorder and aggression in the worlds that all of us inhabit, law, as we know it, would be unnecessary.[4] And what is law, after all, but a partially realized promise[5] to overcome disorder and aggression, tame and domesticate force, and subject action and instinct to reason and will?[6]

Violence stands before the law, unruly; it defies law to protect us from its cruelest consequences.[7] It demands that law respond in kind, and requires law to traffic in its own brand of force and coercion.[8] It is thus that point of departure from which complete departure is impossible.[9] It is the task of law and of much legal theory to insist, nonetheless, on the difference between the force that law uses and the unruly force beyond its borders.[10] Legal theorists name the superiority of the former by calling it legitimate.[11] Such naming suggests that violence can be cleansed, if not purified, by its contact with law.[12]

Yet the violence that calls law into being and becomes part of its arsenal makes law, or at least the achievement of particular kinds of law, impossible. It both provokes the hope of law and defeats the hope that law can be other-than-violence.[13] Violence, indispensable as it is to the generation of law, casts a persistent shadow over it. Violence requires us to ask how, if at all, the force of law differs from the force it is called into being to regulate, as well as whether law can accommodate and control violence without becoming a captive of its own violent instincts. While the threat of force provides a constant justification of and apology for law, it is also a constant reminder of what all law really is. "[I]n this very violence," Benjamin writes, "something rotten in law is revealed."[14]

All too often, all too much legal theory has asserted and attended to the alleged legitimacy of law's violence without paying heed to the "rottenness" that violence reveals and to the price that it exacts from law.[15] In this chapter we attend, in particular, to that price; we ask what difference violence makes to, and in, law, and whether law can ever make peace with violence. Can law do homicidal deeds[16] without itself being "jurispathic"?[17] What possibilities for law are precluded by its continuing reliance on force and coercion? Against those who believe that law can tame and conquer violence, we attend to the ways in which law is conquered by violence. We do so by carefully examining the work of Robert Cover.[18]

We focus on Cover because he was both a visionary legal thinker who saw law as a bridge between the world-of-the-present and the world-of-our-imaginings and our aspirations,[19] and someone who nonetheless provided the most compelling contemporary account of the relationship between law and violence. In Cover we find both a critic of and an apologist for law's violence; we find an insistence that law be different from, and more than, violence—and that law lead human society toward toleration, respect, and community, combined with a reluctant embrace of legal force. In Cover we find a self-proclaimed anarchist, "with anarchy understood to mean the absence of rulers not the absence of law,"[20] nonetheless seeking to identify the conditions for the *effective*, but domesticated, organization and deployment of law's violence.[21]

Cover was hopeful about law even in the shadow of violence. We are much less hopeful. He sought to acknowledge law's violence and temper or domesticate it in a reconstruction of the premises of law's relationship to society. We, however, fear that the violence of law stands in the way of such a reconstruction. To use his own language, he believed that law could be homicidal without being "jurispathic." We do not share his belief. While we admire Cover for taking the violence of law seriously and for facing up to the way that violence is both an indispensable feature of law and, at the same time, deeply antagonistic to it, we do not think that he saw fully the difficulties of accommodating violence and law.[22]

How could this self-proclaimed "anarchist" and visionary legal thinker nonetheless embrace and defend the violence of law?[23] How could Cover so clearly understand the dangers of organizing and deploying violence and not recoil from the danger that such violence would destroy any normative vision that opposed it? How could he make peace with law's violence? These are the questions that we seek to answer about Cover, and, through Cover, about the violence of law itself.

THE EMERGENCE OF "LAW'S VIOLENCE": A CONCEPTUAL REVISION

Despite the obvious importance of the relationship between law and violence, it is a subject about which little is written and little is known.[24] Though there are several famous explorations of the coercive and the punitive dimensions of law,[25] contemporary jurisprudence, at least until Cover, largely avoided the subject.[26] Cover, in essence, reinvented the subject of violence and its relationship to law; indeed, it may seem odd, but we think it is not too much of an exaggeration, to claim that before Cover's writings on law's violence, the topic was in danger of being lost to contemporary legal theory.[27] By this we mean not only that prior to his work, contemporary writers had largely lost their taste for the subject. Though it is true that law's violence was receiving little attention in legal theory, this was hardly the result of mere inadvertence or neglect. Rather, it was a consequence of a purposive effort to free thought about law from its fixation on law-as-force, to kill once and for all the distracting ghost of Leviathan. Meaning and normativity, not physics and force, were, before Cover's intervention, fast becoming the centerpieces of law-talk.[28] Violence, where it was noted at all, was treated as marginal or vestigial.[29] In this setting, it was no easy matter to celebrate the death of Hobbes's beast and yet resurrect for renewed study the continuing and unavoidable reality of law's violence. But such was part of Cover's accomplishment.

Cover, though he did not believe that law was force and only force, insisted that law's violence was neither vestigial nor marginal. He claimed that all "legal interpretive acts signal and occasion the imposition of violence upon others: A judge articulates her understanding of a text, and as a result, somebody loses his freedom, his property, his children, even his life."[30] This is certainly not news to even the most casual observer of the legal system. As Karl Olivecrona put it almost fifty years before Cover,

> According to an old and well-known line of thought, law and force are regarded as opposite things. Force as such is put in opposition to law. In view of the extensive use of force, under the name of law, in the state organization, the contrast is, however, obviously false. Law as applied in real life includes a certain kind of force. It is organized, regulated force used against criminals, debtors and others according to patterns laid down by law-givers.[31]

Indeed, by Cover's own account, to observe that "neither legal interpretation nor the violence it occasions may be properly understood apart from one another," is merely to state the "obvious."[32] Yet he wrote about violence, about the violence in and around law, and its inseparable connection to interpretation[33] as a bracing reminder of what he knew would seem obvious once stated. He sought to bring to mind what he feared would be too easily forgotten in the rush to assimilate law into humanistic scholarship,[34] namely what he called, "the organized social practice of violence."[35]

When Cover contemplated that practice, he confronted a fault line that gave law a shape and character not replicable in any interpretive activity that did not make its mark on bodies.[36] When Cover contemplated violence he understood the fancy, some might say fanciful, way in which interpretation, because it is never entirely innocent nor entirely harmless, does violence;[37] he understood and acknowledged how contests over meaning always carry the possibility, and the danger, that one will prevail and extinguish all others. But, the violence that most sustained and engaged his interest (and the violence discussed in this chapter) was the brute physical force available to, and used by, the state against those who disobey or defy its authority.[38]

Such force translates routinely—though not without studied and careful organization, the marshaling of strong justifications, and reliance on recognizable roles and structures—into pain, blood and death, words that Cover himself used as if they were synonyms for violence. "In this," Cover insisted, judges and others who wield the power of the state "are different from poets, from critics, from artists."[39] Showing impatience with those who insist on a strong resemblance between the violence done by judges and the interpretive violence done by poets, critics, and artists, Cover warned that "it will not do to get precious—to insist on the violence of strong poetry, and strong poets. Even the violence of weak judges is utterly real—in need of no interpretation, no critic to reveal it—an immediate, palpable reality. Take a short trip to your local prison and see."[40] The violence highlighted by Cover in this passage is a violence in need of no mediating representation; it is transparent, and it speaks for itself. Such violence renders all representation both unnecessary and inadequate.[41] It is a violence that can be seen and felt directly, a violence quite unlike the "psychoanalytic violence of literature or the metaphorical characterization of literary critics and philosophers."[42]

Cover was not much interested in splitting epistemological hairs when it came to the conversation about violence. He appealed to something more immediate, more authentic, than a debate about the relationship between violence and its representation. Go "see" is what he said. In that simple, innocent admonition he identified what was, for him, beyond question a central experience with and knowledge about law, an experience and a knowledge instantiated in police and their weapons, jailers and their prisons. He warned legal scholars of the "danger in forgetting the limits which are intrinsic to . . . legal interpretation, in exaggerating the extent to which any interpretation rendered as part of the act of state violence can ever constitute a common and coherent meaning."[43] He wanted them to open their eyes and see what he, Cover, believed could only be ignored in a perilous act of willful blindness.

For Cover, the continuing tragedy of law is the way in which violence "distorts" meaning. Meaning in the shadow of a violent reality can never be pure. But to make this stick as a statement about legal practice, Cover was committed to the search for pure or undistorted meaning. As he put it,

> [F]rom the mundane flow of our real commonalities, we may purport to distill some purer essence of unity, to create in our imaginations a *nomos* completely transparent—built from crystals completely pure. In this transparent *nomos*, that which must be done, the meaning of that which must be done, and the sources of common commitment to the doing of it stand bare, in need of no explication, no interpretation—obvious at once and to all. As long as it stands revealed, this dazzling clarity of legal meaning can harbor no mere interpretation.[44]

In the face of such a commitment, one might ask Cover to identify some, any, realm in which meaning is, or can be, pure.[45] Because even poets and critics exist within communities and conventions that "leave traces" on their interpretive activity, the search for pure meaning is a search in vain; our focus must be not on the fact of distortion that violence introduces, but the *way* in which violence distorts when compared to other distorting factors. This is a question that Cover's work raises but does not address.[46]

Cover's interest in the violence of law was, however, not just the product of an arid academic debate. It emerged as a somewhat surprising expression of his utopian imaginings as well as his own deep doubts and anxieties. His writing about law's violence displays a profound engagement with the possibilities of law itself.[47] He wrote as if by insistence and repetition he could help his readers know and feel the possibilities for human social life that are all too often erased by law's violent impositions. But he also wrote about law's violence as a way of noting and taking seriously the unreconstructed everyday reality of despair and pain to which the law responds and contributes.[48]

Cover achieved a crucial conceptual breakthrough, penetrating a venerable intellectual deposit that nearly succeeded in completely concealing law's violence as violence. According to this accretion, when violence is made part of law, it is transformed by being made orderly and predictable. It becomes something other than violence, something perhaps more properly called "legitimate force."[49] This transformation, this remarkable alchemy—while now commonly viewed as a questionable consequence of equally questionable views in legal and moral theory—threatened to become imperviously protected as a definitional truism, as if it were true by meaning alone that law's force is never the same as violence.[50] In this view, while explosions, storms, and persons can be violent, law, no matter how great, vicious, and wanton its use of force, cannot (*by definition*) be violent.[51]

Of course, law's force remains in full view—no semantic gerrymandering can make it vanish—so whether legal coercion is called "force" or "violence" hardly matters, or so it might seem. Yet it is, then, an achievement of considerable importance that Cover was able to rescue the phrase "legal violence" from the status of near-oxymoron and almost single-handedly reverse received assumptions regarding law and its own violence. However, his success in reviving the subject of law's violence did not come solely from engaging in what must have struck some of his readers as a vaguely churlish if not perverse abuse of language.

This abuse of language, however, obviously mattered to Cover; why did he so pointedly and repeatedly write not of law's legitimate force but of its violence? We think it was to call attention to, and challenge, the easy and apparently widespread assumption that there is something automatically (or prima facie) legitimating about law's force, that law's force is normatively different, that it is entitled to at least a presumption of warrantability. Contrary to any such presumption, Cover believed that law's violence is deeply anomalous. In Cover's view, then, there is no "natural" reason to regard law's violence as different, as being entitled to a favorable presumption regarding its legitimacy. To the contrary, there are much stronger reasons to be ill at ease with law's violence, to regard it as an inharmonious feature of law, one that unavoidably wars with law's constructive purposes and its desperately needed contributions to social and cultural meanings.

"[B]etween the idea and reality of common meaning," Cover wrote, "falls the shadow of the violence of the law, itself."[52] This one sentence reveals, with great simplicity and directness, Cover's awareness of the world-altering reality of law's violence, a reality so disturbing that its mere "shadow" stands as a barrier between present experience and the realization of an "idea." Yet Cover accepted and defended, rather than denounced, the violence of law,[53] and he attempted to reconcile that violence with law itself.

Thus, to read Cover on violence is to be pulled in different directions. In his work one finds a mournful story of inescapable violence set against utopian possibility, and an appeal to scholars to enter the shadows and explore law's violent underside.[54] One also finds an acknowledgment that the violence of law is, despite its tragic character, an aspect of law than can and should be tolerated. Cover refused to give in to the violence that he believed was an inevitable part of law. He refused to recognize, as we believe one inevitably must recognize, the way in which violence distorts law and limits the possibilities/prospects of law itself. To understand why and how he did so we first take up his thoughts about the nature of law and its place in social life, and then we consider his writing on the need and justification for an apparatus of force that claims the name law.

Law in a Normative Universe

Cover's confrontation with and description of law's violence is part of a larger project in which he advanced a distinctive conception of law while exploring classic themes in political and legal theory—meaning and power, freedom and order, community and state.[55] Cover's political and legal theory begins with the proposition, "We inhabit a *nomos*—a normative world. We constantly create and maintain a world of right and wrong, of lawful and unlawful, of valid and void"[56] "*[N]omos*," Cover continued, "is as much a part of 'our world' as is the physical universe of mass, energy, and momentum. Indeed, our apprehension of the structure of the normative world is no less fundamental than our apprehension of the structure of the physical world."[57]

This image of normativity as the basic condition of human social life stands in stark contrast to the liberal image of society without law as a relentless war-of-all-against-all.[58] For Cover, the world outside law is an already constituted social world of communities and associations, each articulating a distinct vision of the good and encouraging commitment to that vision, rather than a world of isolated or alienated individuals.[59] It is a world of vision and commitment, of shared values and shared aspirations rather than opposed interests; it is a nomos. The task of law is to participate in that nomos, and to support the generation of normative vision and the life of commitment; the task of law is to tolerate, respect, and encourage normative diversity even when that diversity generates opposition to the rules and prescriptions of law itself. The danger of law is that, faced with such diversity, it will insist on the superiority of its rules and prescriptions and, in so doing, that it will circumscribe the nomos.

For Cover, law is more than the rules and prescriptions enacted by state institutions.[60] State law should itself embody and articulate a normative vision. This is the particular strength of a constitutional legal order like that of the United States since, in Cover's view, its constitution is a statement of values rather than a body of rules.[61] Law, properly understood, contributes to the articulation of present ways of being as well as to the identification of future possibilities. It arises neither in contract, in the arms-length relations of persons seeking to forge common goals, as liberals would have it,[62] nor in the commands of governments, rulers, or sovereigns.[63]

Law, Cover claimed, links nomos with narrative.[64] As Cover put it, "[L]aw and narrative are inseparably related."[65] Associated with every prescription is an insistence that it be located in a discourse, that it be supplied with "history and destiny, beginning and end, explanation and purpose."[66] Law, then, "includes not only a corpus juris, but also a language and a mythos—narratives in which the corpus is located," and narratives that "establish paradigms for behavior" and describe "a repertoire of moves—a lexicon of normative action."[67] The narratives in which law is embedded include, too, images and ideals and counterfactuals about what is not the case but what might or should be: "A nomos is a present world constituted by a system of tension between reality and vision."[68]

Cover believed that, insofar as the health of the nomos is concerned, there need be "no state."[69] State law provides, for Cover, but one among many sources of meaning, a source that cannot simply by virtue of its connection to the state claim that its normative vision is correct, or superior to visions articulated in other places.[70] It provides just one among many visions of the good, one among many bridges between the world as it is and the alternative realities that comprise the human image of the future.[71] Thus, when a judge interprets the law of the state and gives it meaning that counters interpretations and meanings identified in communities beyond the state, what makes the meaning provided by the judge work in the world is something other than its hermeneutic superiority. Such status cannot be guaranteed in advance, and is, in Cover's view, not regularly achieved.

If we are to accept and defer to the interpretations of judges, the reasons for so doing must be found elsewhere. In this search for other reasons, Cover held up a high standard for measuring the impact of state law even as he began to anticipate tensions between the state and other sources of law. "A great legal civilization," he maintained, "is marked by the richness of the *nomos* in which it is located and which it helps to constitute."[72]

But a great legal civilization is made rich, as we have already seen, by the diversity of the visions and commitments it contains. And in every nomos "[i]t is the multiplicity of laws, the fecundity of the jurisgenerative principle, that creates the problem to which the court and the state are the solution."[73]

For Cover, it is not too little order but too much order, not too thin a moral world but too thick a moral world, that, in his view, creates the problematic of state and law. Nevertheless, the problematic of the state and its laws begins, as it does in liberal political thought, with the specter of conflict. In such a world Cover believed that state law should play a modest, a restrained, a "system-maintaining" role.[74] It should be tolerant and respectful of alternative normative systems rather than trying to make them bend, lest they be destroyed by the ferocious force that the state routinely deploys.[75]

In such a world, law, and more precisely state law, is, according to Cover, always pulled in two directions, and, as a result, there is "an essential tension in law."[76] On the one hand, state law participates in the generation of normative meaning; on the other, state law plays in the domain of social control and uses violence to enforce just one (namely its own) conception of order.[77] Meaning-making, meaning-generating normative activity in plural communities and associations, sits uneasily and complicates the task of maintaining order. Thus, as Cover put it, "[T]here is a radical dichotomy between the social organization of law as power and the organization of law as meaning. . . . The uncontrolled character of meaning exercises a destabilizing influence upon power."[78] Meaning is always greater than power can accommodate, and where the law resorts to power, it acknowledges the limits of meaning.

This formulation is in many ways quite typical of Cover's work. Meaning is, by definition, "uncontrolled"; power, left to itself, is stable. Thus meaning and power, or interpretation and violence, exist separately, as forces in tension, working on and against each other. Meaning, because it is "uncontrolled," is the domain of freedom; "the social organization of law as power" is the domain of *order*. The basic problem of society, politics, and law remains—despite Cover's effort to distance himself from this formulation—the problem as defined by liberalism,[79] the problem of freedom and order, restated and redescribed no doubt, but reinscribed nonetheless.[80]

The internal coherence of systems of meaning and the order already within freedom, as well as the fragility of power and the possibilities of freedom already within the domain of order, seem to escape Cover's gaze just as they escape the gaze of liberalism. For Cover, only the realm of meaning and interpretation is fluid; it, and only it, is, or can be, the realm of the plural, the possible, the imagined, the free. Yet we know, following Foucault,[81] that hierarchies of power proliferate in all meaning-generating activities.[82] Moreover, despite Cover's own efforts to interpret and give meaning to the domain of legal violence, power and violence seem, on his account, to exist outside meaning and interpretation. Thus, the social, political, and legal world can only be a world in tension, moving now toward one pole, and then toward another, a world where meaning is always a threat to power, and where power is always the death of meaning.

Judges, it turns out, play a central role in the achievement of Cover's vision of a diverse, normatively rich culture and a restrained state, and they are crucial, in Cover's understanding, to the place of violence in law. They sit at the fault line between meaning, the interpretive possibilities of the legal text (freedom), and power, the capacity to take one meaning and through force make it *the* meaning (order). Yet, in all their actions, they are "people of violence."[83]

There are two linked senses in which Cover thought of judges as people of violence. The first involves the literal deployment of force that is available to judges as state officials.[84] Judges are people of violence because they are able to bring physical force to bear in making their interpretive acts work in the world.[85] In a second sense, however, judges become people of violence when they repress and reduce the rich normativity of the social world: "Because of the violence they command, judges characteristically do not create law, but kill it. Theirs is a jurispathic office. Confronting the luxuriant growth of a hundred legal traditions, they assert that *this one* is law and destroy or try to destroy all the rest."[86] Cover called upon judges, and the law they represent, to be less "jurispathic," to be less insistent on singularity or hierarchy among normative visions; he called on them to stop circumscribing the nomos, and to "invite new worlds."[87]

Seen from the outside, from the perspective of the nomos, and from the perspective of worlds yet to be, the violence of state law is a strong impediment and an important barrier. That force is, by Cover's account, unnecessarily destructive of the world-affirming, world-building normative activities and commitments of communities and associations outside the state. It is, in addition, incompatible with narrativity, with the evolving network of beliefs, practices, and understandings that constitute or make possible a nomos. It puts an end to interpretation and meaning-construction; it cuts off conversation. It does not elicit and evolve; it concludes. Violence puts an end to the hermeneutic impulses that generate narrative.[88]

Law's violence is, as a result, a continuous threat to law's principal involvement in the production and maintenance of meaning in diverse normative communities. State law, because of its peace-making and boundary-keeping roles, especially threatens to become imperial in character; its prescriptions purport to be general and universal, requiring or forbidding what must or must not be done if there is to be law at all. It is easy for statist judges to become so intent on order, so insistent that only one law, the state's own, shall prevail, that the efforts and commitments of other rich sources of meaning, other normative enclaves, are needlessly limited or destroyed. Here law's violence threatens law itself by being immoderate in its regulation of the sources of law.[89]

Law's violence signals, at some level and to some degree, a normative insufficiency, an inability of the controlling narratives to control. Or, it may signal the inability to generate and maintain a unified nomos in a world of competing nomoi. In either case, the employment of force to retain control immediately raises questions about the normative basis, or the justification, for that force. For if the use of force is required because of an indeterminacy or erosion in normative understandings, it would appear that those understandings are unavailable to ground and justify violence.

Legal force is perhaps most transparently problematic when it is used against opposing normative orders, since it is clear that taking refuge in what Cover calls "(t)he self-referential supremacy of each system" contributes nothing to resolving the normative issue at hand. Far from being a genuine justification, an appeal to such supremacy is only an artless refusal to engage the justificatory question. The "hermeneutic of jurisdiction" simply insists on order above all else.[90] It does nothing to establish normative superiority. It is difficult to see how law's violence, which lacks this quality, is to be justified to those against whom it would be used. It appears, then, that by Cover's account of law, force used against competing normative orders is inescapably questionable and in a certain sense lawless.

Too often, too routinely, judges defer to that violence; too often, too routinely, judges aggressively assert the supremacy of state law. In either posture, Cover believed that jurispathic state law is needlessly destructive of the nomos it is required to regulate. Such excess constitutes a serious danger to the world of meaning. Despite the "radical instability" of the paedeic world, "warring sects" are the wellspring of normative commitment; they make life normatively significant. To destroy or limit them is to threaten the principal sources of articulated value, commitment, and aspiration. Law threatens to kill off what its very existence presupposes— a world that is normatively rich, normatively diverse, and normatively inventive. That violence stands in the way of tolerance, if not respect. Given Cover's commitment to tolerance, respect, and plurality, one expects a rejection of violence and a vision of law without force or coercion.

In Cover's exploration of the relationship between law and other normative orders, one does indeed find dark moments of sadness, of concern, and of critique. Yet Cover cannot imagine law without violence. On the contrary, Cover insists that "the jurisgenerative principle by which legal meaning proliferates in all communities never exists in isolation from violence."[91] And the shadow of that violence is cast as much by the "radical instability" of contesting, meaning-producing normative communities as by self-interested actors in an imaginary state of nature.

The language Cover used to describe a nomos that was unregulated, ungoverned, makes unmistakable his fear of such a place: "Let loose, unfettered, the worlds created would be unstable and sectarian in their social organization, dissociative and incoherent in their discourse, wary and *violent* [emphasis added] in their interactions."[92] Note, too, how he described "*[w]arring* [emphasis added] sects" that wrap themselves in their own special law, in normative worlds where "not all interpretive trajectories are insular."[93] In the presence of such volatile dynamics, the enterprise of "(m)aintaining the world . . . requires no less energy than creating it."[94] In this process, judges, even as they deploy violence, became, for Cover, "people of peace."[95]

Thus, the legal violence that initially seemed so inhospitable to the "nomos" and to the jurisgenerative work of communities and associations within that nomos is imaginatively tamed and transformed. Law's violence is neither an impediment to restraint nor a guarantee of excess. The danger is dissipated and no price is paid for law's intimacy with violence.[96] In this imagined transformation of violence into peace, Cover moved away from critique to restate the liberal apology for the law and its reliance on force.[97]

THE SOCIAL ORGANIZATION OF LAW: ON THE ACHIEVEMENTS OF AN ORDERLY VIOLENCE

Having imaginatively transformed violence into peace, Cover could further imagine that he had made peace between law's violence and the restraint and toleration he thought was so essential to law. Thus, it is not surprising that Cover's other two treatments of law's violence— "Violence and the Word" and "The Bonds of Constitutional Interpretation"—would identify the conditions that make it effective in the world. In those articles, he paid particular attention to the judge now as an important role player in law's social organization, and he described judges "from John Winthrop to Warren Burger . . . [sitting] atop a pyramid of violence. . . ."[98]

As suggested by the metaphor of the pyramid, the conception of social organization at work in "Violence and the Word" is rigidly hierarchical and "formalist in its apparent assumption that the hierarchy of state violence has the same contours as the hierarchy of legal institutions."[99] Given this picture of judges seated at the apex of such a hierarchy, the question almost naturally becomes not so much how judges interpret legal texts, and whether their interpretations circumscribe or invite new worlds, but rather what happens to their interpretations, what happens when the interpretive act is completed. Does anybody listen? Does anybody care? Does anybody respond?

If the answer to those questions were to be no, then we would face a situation in which law could not, or would not, deploy its coercive force, a situation perhaps welcome within the nomos, but quite unwelcome once it is acknowledged that violence and death are already within our society and polity. As Cover himself put it, "To stop short of suffering or imposing violence is to give law up to those who are willing to so act."[100] Or, alternatively, if the answer is no, then it may be that others down the chain of command, deploy coercive force as independent operators, themselves undisciplined, lawless. It is, of course, against both of these possibilities—uncontrollable violence at large in society, or the state as renegade—that the liberal vision of law arrays itself.[101]

If in "*Nomos* and Narrative" Cover seems to ally himself with meaning against power, in "Violence and the Word" and "The Bonds of Constitutional Interpretation " the alliance is at least destabilized and perhaps reversed. "So let us be explicit," Cover states,

> "[i]f it seems a nasty thought that death and pain are at the center of legal interpretation, so be it. It would not be better were there only a community of argument, of readers and writers of texts, of interpreters. As long as death and pain are part of our political world, it is essential that they be at the center of law. The alternative is truly unacceptable—that they be within our polity but outside the discipline of *collective* decision rules and the individual efforts to achieve outcomes through those rules."[102]

In these sentences we see no glimpse of the "nomos," no bold assertion of the possibilities and virtues of a plural society where the threat of conflict is relegated to interactions at the boundaries separating normatively integrated communities. Instead we see in Cover's work the evocation of a Hobbesian nightmare of death and pain undisciplined, inside the body polity but outside the reach of rules.[103] Order, and some semblance of peace, can be achieved only where legal interpretation is embedded in, and is attentive to, what Cover called, conditions of "effective domination."[104] Where such domination is not achieved we face the prospect that people will find themselves in "conditions of reprisal, resistance and revenge."[105]

In Cover's praise of "collective decision rules," and persons seeking to achieve results through "rules," there is a move from Hobbes to Locke, from power against freedom to rules against disorder. Here, too, we see the imagining of a world outside of law used to conjure up and justify the "discipline" of "rules."[106] From this point, with a Hobbesian nightmare as a background condition, the next step in Cover's exploration of law's violence is to inquire about its own discipline, to ask about the adequacy of the Lockean "discipline of *collective* decision rules," and, in addition, to applaud that discipline where it is found.

Such discipline, in which the deployment of force is controlled and coordinated by judges through their interpretations of legal texts, stands in stark contrast to situations of uncontrolled private violence—lynching is the example to which Cover himself referred[107]—and to lawless states in which people "disappear . . . die suddenly and without ceremony in prison, quite apart from any articulated justification and authorization of their demise."[108] Seen from the inside, against the specter of an undisciplined violence, the discipline of collective decision-rules is an achievement to be respected, if not cherished and admired. In Cover's own words, "[w]e have come to expect near perfect coordination of those whose role it is to inflict violence subject to the interpretive decisions of judges. . . . Such a well-coordinated form of violence is an achievement."[109]

Cover's concern was to understand that "achievement" by understanding how judicial interpretations of legal texts get translated into deeds, how judicial words become violent acts. The doing of such deeds and acts means that when judges confront an interpretive problem they really confront two problems not one. The first is, of course, the problem of meaning itself, namely, how to identify and justify a hermeneutically satisfactory, if not superior, rendering of a text.[110] The second is the problem of implementation, namely, how to insure that others act on the basis of, and in the ways prescribed by, an interpretive act.

With respect to the first of these problems—the problem of meaning—Cover again took cognizance of the social organization of law, only this time the social organization of interpretation and justification. No judge, Cover writes, "*acts* alone. . . . The application of legal understanding in our domain of pain and death will always require the active or passive acquiescence of other judicial minds."[111] Before judicial words can be translated into deeds, other judges, whether appellate judges reviewing a trial-court decision or other members of a collegial court, must be convinced that those words represent a reasonable interpretation of a legal text. They must be convinced, in other words, that the mandate for action is justified, that the words supply sufficient justification for violent acts. The community of judges is always a community of interpretation and justification. As Cover put it, "[F]or those who impose the violence, the justification is important, real and carefully cultivated."[112]

Because judges do not themselves do the deeds that their acts authorize, they are dependent on others in preexisting institutional roles to carry out their orders and make their decisions work in the world. Cover illustrates this familiar fact by considering the act of criminal sentencing, an act in which judges are "doing something clearly within their province."[113] That act, however, depends upon a "structure of cooperation" in which "police, jailers or other enforcers . . . restrain the prisoner . . . upon the order of the judge, and guards who will secure the prisoner from rescue and who will protect the judge, prosecutors, witnesses and jailers from revenge."[114] That structure of cooperation must work to overcome substantial cultural and moral inhibitions that curb "the infliction of pain on other people."[115] For Cover, the key fact is that those inhibitions could be overcome "upon the order of the judge."

In such a structure of cooperation, judges do the interpretive work that renders law's deeds of violence "intelligible."[116] In return for their "relatively automatic heed" of the orders of judges,[117] those who carry out those orders are able "to shift to the judge primary moral responsibility for the violence which they themselves carry out."[118] Cover believed that the institutional context of legal interpretation provides, and should provide, a predictable, "though not logically necessary,"[119] set of responses to judicial decisions. It is in the gap between the necessary and the merely predictable that Cover looked to see the way in which interpretation is itself tutored by the need both to activate and, at the same time, control those who actually do law's violence.[120]

As we move from thinking about interpretation to thinking about implementation, one might contemplate two possibilities. In the first, the problem of implementation would be resolved in the interpretive act itself and in the justifications that it provides. Readings of texts would be authoritative, even compelling, providing analyses with which no rational person could disagree. Implementation would be assured as a series of successive readers: first the judge, then the marshall, then the warden, then the executioner—all, albeit independently, read the text in the same way, all embraced the same justifications, and, as a result, all embraced the same commitments. But given Cover's own theory of interpretation, a theory in which the realm of meaning is the realm of freedom rather than authority,[121] it is not surprising that Cover explored a second possibility to understand how judicial readings get translated into deeds.

For him the answer was to be found, in the first instance, in the way judges alter their readings to take into account the likely reactions of others in the chain of command, and, in the second instance, in a structure of offices and roles that assures relatively automatic compliance with any reading that emanates from someone exercising judicial power.[122] With respect to the former, if judges were poets, or literary theorists, their attention to meaning might be innocent. They would be free, like Ronald Dworkin's proverbial Hercules, to act on their own sense of the best theory of meaning or political morality.[123] In so doing they might rescue meaning at the risk of relinquishing control over the apparatus of state violence.

However, judges in the usual, ordinary performance of their duty seek to insure that that apparatus will respond, because, in Cover's view, interpretive acts mean nothing in a legal sense if they have no purchase in the world. Thus judges ordinarily are not free;[124] they can never engage in poetic inattention to things outside the text. Judicial interpretation and the justifications judges provide are always, and must always be, attentive to the organizational context in which they will be received and translated into action. As Cover argued, "The practice of interpretation requires an understanding of what others will do with . . . a judicial utterance and, in many instances, an adjustment of that understanding, regardless of how misguided one may think the likely institutional response will be. Failing this, the interpreter sacrifices the connection between understanding what ought to be done and the deed, itself."[125]

"[R]egardless of how misguided"—here Cover was clearly thinking about the those who are responsible for the deed rather than the word. For that audience there is, and must be, a low threshold for influence; indeed Cover might just as well have said that the rational judge, remembering that he is a judge and not a poet, will always take into account likely institutional responses to insure that his readings will be persuasive if not pure, efficient if not excellent. Legal interpretation, on this account, is deeply and profoundly shaped by an awareness of the contingent character of implementation; meaning is altered and transformed in order to insure that action follows utterance. An excellent reading of a legal text is one that garners not just the praise of critics, but also triggers necessary responses in those charged with carrying out acts of violence it authorizes.

When he considers the vertical organization of law, the lower ranges of the pyramid that judges rule from the top, the anarchist Cover sounds suspiciously Weberian. "When judges interpret the law in an official context, we expect a close relationship to be revealed or established between their words and the acts that they mandate. That is, we expect the judges' words to serve as virtual triggers for action. We would not, for example, expect contemplations or deliberations on the part of jailers and wardens to interfere with the actions authorized by judicial words."[126] Judges who take into account the likely reaction of others in the chain of command, "regardless of how misguided," can, in this picture, expect the favor to be returned.

The language in which Cover described the translation of judicial words into legal acts is particularly slippery, and notably atypical of Cover. Who is the "we" that expects a close relationship between the words judges utter and the acts others perform? Is the reference to what we "expect" empirical? Or, does it instead (or in addition) have a normative dimension and refer to what we should expect? And why shouldn't "we expect" contemplation or deliberation to "interfere"? The imagined alternative that generates "our" preferences and expectations seems to be an apparatus of violence—the state—uncontrolled, undisciplined, unresponsive.

"When judges interpret, they trigger agentic behavior within . . . an institution or social organization. On one level judges may appear to be, and may in fact be, offering their understanding of the normative world to their intended audience. But on another level they are engaging a violent mechanism through which a substantial part of their audience loses its capacity to think and act autonomously."[127] At this point, in the face of his own image of such rigid and unthinking bureaucratic behavior,

Cover, one might expect, would have rebelled against his own insights, rebelled against any use of interpretive authority to suspend the "capacity to think and act autonomously." Cover the anarchist, or Cover the normative pluralist, might have been expected to embrace and to praise a theory of social organization that allowed for and encouraged multiple sites of interpretation, sites in which alternative readings might prevail, sites of resistance. In this way, the deployment of violence would be greatly tempered by problems of coordination within law's complex chain of command. To the extent that interpretive authority is fragmented and dispersed, that rival centers of power enter competing interpretations, the literal violence of the law might be reduced.

But there is, in fact, no rebellion, no endorsement of a loosely coupled bureaucratic structure; there is, instead, first silence, and later an approving, if stark, description of wardens, guards, and doctors engaged in the process of carrying out a death sentence who "jump to the judge's tune."[128] The world of interpretation is altered by a consideration of the requisites of order; meaning (freedom) gives way to insure that an orderly violence is done. Meaning is disciplined, in Cover's analysis, by the requisites of discipline itself. From the inside of law, and against the possibilities of undisciplined force and aggression, legal interpretation and law's social organization are looked to by Cover as the domain to achieve "whatever achievement is possible in the domesticating of violence."[129]

Violence domesticated, force turned into persuasion, war turned into peace—it is not particularly surprising that Cover, given this hope, accepts law's violence,[130] and writes as if that violence would have no price for law itself. Combined, the instructions regarding state law expressed in "Nomos and Narrative" and "Violence and the Word" appear to be,

> Wherever possible, withhold violence; let new worlds flourish. But, for the sake of life, do not forget that law's violence is sometimes necessary and that its availability is not automatic but must be provided for. And finally, effective violence that is also temperate and controlled is a considerable achievement, requiring "an organization of people" that is as complex as it is fragile.

The insistence that legal violence be used sparingly is explained by his conviction that "(w)e inhabit a nomos—a normative universe" that is easily destroyed by such violence even though some measure of it is needed to maintain normativity. The restraint called for at the end of "Nomos and Narrative" refers principally to instances or kinds of instances in which the use of force is justifiable or appropriate; to insist that such instances are relatively rare and that legal force should be used sparingly is, of course, perfectly compatible with the conviction that *some* use is actually necessary and, on those occasions, it should be applied efficiently. To do its job, then, law *must* be violent, but as minimally as possible. Cover's attention to law's violence in "Violence and the Word") signals his recognition that despite the normativity that precedes law, and partly because of it, there is need for law's violence and need also to secure the conditions of its effective use.

But again we ask, can Cover have it both ways? Can he (and we) provide those conditions for the effective use of force that he so insightfully identified and, at the same time, develop a legal system that is restrained, tolerant, and encouraging in its attitude toward alternative normative visions? Can law be homicidal without being jurispathic?

THE DIFFERENCE VIOLENCE MAKES

Cover believes that it is indeed possible to limit the jurispathic characteristic of law while making peace with a legal order that is "homicidal," and for law to escape the imperatives of violence;[131] we do not.[132] Cover could imagine judges gearing up and governing an apparatus of pain-imposing, death-dealing force in one moment, and then judiciously tolerating diverse and provocative normative visions the next; we cannot. Violence and law can never adequately and satisfactorily be reconciled. They are conflicting social facts that no amount of theoretical ingenuity can harmonize.[133]

While we grant that the central messages of "*Nomos* and Narrative" and "Violence and the Word" are not formally or logically incompatible, they are, we believe, antagonistic to one another at the level (to borrow Cover's phrase) of practical activity. The forces at work in the arrangements described in "Violence and the Word" undercut and oppose any self-limitation on the impulse of statist judges to be jurispathic. The first of those forces is a disposition of which the initial impetus is the supposed demand of rationality to universalize or objectify judgments and decisions,[134] to be governed, that is, by the maxim of "treating like cases alike and different cases differently." Such treatment is a purely formal requirement that is subsequently given direction—at least by Cover's account of judges' circumstances—in favor of finding similarity, not difference. Other forces derive largely from the interaction between the members of that fragile "organization of people" required, Cover contends, to make legal violence both doable and domesticated.

We begin our exploration of these forces by noting, with Cover, the familiar but unfathomable distance between thought and action, especially between the judgments and decisions of some and the uncoerced but reliably certain deeds of others. In the case of law, this distance is at once a blessing and a difficulty. It is a blessing because if there were virtually no distance between a judicial decision and its actualization on another's body—that is, if judges themselves were required to impose the pain and death that their judgments demand—too little violence would be done, according to Cover, and law would fail in its contest with the violence that is its origin. On the other hand, the distance is a difficulty, because a way must be found to traverse the gap between the judge's thought and the material act of, say, the executioner. For the reason just noted, it obviously will not do simply to force others to do law's violence; between the legal word and the deed there has to be something like a transmission capable of linking word and action, capable of activating the deed but not causing it.

The transmission, then, does two things: first, it keeps the judge separated—distanced—from the deed itself (so that decisions that need to be made will be made), but also connected to it (so that meaning is conferred on the deed and so that, in ways yet to be described, the judge is to some extent morally implicated in that deed). Second, it connects the deed to the word by linking the agent of law's violence (for example, the executioner) to the judicial decision in some manner that overcomes cultural and moral inhibitions against inflicting pain and death. These, it appears, are the basic pathways that make possible "the organization of people" required for law to function as a practical activity, as thought-in-action. But to these formal routes matters of substance must now be added.

To begin from the perspective of the active agent, the actual doer of law's violence—the executioner—we can ask what is required to trigger such conduct, to make it possible for these persons to act in a manner that seems virtually "agentic" in character, that does not involve independent review or judgment of the merits of the judicial decision.[135] Here Cover refers us to two possible accounts, one that ascribes evolutionary value to obeisance within hierarchical structures (the Milgram studies) and another (in Anna Freud) that suggests, contrary to Milgram, that a disposition to do such violence is the *natural* condition of human beings and that, except for institutionally specified occasions (as in law) where outlets for this natural aggression can be expressed, the impulse is firmly restrained.[136]

There is, of course, another story that might be told, not a causal account as the others are, but one that sounds in the language of justification, moral or otherwise. Surely it is just such a story that officers and agents of the law tell themselves and one another: they believe or appear to believe that they are justified in what they do, and it is this conviction that explains their capacity to set aside the customary inhibitions against doing violence. Somewhat more specifically, they presumably believe that acts of the kind that they perform are indeed necessary and that they, unlike others, are specifically authorized to carry them out.

But that they are disposed to act "agentically," in immediate, largely unquestioning response to the judicial decree is perhaps still both puzzling and problematic.[137] It is one thing to believe that acts of the kind being contemplated here are necessary and in some sense justified; it is, we understand, one thing to suppose that a certain *system* of rules and sanctions is justified, and another, albeit related, thing to believe that particular applications of force are justified. To bridge the latter gap, we need reasonable assurance of the correctness of the intervening determinations, or we need the interposition of other responsible agents, or both.

Because, in Cover's view, law is not a formal system but is inescapably an interpretive enterprise,[138] it is apparent that the merit of any particular judgment is never entirely separable from the agent who makes it.[139] It does not follow that such judgments can be judged as neither correct nor incorrect; it means only that their warrantability is not fully determined by reference to the rules of the system alone.[140] Wielders of the rules always have the option to understand them anew, to see them in new light, to interpret them in new, yet fully cogent, ways.[141] Assuming this to be so, legal officials, and judges especially, are never justified in behaving agentically with respect to their texts. They must construe and measure and balance, and construe again, in ways that are never and can never be tied down fully. Such judgments need not be subjective (that is, products of mere whim or bias or unsupported preference), but they *are* ineliminably personal.[142] By this we mean they bear the marks of their author, they bespeak a perspective, a set of assumptions, a point of view that is the decider's own and that cannot help influencing the content of the judgments made.

That *this* defendant is to be executed for *this* crime under *this* body of law is the result of this judge's sentence—a sentence that, but for the predilections, perceptions, and turns of mind of this particular judge, could, with full warrant, have been different from what it turned out to be.[143] It does not follow, of course, that judges must bear full responsibility for the decisions they make since what they decide is powerfully shaped by considerations (pertinent statutes, previous decisions, the conduct being censured) over which they have no control.[144] But especially in an interpretivist account of law, judges are deeply implicated in the decisions they make; moreover, it is to be expected that the capacity of these judgments to endure will depend in large measure on the practical activity, the arguments and analyses, their authors are prepared to marshal in behalf of those decisions.

Presumably, the responsibility borne by interpretivist judges in every decision they make is part of what Cover had in mind when he imagined that law's violence might be domesticated. These judges, it seems, are "the transmission" between the standing system of rules and the inscription of pain and death on the bodies and souls of other human beings. Their responsibility is not so great that they are unable to do what needs to be done, but it is great enough to implicate them as moral agents and to give them ample reason to behave thoughtfully.[145] It surely suffices to test "the faith and commitment" of deciding judges.[146]

Correspondingly, judges thus implicated in the "organization of people" that is required to carry out law's violence, would appear to meet the conditions set out earlier for authorizing agentic behavior on the part of others, namely by offering reasonable assurances regarding the correctness of the decisions to be implemented, or by overseeing the interposition of responsible agents, or by doing both. Because judges are personally implicated in the decisions they make (so there *is* an intervening responsible agent), they have compelling reasons (at least to try) to get it right. Perhaps it is not surprising that others, given the specific character of their involvement, feel at ease "jump(ing) to the judge's tune." Here, then, is another way in which judges are implicated in law's violence: they contribute to the justificatory story that induces or allows others to behave agentically.

Cover's work thus pointed toward a troublesome impediment to his own reconstructive project. That problem arises from the difficulty that judges and other legal officials face in marshalling the conviction necessary to use and deploy law's violence. Faced with that difficulty they need, Cover argued, to provide compelling reasons and justifications—for themselves and within their own interpretive communities—for the violence that they authorize.[147] Without such reasons and justifications law's violence could/would not be effectively organized and deployed.

So the presence of violence requires what might be called strong justification for legal acts.[148] The consequence of this fact is transformative; it promotes an imperialistic relationship between the legal order, in which one constant need is the generation of strong justifications, and normative communities whose ideas of the right and the good are at odds with what the law requires. In the face of such challenges, and spurred on by the strong justifications generated to sustain its own violence, the legal order becomes aggressive in its insistence that what it proclaims as right is *the* only acceptable version of right. As Hadley Arkes puts it,

> "When we invoke the language of morals, we praise and we blame, we commend and condemn, we applaud and deride, we approve and disapprove. It would make no sense, however, to cast these judgments on other people unless it were assumed that there are standards of judgment, accessible to others as well as ourselves, which allow these people to know that what they are doing is right or wrong. . . . When we invoke the language of morals . . . we move away from statements of personal taste and private belief; we offer a judgment about the things that are universally right or wrong, just or unjust."[149]

Legal interpretation that contemplates violence must tell a story that tends to "objectify" the demands it would enforce.[150] That is, legal interpretation seeks to show not only that its decisions are technically sustainable, but that they merit *imposition* against those who might resist, that they are worthy of being lived in and through the pain that is done in their name.[151] This, as Cover noted, "escalates the stakes of the interpretive enterprise."[152] To meet them, judges must generate a normatively enriched story, one that suffices to overcome reticence and to persuade other officials not to intervene. Such a story will be difficult to restrain; it will tend to assert itself in new domains, and to promote intolerance in the face of challenges.[153]

It is difficult to contemplate such stories without recalling Cover's discussion of the creation of legal meaning, a process, he said, that involves commitment, identification, and objectification. As he put it, "Creating legal meaning . . . requires . . . dedication and commitment, but also the objectification of that to which one is committed."[154] Here it seems Cover had in mind the attitudes and behavior of members of various insular and redemptive communities, but it would be strange to posit any radical disjunction between those persons and a community of statist judges, whom Cover expects to admit the contingency of the meanings and justifications generated in that community. Violence cannot be done without a sense that it is justified, and, once generated, justification is unlikely to be self-limiting.

But matters are more complicated still, as Cover emphatically reminds us. The judge, as we have seen, contributes to the emergence of agents who feel themselves morally "free" to do law's violence. But these actors are not utterly without effect on the law that they enforce. Though they do not review a judge's order on its merits—if they did that they would not be behaving agentically—there are limits to what they are prepared to do and the circumstances under which they will do it. The judge who would issue orders and decisions in hopes of having them acted on must be attentive to such limitations and fashion decrees accordingly.

Legal interpretation is never free; it is reciprocally bonded to the roles from which it issues and at which it is directed. It follows that there is always a tension between producing the most coherent legal meaning (in the manner that Dworkin might applaud) and (to quote Cover) "generating effective action in a violent context."[155] But precisely this constraint on legal interpretation, while it has the virtue of perhaps domesticating and tempering law's violence, puts in play the very logical, socio-pragmatic, and moral forces that dispose statist law to be jurispathic, to kill other normative orders, contrary to Cover's appeals at the end of "*Nomos* and Narrative."

We thus return to where we began, when we suggested it is a mixed blessing that "the organization of people" described in "Violence and the Word" is necessary if law is to deal pain and death. Inside, it makes available devices by which thought might effectively be transformed into action and law's violence might be done in a way that it is generally controlled and temperate. But in its interactions with competing normative visions, a statist legal order that is bonded to local practices—an order in which judges are not free to do the work of pure, unimpeded legal interpretation but whose decisions must cater to the conditions of doing violence—will be limited by those conditions. Thus a judge who, for example, lives in a world that includes a statute against bigamy might find cogent legal reasons for carving out an exception for a particular insular community and its embrace of plural marriages. But if the "right" or "best" decision is one that is suitably responsive to the social organization of violence it is less likely that such an exception would be made. The lesson of "Violence and the Word" is that thought cannot issue in action without being transformed by it, that interpretation is tutored and transformed by the imperatives of its violent context.

Violence changes things; violence changes law. At issue is the capacity of people who have imposed their will on some—who have used force to assure conformity among themselves—to find reasons now, but not then, to respect multiplicity and difference in their midst. New distinctions may weaken if they do not refute old justifications. An excess of casuistry is surely contrary to the demands of solidarity, and if Cover is right, solidarity, not subtlety of thought, is the *sine qua non* of effective legal violence.

Poets and philosophers, Cover would have us believe, unencumbered by the need to act, are free to proliferate distinctions and cultivate a taste for incompatible views. But the need to do violence, as we have said and as Cover himself recognized, makes a difference. Where pain and death are to be done, irreversible stands must be taken. When death and pain are involved, what is done cannot be undone, and judges especially are responsible for it. In the interpretive world of law, texts and reason alone do not dictate the result; on the contrary, in a world that requires legal violence, the "right result" is shaped in part by the shared commitments and common meanings that make the cooperative enterprise of law possible.

These commitments and meanings, while never wholly cogent nor wholly shared and common, must be respected if law's fragile capacity to do (controlled and temperate) violence is to be sustained. The price of this capacity, we have argued, is a disposition to be hostile to the visions of other normative orders, contrary to the plea at the end of "*Nomos* and Narrative" "to stop circumscribing the nomos" and "to invite new worlds." It appears, then, that violence ties thought to action and, as a consequence, makes law less tolerant of multiplicity and difference. Law's capacity to be homicidal tends, against Cover's fervent hope, to make it jurispathic as well.

NOTES

We are grateful for the helpful comments of Lawrence Douglas. An earlier version of this essay appeared in Austin Sarat and Thomas R. Kearns, eds., *Law's Violence* (Ann Arbor: University of Michigan Press, 1992). Reprinted by permission.

1. "Critique of Violence," in *Reflections*, trans. Edmund Jepchott (New York: Harcourt, Brace, 1978), 286. For an important commentary on Benjamin and the search for the origin of law, see Jacques Derrida, "Force of Law: The 'Mystical Foundation of Authority,'" trans. Mary Quaintance, *Cardozo Law Review* 11 (1990): 919.

2. See Friedrich Nietzsche, *The Birth of Tragedy and The Genealogy of Morals*, trans. Francis Golffing (Garden City, N.Y.: Doubleday, 1956). See also Benjamin, "Critique of Violence," 277.

3. As Nietzsche puts it, "I take bad conscience to be a deep-seated malady to which man succumbed under the pressure of the most profound transformation he ever underwent—the one that made him once and for all a sociable and pacific creature. Just as happened in the case of those sea creatures who were forced to become land animals in order to survive, these semi-animals, happily adapted to the wilderness, to war, to free roaming, and adventure, were forced to change their nature." *The Birth of Tragedy*, 217. Benjamin also suggests that while natural law regards violence as a product of nature, positive law sees violence as a product of history (see "Critique of Violence," 278).

4. See Thomas Hobbes, *Leviathan*, ed. C. B. MacPherson (New York: Penguin Books, 1986). As Mark Taylor argues, "Force is comprehended in law. Since the structure of force is isomorphic with the structure of law, each perfectly mirrors the other" ("Desire of Law/Law of Desire," *Cardozo Law Review* 11 [1990]: 1269–70).

5. Laws, Paul de Mann argues, "are future-oriented and prospective; their illocutionary mode is that of the *promise*. On the other hand, every promise assumes a date at which the promise is made and without which it would have no validity; laws are promissory notes in which the present of the promise is always a past with regard to its realization" (*Allegories of Reading: Figural Language in Rousseau, Nietzsche, Rilke, and Proust* [New Haven: Yale University Press, 1979], 273).

6. In the well-known case of *United States v. Holmes*, this promise is described in the following terms: "The law of nature forms part of the municipal law; and in a proper case . . . , homicide is justifiable, not because the municipal law is subverted by the law of nature, but because no rule of the municipal law makes homicide in such cases criminal." See 26 *Fed. Cas.* 360 (C.E.D. Pa. 1842), reprinted in Joseph Goldstein, Alan Dershowitz, and Richard Schwartz, *Criminal Law: Theory and Process* (New York: Free Press, 1974), 1028. Yet the promise is at best partially realized because law itself is a disordering force in social relations.

7. For a fuller description of how the image of a defiant, unruly violence works in legal theory, see Austin Sarat and Thomas R. Kearns, "A Journey Through

Forgetting: Towards a Jurisprudence of Violence," in *The Fate of Law*, ed. Austin Sarat and Thomas R. Kearns (Ann Arbor: University of Michigan Press, 1991).

8. Taylor, "Desire of Law/Law of Desire."

9. As Derrida puts it, "If the origin of law is a violent positioning, the latter manifests itself in the purest fashion when violence is absolute, that is to say when it touches on the right to life and death" ("Force of Law," 1005).

10. See Sarat and Kearns, "A Journey Through Forgetting." Robert Paul Wolff contends that in the eyes of law and legal theory, "murder is an act of violence, but capital punishment by a *legitimate state* is not; theft or extortion is violent, but the collection of taxes by a *legitimate state* is not" ("Violence and the Law," in *The Rule of Law*, ed. Robert Paul Wolff [New York: Simon and Schuster, 1971], 59).

11. See H. H. Gerth and C. Wright Mills, eds. and trans., *From Max Weber: Essays in Sociology* (New York: Oxford University Press, 1946), 78. Also, Robert Paul Wolff, "Violence and the Law"; Edgar Friedenberg, "The Side Effects of the Legal Process," in *The Rule of Law*, 43; and Bernhard Waldenfels, "Limits of Legitimation and the Question of Violence," in *Justice, Law, and Violence*, ed. James Brady and Newton Garver (Philadelphia: Temple University Press, 1991). For an interesting examination of the way law legitimates itself, see Samuel Weber, "In the Name of the Law," *Cardozo Law Review* 11 (1990): 1515.

12. Karl Olivecrona calls for an explicit recognition that the violence of law is neither transformed nor purified. As he argues, in most writing about law, "[a]ctual violence is . . . kept very much in the background. . . . Such a state of things is apt to create the belief that violence is alien to law, or of secondary importance. That is, however, a fatal illusion. . . . [Law's] real character is largely obscured and this is done by metaphysical ideas and expressions. It is not bluntly said, e.g., that the function of the courts is to determine the use of force. Instead their function is said to be the 'administration of justice' or the ascertaining of 'rights' and 'duties' " (*Law as Fact* [Copenhagen: E. Munksgaard, 1939], 125).

13. As Sarat and Kearns argue, "Force is disdainful of reason; it pushes it aside; it takes over completely. Reason and force have no way to share control of human agency. Where the two meet in battle only one can win, and given the levels of force, pain, and violence at law's disposal, law, wherever it wants, is assured of victory. It appears, then, that law's violence does not sit well with—indeed, it wars with—the conception of human agency that is built into, and held out to us by, a jurisprudence of rules" ("A Journey Through Forgetting," 269).

14. Benjamin, "Critique of Violence," 286. In this phrase, Derrida contends, Benjamin meant to suggest that "law is a violence contrary to nature" ("Force of Law," 1005).

15. A good example of this tendency in legal theory is provided by Ronald Dworkin, who treats the occasion of law's violence as that which requires an examination of the adequacy of the "principles" that justify it. See Dworkin's *Taking Rights Seriously* (Cambridge: Harvard University Press, 1977), 15.

16. The most striking and important example of such homicidal deeds is the death penalty. As Benjamin puts it, "[I]n the exercise of violence over life and

death more than in any other legal act, law reaffirms itself" ("Critique of Violence," 286).

17. This phrase is used by Robert Cover to describe the tendency to kill or destroy legal meaning. See "The Supreme Court, 1982 Term—Foreword: *Nomos* and Narrative," *Harvard Law Review* 97 (1983): 4, 40. All subsequent notes will refer to this work by its shortened title, "*Nomos* and Narrative."

18. We focus on three articles in particular; "*Nomos* and Narrative," "Violence and the Word," *Yale Law Journal* 95 (1986): 1601, and "The Bonds of Constitutional Interpretation: Of the Word, the Deed, and the Role," *Georgia Law Review* 20 (1986): 815.

19. For a discussion of Cover's vision, see Ronald Garet, "Meaning and Ending," *Yale Law Journal* 96 (1987): 1801.

20. Robert Cover, "Folktales of Justice: Tales of Jurisdiction," *Capital University Law Review* 14 (1985): 179, 181.

21. Mark Tushnet explains this by saying, "I doubt that Cover was a romantic anarchist who believed that the practice of individual violence would disappear in a well-ordered anarchy" ("Reflections on Capital Punishment: One Side of an Uncompleted Discussion," *Journal of Law and Religion* 7 [1989]: 21, 25).

22. We worry that he did not see the way in which an acceptance of the violence of law imprisons legal theory and limits the legal imagination. Describing tensions and limitations in Cover's thought about law and violence is one way of getting a handle on the tensions and limitations that plague law whenever it traffics in violence, as inevitably it must.

23. For a similar question asked about Cover in the context of capital punishment, see Tushnet, "Reflections on Capital Punishment."

24. There are, of course, notable and important exceptions. See Gerth and Mills, *From Max Weber*; Hans Kelsen, *General Theory of Law and the State*, trans. Anders Wedberg (New York: Russell and Russell, 1945); Noberto Bobbio, "Law and Force," *Monist* 48 (1965): 321. Also, James Brady and Newton Garver, eds., *Justice, Law, and Violence* (Philadephia: Temple University Press, 1991).

25. For a useful overview and summary of this work, see Jack Gibbs, *Crime, Punishment, and Deterrence* (New York: Elsever, 1975).

26. Contemporary scholars treat the violence of law as too obvious to merit sustained attention and choose instead to emphasize the ideological, interpretive, meaning-affirming qualities of law. While no one pretends that law does not coerce and punish, many push such facts to the margin or claim that the violence in and around law is vestigial and incidental to our understanding of what law is. For one explanation of this development, see Robert Gordon, "New Developments in Legal Theory," in *The Politics of Law: A Progressive Critique*, 2nd ed., edited by David Kairys (New York: Pantheon, 1990).

27. Since Cover wrote "Violence and the Word," there has been a revival of interest in the subject of violence and its connection to law. See, for example, Derrida, "Force of Law."

28. This is not to suggest that his intervention derailed, or was intended to derail, this development. For recent examples of the emphasis on meaning and

normativity see James Boyd White, *Justice as Translation* (Chicago: University of Chicago Press, 1990), and Robert Post, ed., *Law and the Order of Culture* (Berkeley: University of California Press, 1991).

29. This is a point amply illustrated by Michel Foucault. See *Discipline and Punish: The Birth of the Prison*, trans. Alan Sheridan (New York: Pantheon, 1977; paperback, Vintage Books, 1979).

30. Cover, "Violence and the Word," 1601.

31. Olivecrona, *Law as Fact*, 126, 134.

32. Cover, "Violence and the Word," 1601.

33. "In law to be an interpreter is to be a force, an actor who creates effects even though or in the face of violence" (Cover, "The Bonds of Constitutional Interpretation," 833). See also Drucilla Cornell, "From the Lighthouse: The Promise of Redemption and the Possibility of Legal Interpretation," *Cardozo Law Review* 11 (1990): 1687.

34. Though Cover lent his own considerable intellectual energy to the project of opening legal scholarship to humanistic impulses and to the materials of humanistic disciplines—history, literature, philosophy, and religion—he believed that law would neither sit comfortably with those materials nor be easily reconciled with those impulses. While he was eager to explore similarities between law and the humanities, as well as the interpretive dimensions of legal activity and the community-building, meaning-making aspects of law, he worried that an exclusive focus on those things would produce a distorted view, and that this view would, even if unintentionally, encourage or tolerate the violence of law, or worse yet, make it possible for us to live easily, complacently, with that violence. Cover candidly acknowledged that exploration of differences, tensions, and discomforts in the relationship between law and the humanities might, given the nature of his own earlier work, seem "surprising, even contradictory" ("The Bonds of Constitutional Interpretation," 815). Yet it is perhaps characteristic of his love of the plural, the diverse, and the contested that he would take issue with scholars who sought to identify an essential "unity" between the meaning-making, interpretive activities of law, and the work of the humanities (ibid., 815). And it is in this effort to deny the unity of law and the humanities where Cover's interest in violence found its location and its home.

35. See Cover, "Violence and the Word," 1602, note 2.

36. Cover's exploration of differences between law and other interpretive enterprises, and the nature of his disagreement with others in the effort to promote interdisciplinary legal scholarship, are perhaps best glimpsed in a long footnote to "Violence and the Word" (note 2, 1601–02). Here Cover observes that "there has been a recent explosion of legal scholarship placing interpretation at the crux of law"; he acknowledges the rhetorical, interpretive, meaning-making quality of law, and, in this way, allies himself with Ronald Dworkin (see "Law as Interpretation," *Texas Law Review* 60 [1982]: 527), James Boyd White, and other humanist scholars of law. At the same time, however, he notes, with some alarm, that "the violent side of law and its connection to interpretation and rhetoric is systematically ignored or underplayed . . . " in humanist scholarship ("Violence and the Word," note 2, 1602). Because of law's tie to violence, because of the

painful consequences of all legal activity, because its interpretations and meanings are inscribed on bodies, law, Cover claimed, could never be just another domain of meaning making and interpretation.

37. On the violence of interpretation, see Harold Bloom, *The Anxiety of Influence: A Theory of Poetry* (New York: Oxford University Press, 1973).

38. This is not to suggest that Cover denied the interpretive violence of the legal act. As he put it, "My point ... is not that judges do not do the kind of figurative violence to literary parents that poets do, but that they carry out—in addition—a far more literal form of violence through their interpretations that poets do not share" ("Violence and the Word," 1609, note 20).

39. Cover, "The Bonds of Constitutional Interpretation," 818.

40. Ibid., 818.

41. On the inadequacies of representation in the realms of pain and violence, see Elaine Scarry, *The Body in Pain: The Making and Unmaking of the World* (New York: Oxford University Press, 1985), 3–11.

42. Cover, "The Bonds of Constitutional Interpretation," 818–19.

43. Cover, "Violence and the Word," 1628.

44. Cover, "*Nomos* and Narrative," 14.

45. As Richard Sherwin claims, "I submit that *every* meaning contains within it the contingency and deceit of social structure. Put differently, within the realm of human history and understanding, a decontextualized (or ahistorical) utterance is unthinkable. On this view, then, the deceit (or 'made-up' aspect) of meaning and its conceit (viz. the denial of partiality) are present in discourse even when interpretation falls short of coercive (or imperial) enactment" ("Law, Violence, and Illiberal Belief," *Georgetown Law Journal* 78 [1990]: 1785, 1808).

46. This criticism of Cover was suggested to us by Lawrence Douglas.

47. Thus, it is not surprising that he asked his readers to see the world of law from the perspective of those deeply attached to normative visions quite at variance with law's own; he asked us to see the world of law from the perspective of the resister and the civil disobedient, and he wrote movingly, eloquently, and even admiringly of the miracle of martyrs, of those who hold onto a normative vision, an imagining of other worlds, in the face of world-destroying, world-shattering pain (see "Violence and the Word," 1604). What is somewhat more surprising is that he also asked us to see the world of law from the perspective of the ordinary criminal defendant and the death-row inmate for whom questions of justification, of meaning, and of interpretive authority fade from view (see ibid., 1608).

His intent in so doing was not to equate the ordinary criminal or the death-row inmate with the resister or the martyr. As he put it in talking about those sentenced, "If I have exhibited some sense of sympathy for the victims of this violence [the violence of criminal sentencing], it is misleading. Very often the balance of terror in this regard is just as I would want it" ("Violence and the Word," 1608). Or, as he put it elsewhere in talking about capital punishment, "I am not an abolitionist. If the death penalty is constitutional, and it is, ... there must be deaths. Ours is not a Platonic Constitution. We do not adjudicate the nature of pure forms of the death penalty that can never be realized materially" ("The Bonds of Constitutional Interpretation," 831). In the request that we see the world of law as the criminal and the condemned see it, Cover takes us back to his concern about the interpretive turn in legal scholarship; for in humanist scholarship on law we are much more likely to be drawn to the articulate voice of those engaged with legal texts than to the inarticulate, almost inaudible voice of those subject to law's violence. See *McCleskey v. Kemp*, 107 S.Ct. 1756, 1794 (1987), Justice Brennan dissenting.

48. See Cover, "Violence and the Word." In Elaine Scarry (*The Body in Pain*), Cover found someone who courageously wrote about the knowledge and experience of pain even as she acknowledged the limits of our ability to know and experience someone else's pain. It was a courage that he himself emulated as he tried to communicate about the hurts done and pain experienced in the most mundane as well as in the most dramatic of legal acts. He wrote about violence and pain as someone who was fully aware of the limits of his own ability to communicate. But he wrote about violence and pain nonetheless, and, in so doing, expressed his own deep faith in the human capacity to bridge worlds, to move from the world of experience to the world of possibility, from the present to the future.

49. See Wolff, "Violence and the Law." Also, Jan Narveson, "Force, Violence, and Law," in *Justice, Law, and Violence*.

50. See Bobbio, "Law and Force."

51. See Wolff, "Violence and the Law," 59.

52. Cover, "Violence and the Word," 1629.

53. See Sherwin, "Law, Violence, and Illiberal Belief," 1797.

54. This is an invitation that others are taking up. See, for example, Derrida, "Force of Law."

55. In that exploration (see "*Nomos* and Narrative," 4) Cover both departs from, and remains tied to, the premises of liberal political thought. His departure from liberalism is seen in his emphasis on community over individualism, and in his insistence on the priority of values over interests. His ties to liberalism are seen in his use of the polarities of freedom and order to describe the tensions of human social life, and in his reluctant apology for, and endorsement of, the violence of state law. For an interesting point of comparison, see Judith Shklar, "The Liberalism of Fear," in *Liberalism and the Moral Life*, ed. Nancy Rosenblum (Cambridge: Harvard University Press, 1990).

56. Cover, "*Nomos* and Narrative," 4.

57. Ibid., 5.

58. See Hobbes, *Leviathan*, 184–85. As Shklar argues, "Of fear it can be said without qualification that it is universal as it is physiological. . . . To be alive is to be afraid. . . . The fear we fear is of pain inflicted by others to kill and maim us" ("Liberalism of Fear," 29).

59. See also Michael Sandel, *Liberalism and the Limits of Justice* (Cambridge: Harvard University Press, 1982).

60. Cover worried lest students of law "identify the normative world with the professional paraphernalia of social control," and he contended that "the formal institutions of law . . . are . . . a small part of the normative universe that ought to claim our attention" ("*Nomos* and Narrative," 4). See also Garet, "Meaning and Ending."

61. See Robert Post, "Theories of Constitutional Interpretation," in *Law and the Order of Culture.*

62. For a discussion of the place of contract in liberal thought, see Vicente Medina, *Social Contract Theories: Political Obligation or Anarchy* (Savage, Md.: Rowman & Littlefield, 1990). Also, Michael Lessnoff, *Social Contract* (Atlantic Highlands, N.J.: Humanities Press, 1986).

63. See John Austin, *The Province of Jurisprudence Determined,* reprinted as "Law as the Sovereign's Commands," in *The Nature of Law: Readings in Legal Philosophy,* ed. M.P. Golding (New York: Random House, 1966).

64. The "imposition of a normative force" upon a real or imagined state of affairs is, Cover contends, the act of creating narrative. All "genres of narrative—history, fiction, tragedy, comedy—" (and not just the law) are accounts of states of affairs that have been subjected to various "normative force fields." All of them, including law, are "models" of a socially constructed world that has been screened, shaped, and transformed by some relatively stable set of normative commitments and aspirations. In sum, "[t]he codes that relate our normative system to our social constructions of reality and to our visions of what the world might be are narrative" (*"Nomos* and Narrative," 10). For other discussions of the nature and possibilities of narrative, see Robert Scholes and Robert Kellogg, *The Nature of Narrative* (London: Oxford University Press, 1966), and D. A. Miller, *Narrative and Its Discontents: Problems of Closure in the Traditional Novel* (Princeton: Princeton University Press, 1981).

65. Cover, *"Nomos* and Narrative," 5. This point is now widely recognized. See "Symposium on Legal Storytelling," *University of Michigan Law Review* 87 (1989): 2073–2496.

66. Cover, *"Nomos* and Narrative," 5.

67. Ibid., 9.

68. Ibid.

69. Ibid., 11. Here again one hears echoes of Cover's anarchism. See his "Folktales of Justice," 181.

70. Describing the position of the Mennonite Church in *Bob Jones University v. U.S.* (103 S. Ct. 2017 1983), Cover argued that "within the domain of constitutional meaning, the understanding of the Mennonites assumes a status equal (or superior) to that accorded to the understanding of the Justices of the Supreme Court. In this realm of meaning . . . the Mennonite community creates law as fully as does the judge" (*"Nomos* and Narrative," 28).

71. Here Cover displays his sympathy for a radical legal pluralism. See Sally Merry, "Legal Pluralism," *Law and Society Review* 22 (1988): 869. See also John Griffiths, "What Is Legal Pluralism?" *Journal of Legal Pluralism* 24 (1986): 1.

72. Cover, *"Nomos* and Narrative," 6.

73. Ibid., 40. For a very different perspective on the same problem, see Martin Shapiro, *Courts* (Chicago: University of Chicago Press, 1981).

74. Cover, *"Nomos* and Narrative," 12.

75. Ibid., 53.

76. Cover, "Violence and the Word," 1602, note 2.

77. This is not to say that violence is only the province of the state. Cover seems to grant that *some* imposition, *some* force, is always a feature of law. Even

the largely paedeic Massachusetts Bay Colony sought to maintain its "holistic integrity" by forcefully *excluding* heretics like Roger Williams and Ann Hutchinson.

78. Cover, "*Nomos* and Narrative," 18.

79. For a rich exploration of the tensions between Cover's work and liberalism, see Sherwin, "Law, Violence, and Illiberal Belief."

80. See Roberto Unger, *Knowledge and Politics* (New York: Free Press, 1975).

81. See Michel Foucault, *Power/Knowledge: Selected Interviews and Other Writings, 1972–1977,* trans. Colin Gordon et al. (New York: Pantheon, 1980).

82. This point was suggested to us by Lawrence Douglas.

83. Cover, "*Nomos* and Narrative," 53.

84. This kind of violence is more fully explored by Cover in "Violence and the Word."

85. Violence, coordinated and controlled in and by the interpretive acts of judges, appears, in Cover's exploration of the internal perspective, as an achievement of considerable social importance. Awareness of the need to coordinate and control violence, in turn, presses on and shapes the interpretive activities of judges who sit atop what Cover called "a pyramid of violence" ("Violence and the Word," 1609). Interpretation is transformed and made different by the presence of violence for, as Cover so vividly put it, "Legal interpretation takes place in a field of pain and death" (ibid., 1601). Or, as if that were not enough to make the point, "[L]egal interpretation occurs on a battlefield—it is part of a battle—which entails the instruments both of war and of poetry. Indeed constitutional law is . . . more fundamentally connected to the war than it is to the poetry" ("The Bonds of Constitutional Interpretation, 817). But law's violence is not just an issue of interpretation; it is, in addition, a question of social organization, of the implementation of judicial decisions, of the translation of words into violent deeds.

86. Cover, "*Nomos* and Narrative," 53. "By exercising its superior brute force," Cover argued, "the agency of state law shuts down the creative hermeneutic of principle that is spread throughout our communities" ("*Nomos* and Narrative," 44). Sanford Levinson argues that in this passage Cover is writing about a "'merely' metaphorical" violence. See Levinson, "Conversing About Justice," *Yale Law Journal* 100 (1991): 1855, 1865.

87. Cover, "*Nomos* and Narrative," 68.

88. As Cover put it, "[T]he coercive dimension of law is itself destructive of the possibility of interpretation" ("*Nomos* and Narrative," 48).

89. Sometimes law's violence damages the source of law not from imperial motives but from excessive deference to the claims of state bureaucracy. While with regard to the normative communities outside the state Cover calls for modesty and restraint, with regard to the state bureaucracy Cover allows himself to imagine the judge-as-resister already inscribed in the sanctuaries of power, as a privileged rescuer of meaning and freedom from the forces of violence and order. In this imagining, he works through what seems like a rather familiar argument about the rule of law in which the office of judge is set apart from the rest of the state's administrative apparatus (see John Norton Moore, "The Rule of Law: An Overview," unpublished manuscript, University of Virginia, 1998) and he

reminds us of Lord Coke's resistance to King James, Taney's resistance to Lincoln, and the resistance of judges in Ghana to the perpetrators of a military coup in the late 1970s. He urges judges to commit themselves to a "jurisgenerative process that does not defer to the violence of administration" ["*Nomos* and Narrative," 59] as the only way to temper law's all-too-close association with violence.

90. It is in the confrontation of the judge with the deep normative commitments of resisters, civil disobedients, and members of communities so dedicated to their way of life that they are willing to suffer for their beliefs, that the violence of law is put to its severest tests. Faced with such tests, and stripped of the illusion that their interpretations are superior, judges usually resort, Cover argued, to systemic rationales for their deployment of violence, to what he called the "principles of jurisdiction" ("*Nomos* and Narrative," 55). Those principles provide "apologies for the state itself and for its violence" (ibid., 54). In his view, however, they overvalue power and order, and undervalue meaning and freedom (see "Folktales of Justice," 180–81). The principles of jurisdiction are premised on a profound fear of differences and the problems that accommodating differences creates. As a result, those principles promote closure and justify intolerance toward normative visions seemingly at odds with the commitments embodied in state law. Jurisdiction is a way of avoiding normative engagement; it allows judges to separate themselves from the violence they authorize and to avoid measuring the strength of their commitment to violence against the persuasiveness of their understandings of law. In this, Cover believed that judges are different from, and often inferior to, resisters whose interpretive commitments cannot be abstracted and are, in Cover's view, measured in and through the willingness of resisters to suffer and die for their beliefs.

91. Cover, "*Nomos* and Narrative," 40. As he wrote about the organization of law's violence, and, in particular, about the way "judicial authority is transmitted through the inferior layers of the administration of justice," Cover, Douglas Hay has recently claimed, "celebrated . . . the fact of the integrity of that power of command of violence" ("Time, Inequality, and Law's Violence," *Law's Violence*, in Austin Sarat and Thomas R. Kearns [Ann Arbor: University of Michigan Press, 1992], 141). Though Hay is onto something important about Cover's work, "celebrate" seems not quite right as a way of describing Cover's attitude toward the internal organization of law's violence. While continuing to press the analytic point about the relationship of violence and legal interpretation that animated his critique of others in the law and humanities movement, Cover's contemplation of the internal organization of law's violence is the contemplation of the sociologist simply investigating the facts rather than of the enthusiast celebrating what he has found. Yet it is nonetheless true that in his sociological guise Cover expressed much less regret about the fact of violence than he did in his reconstructive/utopian mood, and much more resigned acceptance of the need for law to do violence.

92. Cover, "*Nomos* and Narrative," 16.

93. Ibid., 60.

94. Ibid.

95. Ibid., 53.

96. By appealing to judges to resist "mere administration," to avoid acceding to the violence done by others, Cover hoped that he could reconcile law's violence with a legal order hospitable to diverse normative worlds. Here the concern is that judges will violently and *unnecessarily* impose themselves against critique, vision, and aspiration in the normative world beyond state law and, in doing so, will destroy the nomos and narrative on which law itself deeply depends.

97. See Shklar, "The Liberalism of Fear." Also, Unger, *Knowledge and Politics*.

98. Cover, "Violence and the Word," 1609.

99. See Douglas Hay, "Time, Inequality, and Law's Violence," 3–4.

100. Cover, "The Bonds of Constitutional Interpretation," 833.

101. See Sarat and Kearns, "A Journey Through Forgetting."

102. Cover, "Violence and the Word," 1628.

103. For a similar analysis in a different context see Gary Peller, "Reason and the Mob," *Tikkun* 2 (1987): 28.

104. Cover, "Violence and the Word," 1616.

105. Ibid., 1616. See also Susan Jacoby, *Wild Justice: The Evolution of Revenge* (New York: Harper & Row, 1983).

106. See Sarat and Kearns, "A Journey Through Forgetting."

107. Cover, "Violence and the Word," 1624.

108. Ibid., 1624. In one place, Cover seemed to entertain a quite different proposition, namely, that "violence . . . must be viewed as problematic in much the same way whether it is being carried out by order of a federal district judge, a mafioso or a corporate vice-president." Yet even here he quickly retreated, "Please note well, here," he argued, "that I am not saying that all violence is equally justified or unjustified. I am claiming that it is problematic in the same way. By that I mean that the form of analysis that we enter into to determine whether or not the violence is justified is the same. That same method will, of course, if it is any good at all, not yield the same answer with respect to dissimilar cases" (See "Folktales of Justice," 182 and note 15).

109. Cover, "Violence and the Word," 1624.

110. This is, of course, the stuff of much debate in legal and constitutional theory. See, for example, Sanford Levinson, "Law as Literature," *Texas Law Review* 60 (1982), 373; and Ernest Weinrib, "Legal Formalism: On the Immanent Rationality of Law, " *Yale Law Journal* 97 (1988): 949.

111. Cover, "Violence and the Word," 1627.

112. Ibid., 1629. The emphasis on justification is especially great in situations where the violence to be authorized is most severe. Thus, in the case of capital punishment, because "the action or *deed* is extreme and irrevocable, there is pressure placed on the *word*—the interpretation that establishes the legal justification for the act. At the same time, the fact that capital punishment constitutes the most plain, the most deliberate, and the most thoughtful manifestation of legal interpretation as violence makes the imposition of the sentence an especially powerful test of the faith and commitment of the interpreters" (ibid., 1622). Faith and commitment become the ultimate test of interpretation, the ultimate standard against which the persuasive power of justification will be measured.

113. Ibid., 1618.

114. Ibid., 1619.

115. Ibid., 1613. As Cover puts it, "Were the inhibition against violence perfect, law would be unnecessary; were it not capable of being overcome through social signals, law would not be possible" (ibid.). For a useful discussion of the dangers of overcoming that inhibition, see Herbert Kelman and V. Lee Hamilton, *Crimes of Obedience: Toward a Social Psychology of Authority and Responsibility* (New Haven: Yale University Press, 1989).

116. Cover, "Violence and the Word," 1617.

117. Ibid., 1626.

118. Ibid., 1626–27.

119. Ibid., 1611.

120. Because responses are predictable, judges can view their own interpretive acts as having an impact in the world; because responses are not logically necessary, judges must be attentive to the conditions that maintain the predictable quality of administration and implementation.

121. See Cover, "*Nomos* and Narrative," 18.

122. "No wardens, guards or executioners wait," Cover argued, "for a telephone call from the latest constitutional law scholar, jurisprude or critic before executing prisoners, no matter how compelling the interpretations of those others may be. And, indeed, they await the word of judges only insofar as that word carries with it the formal indicia of having been spoken in the judicial capacity" ("Violence and the Word," 1625).

123. See Ronald Dworkin, "Hard Cases," *Harvard Law Review* 89 (1975): 1057.

124. Cover, "Violence and the Word," 1617.

125. Ibid., 1612.

126. Ibid., 1613–14.

127. Ibid., 1615.

128. Ibid., 1623–24.

129. Ibid., 1628.

130. It is apparent, then, that Cover was not so much of an anarchist that he was indifferent to the distinctions among a lynching (or a run-away police machinery), and an execution authorized after a trial, and review on appeal. And this is precisely the point: Cover had neither such a romantic aversion to violence, nor such an unqualified sympathy for freedom over order, that he rejected violence entirely.

131. On the possibilities of such an escape see Tom Dumm, "The Fear of Law," *Studies in Law, Politics and Society* 10 (1990): 29. Also, Drucilla Cornell, "The Violence of the Masquerade: Law Dressed Up as Justice," *Cardozo Law Review* 11 (1990): 1047.

132. To make our case against Cover, we mean to draw on Cover himself, to use the insights of "Violence and the Word" to explain why Cover's toleration of legal violence undermines the vision and hope of "*Nomos* and Narrative."

133. See Taylor, "Desire of Law/Law of Desire."

134. See Thomas Nagel, *The View from Nowhere* (New York: Oxford University Press, 1986); and Richard Rorty, *Philosophy and the Mirror of Nature* (Princeton: Princeton University Press, 1979).

135. See Petres Spierenburg, *The Spectacle of Suffering: Executions and the Evolution of Repression* (New York: Cambridge University Press, 1984); and William Bowers, *Executions in America* (Lexington, Mass.: Lexington Books, 1974).

136. See Cover, "Violence and the Word," 1614–15.

137. But see Kelman and Hamilton, *Crimes of Obedience.*

138. See Stanley Fish, "The Law Wishes to Have a Formal Existence," in *The Fate of Law,* ed. Austin Sarat and Thomas R. Kearns (Ann Arbor: University of Michigan Press, 1991). Also, Ronald M. Dworkin, "Law as Interpretation," *Texas Law Review* 60 (1982): 527.

139. "Interpretation," Stanley Fish argues, "is not the art of construing but the art of constructing. Interpreters do not decode poems; they make them" (*Is There a Text in This Class?* [Cambridge: Harvard University Press, 1980], 327). See also Sanford Levinson, "Law as Literature," 373.

140. For a useful discussion of this point see H.L.A. Hart on formalism and rule skepticism in *The Concept of Law* (Oxford: Clarendon Press, 1961), chapter 7.

141. See Fish, *Is There a Text in This Class?*

142. On the distinction between the personal and the subjective, see Nagel, *The View From Nowhere,* 152–53.

143. For a general treatment of this topic, see John Noonan, *Persons and Masks of the Law: Cardozo, Holmes, Jefferson, and Wythe as Makers of Masks* (New York: Farrar, Strauss & Giroux, 1976).

144. The question of how much constraint is imposed by such legal and polit- ical facts is, of course, at the center of debates in interpretive theory. See Levinson, "Law as Literature" and Gerald Graff, " 'Keep Off the Grass,' 'Drop Dead,' and Other Indeterminacies," *Texas Law Review* 60 (1982): 405.

145. On the imperative of deliberation in moral decision making, see Daniel Maguire, *The Moral Choice* (Garden City, N.Y.: Doubleday, 1978). See also Charles Larmore, *Patterns of Moral Complexity* (Cambridge: Cambridge Univer- sity Press, 1987); and Edmond Cahn, *The Moral Decision: Right and Wrong in the Light of American Law* (Bloomington: Indiana University Press, 1955).

146. As Cover himself put it, "[A] legal interpretation cannot be valid if no one is prepared to live by it" (*"Nomos* and Narrative," 44).

147. Cover, "Violence and the Word," 1627.

148. By a strong justification we mean a justification sufficient to explain an action as having some other origin than an act of will or raw power. For an argument that all justifications, properly so called, are strong justifications, see Hadley Arkes, *First Things* (Princeton: Princeton University Press, 1986), 20.

149. Ibid., 22–24.

150. "The Law of Law calls us to interpretation, and this process of interpre- tation appeals to the promise of a reconciled whole, or the Good, which is itself only an interpretation and not the last word on what the Good of the community actually could be. . . . Yet even so, the Law of Law is that we justify our interpre- tation through an appeal to the Good. . . . [W]hen one legal interpretation is vin- dicated as to what constitutes the Good, it is imposed upon the other as if the Good had been achieved" (Cornell, "From the Lighthouse," 1712).

151. See Martha Minow, *Making All the Difference: Inclusion, Exclusion, and American Law* (Ithaca: Cornell University Press, 1990), 60–65.

152. Cover, "*Nomos* and Narrative," 51.

153. As Minow (*Making All the Difference*, 64–65), puts it, "Legal language seeks universal applicability, regardless of the particular traits of an individual, yet abstract universalism often 'takes the part for the whole, the particular for the universal and essential, the present for the eternal.' . . . Justices to this day fail to acknowledge their own perspective and its influence in the assignment of difference in relation to some unstated norm."

154. Cover, "*Nomos* and Narrative," 45.

155. Cover, "Violence and the Word," 1629.

CHAPTER FOUR

The Silence of the Law

JUSTICE IN COVER'S "FIELD OF PAIN AND DEATH"

Marianne Constable

In "Violence and the Word," Robert Cover argues that "legal interpretation takes place in a field of pain and death."[1] Here Cover describes law in several ways. Law, to him, involves "the projection of an imagined future upon reality";[2] it is a "practice,"[3] a meaning-giving system,[4] a set of resources for claiming significance.[5] Above all, however, "it is those things in the context of the organized social practice of violence."[6] Criticizing scholars of the 1980s whom he believed concentrated too single-mindedly on the interpretive aspects of judging, Cover accused them of systematically ignoring or underplaying "the violent side of law and its connection to interpretation and rhetoric."[7] He himself distinguished between the word or "interpretation," with its suggestion of "social construction of an interpersonal reality through language," and "violence," as "pain and death," with its language– and "world-destroying" capacity.[8] At the same time, he argued that "the 'interpretations' or 'conversations' that are the preconditions for violent incarceration are themselves implements of violence" and key to law.[9] "Legal interpretation," he wrote, "is either played out on the field of pain and death or it is something less (or more) than law."[10]

At one level, Cover's argument appears unexceptional. There seems little here with which to disagree and there are few who seem to do so: yes, legal interpretation is different from literary interpretation; yes, judicial decisions may trigger institutional responses of violence; yes, a defendant experiences the violence of the system differently than does a judge. Why then was—or is—the essay important? It is doubtful that law professors in the late 1980s were in need of another legal realist reminder; despite their ostensible focus on doctrine, interpretation, and application, law professors then as now seemed all too aware of what they took to be the social and economic realities governing life and constraining possibilities of law in the United States. Certainly many of the scholars whom Cover mentions—as he acknowledges in his footnotes—have located law in a context of social control and state coercion and many have gone so far as to make coercion central to law. Ronald Dworkin acknowledges that legal interpretation occurs in the context of a state monopoly of legitimate violence;[11] H.L.A. Hart argues that legal rules characterize what is fundamentally a coercive legal system;[12] sociologists of law have long been fixated on law as social control.[13]

This essay suggests that the significance of "Violence and the Word" lies not so much in the aptness of its description of law as in the possibilities it opens to those who would interrogate its conception of law further. The next section summarizes Covers's account of law in "Violence and the Word," analyzing its presuppositions to show how Cover himself—unlike Foucault and Freud—colludes in the loss of self and collective meaning that his essay attributes to a violent law. The essay then suggests that a possible retrieval of the collective meaning that Cover alleges is lost lies in asking how his conception of law as mediated violence has grown from a tradition that long has associated law—and language—with justice and the *limits* of violence. Cover not only associates law with violence, rather than its limits, but argues further that violence in law "is so intrinsic . . . that it need not be mentioned."[14] When Cover aligns both silence and the word with the violence of law, there indeed seems little possibility of justice in the modern law he takes as law. The law of "Violence and the Word" that plays exclusively on the "field of pain and death" precludes the aspirations of justice in law to which Cover gestures in essays that turn to narrative, myth, and folktales.[15] Nevertheless, the final section suggests, one need not understand the "field of pain and death" as simply violent. The field of pain and death can also be understood as a site of human need, where law through language, establishes what Cover calls the "normative" world and aspires to justice. The word of modern law may be violent, as Cover claims, but law that plays upon a field of pain and death may yet appeal to justice precisely in its silences. If, in declaring the violence of modern law, Cover is silent about the possibility of justice, it is to Cover's silence as well as to that of modern law, that one must turn to recall law's aspiration to justice.

LOSS OF SELF

In "Violence and the Word," Cover presents a conception of law as mediated violence. This conception in important ways resembles the conceptions of law of those whom Cover would critique.[16] The resemblance is worth examining, because it helps reveal the substance and limits shared by both conceptions. Both Cover and those he would critique, that is, speak of a positive law in which judges, although not sovereign, nevertheless command or rather trigger a particular response. This response, or carrying out of commands, is an expression of institutional mechanisms. Cover refuses to call the activation of those mechanisms "a matter of will":[17] the "act of legal interpretation" is less "a single mind placed in the admittedly hypothetical position of being able to render final judgments sitting alone" than "products of judges acting under the constraint of potential group oversight of all decisions that are to be made real through collective violence." Legal interpretation, he goes on to say, is "the violent activity of an organization of people."[18]

In this activity, according to Cover, "a substantial part of [the judges'] audience loses its capacity to think and act autonomously."[19] Judges speak—from them issue "words," "utterances," "language"[20] but they cannot "act" alone.[21] Instead, the social mechanism of which they form part deploys the violence of the law in restraining, rendering helpless, or otherwise hurting defendants.

In some sense like Michel Foucault, then, Cover presents a modern penality that involves something other than the direct laying of hands on a body by the representative of a sovereign.[22] Cover argues, like Foucault, that traditional concepts of sovereignty no longer serve as privileged descriptions of power insofar as many others necessarily accompany a judge in the deployment of law. But Foucault's critique of the Enlightenment subject-who-wills is in the service of a critique of certain metaphysical distinctions—between ideal truth and real power, discourse and practice, mind and matter. In his appeal to the circulation of what he calls power-knowledge, Foucault refuses to allocate agency to any determinate site.[23] Instead, he explores what might be considered, in the parlance of contemporary philosophy of language, the "performative" aspect of speech that has been stripped of a controlling or sovereign subject.[24] For Foucault, it makes little sense to speak of a "gap," as Cover calls it, between word and deed;[25] the problem is to grasp how particular sorts of discourse lend credence to, reinforce, and/or produce particular practices and, conversely, how particular practices structure, reinforce, and/or produce particular sorts of discourse.[26]

By contrast, Cover displaces the notion of will from judge to grander "social" entity in an argument that reiterates the very dualities between mind and deed, thought and action, speech and behavior, that Foucault aimed to disrupt. As Cover puts it,

> Bridging the chasm between thought and action in the legal system is never simply a matter of will. The gap between understanding and actions roughly corresponds to differences in institutional roles and to the division of labor and of responsibility that these roles represent. Thus, what may be described as a problem of will with respect to the individual becomes, in an institutional context, primarily a problem in social organization.[27]

For Cover, the sociological relocation of agency from willing actor to institutional role-player fills a "gap": it explains the transformation of legal interpretation or of the judicial word into violent deed.[28] Legal interpretation, Cover writes, "must be capable of transforming itself into action; it must be capable of overcoming inhibitions against violence in order to generate its requisite deeds; it must be capable of massing a sufficient degree of violence to deter reprisal and revenge."[29] Citing Milgram's experiments, Cover explains that in an agentic state, institutional systems of authority provide the cues needed to cause a "shift from autonomous behavior to the agentic behavior cybernetically required to make hierarchies work." Law, he goes on to say, operates "as a system of cues and signals to many actors who would otherwise be unwilling, incapable or irresponsible in their violent acts."[30]

Taking law as "cue" and "signal," then, Cover argues that law transforms "actors" (now "unwilling" rather than nonwilling) into nonwilling "agents." This "shift" involves a loss of self, he argues, in which the prior "self" is distinguished from the "institutional roles" produced by the system of legal interpretations that call for violence.

For Cover, adopting agentic and institutional roles threatens and destroys the autonomous self. It destroys the self of all partipants. Not only do interpretive agents lose autonomy and judges lose the ability to act, but defendants, too, lose themselves. The defendant's "civil facade" is a role, according to Cover; it is "grotesque" to think it "voluntary," except insofar as it represents the defendant's so-called "autonomous recognition of the overwhelming array of violence ranged against him."[31]

Furthermore, Cover argues, the loss of self is accompanied by betrayal of a normative world. The defendant's experience of pain reveals this most explicitly, he writes, drawing on Elaine Scarry's work on torture.[32] But loss of a normative world is not limited to the defendant. Rather the deployment of violent law entails the loss of everyone's normative world, Cover explains, as commonality and coherence of meaning are limited in two ways.

First, according to Cover, the absence of a singular sovereign or will makes unified or coherent meaning improbable. This "practical" limit, as Cover puts it, "follows from the social organization of legal violence [in which no] single individual . . . renders any interpretation operative as law—as authority for the violent act." The legal system requires the interpretations of many individuals, but convergence of meaning by various individuals is "unlikely," writes Cover. Identifying, in effect, commonality with aggregation of differences and coherence with identity or unity, Cover maintains that meaning is unlikely to be coherent if it is common; it is not common if it is coherent.[33]

The second—"tragic"—limit to common meaning for Cover is due to the unbridgable gap between the experiences of the victim and the perpetrator of violence. The "pain and fear" of the victim is to the perpetrator "remote, unreal and largely unshared. [Pain and fear] are, therefore, almost never made a part of the interpretive artifact, such as the judicial opinion." The violence experienced by the victim contrasts with the interpretation that concerns the perpetrator: "[F]or those who impose the violence, the justification is important, real and carefully cultivated. Conversely, for the victim, the justification for the violence recedes in reality and significance in proportion to the overwhelming reality of the pain and fear that is suffered."[34]

The limits to coherence and commonality of meaning that Cover describes suggest that his sociological account holds out no hope for the recovery of what he calls a "normative world," the shared world that is betrayed with the loss of self required by a violent law. In some sense like Foucault's Benthamite Panopticon, Cover's legal system involves an incorporation or loss of self in the service of judicial interpretation as societal command.[35] Yet if Foucault's Panopticon is an external projection of a Freudian superego in which a subject/ego internalizes the demands of authority,[36] Foucault—and Freud—unlike Cover, do hold out possibilities other than loss. For Foucault, resistance at a local level is itself an exercise of power and a possible political strategy.[37] For Freud, recovery of self or ego development may occur through analysis.[38] But Cover's sociological account precludes recovery of autonomy or production of common worlds. Ironically, then, Cover's account, which least disrupts the traditional metaphysics of will, also holds out least hope for recovery of self or world.[39] His account relies on a strong subject-object (or autonomous actor-productive agent) distinction, even as it claims to deny the centrality of the subject or will. Like much of contemporary sociology, Cover's account transforms subjects into objects and then refuses to acknowledge the commonality or coherence of the former subjects' normative world. Thus it turns out to be more radical in its foreclosure of possibilities than the accounts of either Foucault or Freud.

In other words, unlike Foucault's appeal to resistance and Freud's to analysis, Cover seems resigned to what is lost. His resignation reinforces the loss that his essay describes.

In sum then, Cover describes the field of pain and death in which law plays, however subjectively experienced, as an empirically ascertainable and socially organized violence that not only transforms language into action and word into deed, but also limits the possibilities of collective meaning for all parties. The "achingly disparate significant experiences" of victim and perpetrator mean that both are alienated from "normative worlds" and unable to share in a "reality of common meaning." Not only the "victim" of the organized violence of the legal system, but also the "perpetrator" of that violence, undergoes a loss of self through alienation from collective meaning and a common world. Cover's ostensible resignation to a situation of limited possibilities of common and coherent meaning reveals his own alienation from a normative world. Under his account, this inability to share in a normative world is no fault of his own. Such inability—whether his own or that of others—is presumably something he deplores elsewhere, for example, in "Folktales of Justice" and "*Nomos* and Narrative." Yet in "Violence and the Word," acceptance of an inability to share in a normative world suggests an even greater alienation and loss of self than that originally described, a growing alienation in which those readers who accept Cover's account, without deploring it, participate.

Modern Law

Cover's account of law as mediated violence may or may not accurately describe the law of modernity. Yet it is important to note that his account seems acceptable or even pedestrian to many. To whatever degree his account is borne out, that is, our acceptance of it—or its inability to shock us—in itself says something about the conditions under which we think about law. Consider, by contrast, the conditions, *unlike* those in which we live, in which an account of law as violence would be shocking.

Whatever the conditions under which one might be shocked at Cover's account of violent law, those conditions are not the conditions in which Cover or his judges or most of his readers or victims find themselves. The current acceptability and familiarity of Cover's description of law suggests that the modern law of the United States may indeed be at least somewhat as Cover describes it. Violence makes "the commonality and coherence that can be achieved" by a collectivity problematic, as Cover correctly claims. If violence is an attribute of modern law, such violence indeed seems to distinguish, as Cover puts it, modern law from poetry, as well as legal interpretation from literary interpretation.

The issue for our times, though, is not why or how modern law is not poetry. Those of us who have been raised on the legal positivism and sociology of law of the modern West know that law is not poetry. The issue for us, for our times—and indeed what it may have been for Cover, before "Violence and the Word," in "*Nomos* and Narrative" or "The Folktales of Justice"—is how law is not violence. We should ask how in a tradition (of meaning) that has strived to identify law with aspirations of (if not the essence of) justice, modern scholars and others all seem to identify what is crucial or essential to law with what was traditionally its opposite: violence and the destruction of a shared world.

Of course, the tradition of law in the West is not unmixed. But, drawing in part on Nietzsche's account of the history of metaphysics, one can certainly read the history of jurisprudence since the Greeks as the story of the unfolding, through reason or the will to truth, of various relations of justice to law.[40] In the early Socratic dialogues, for instance, justice lies in the virtue of the wise citizen of the polis; although not accessible to all, the relatively sensible custom or law of the community is known to and practiced by or enacted in the good man. With Christianity comes the recognition that justice attaches not to the City of Man, but to the City of God. Although the divine and eternal law is temporally unattainable, Christianity holds out to the pious the assurance of participation in a natural law and the promise of a future Justice in a world beyond. Following challenges to the foundations of Christianity, Kant replaces the natural law that was grounded in an inaccessible or undemonstrable God, with a moral law that grounds itself in the autonomy (or "self-law") of persons. It falls to the utilitarians to point out that the categorical imperative and the Kantian absolutely good will are as unknown and undemonstrable as Christian justice and to try instead to ground duty and obligation in what can (actually) be known of human beings in an empirical world. The principle of utility, the positive law of the empiricists and legislators, the social policies of economists and political theorists, all aim for better worlds, too, though. They aim for happiness or fairness or distributive justice or other values that are to come about not in a world beyond but in the future of the actual world.

Since Plato, then, it seems, the history of jurisprudence has been, at least in part, the history of a quest for justice. That the justice law seeks is neither grasped nor graspable in this world is an aspect of the fixation of Western jurisprudence with the question of law. The paradox of law has lain in the simultaneous maintenance of a quest for justice with a founding violence in pursuit of this quest.[41] Cover recognizes this originary violence in his description of the martyrs and the founding of the United States of America. Yet in "Violence and the Word," the paradox of law—of a future justice that grounds itself in violence, of a present violence that grounds itself in a promise of justice—flattens out in an exploration of socially organized violence *as* law. Despite his writings elsewhere, Cover here follows not the tradition that would associate law with an aspiration, successful or not, to justice, but follows rather—with social contract theorists and other sociologists—in the footsteps of the one-sided Thrasymychus and a bastardized Hobbes.[42]

Legal interpretation plays in a field of pain and death where violence is imposed and justified, writes Cover. But so, too, do wars and cat fights and insurance adjusters and movies and the Red Cross play in fields of pain and death where violence is imposed and justified in one way or another. The question—for those of us who have been raised on or in Weberian states that hold monopolies on legitimate violence—is: What, if anything, *distinguishes*, or has distinguished, law from *these*? or from any other internalized coercive and social phenomenon?

The question arises for all who would take law to be positive law, whether as a system of rules, network of social control, or commands of a sovereign. As a tradition of contestation over the association of law with justice, jurisprudence answers one way, Cover and the legal positivists, with their assertions that there is no necessary connection between law and morality, another.[43] Cover suggests that the difference between law and any other internalized coercive and social phenomenon is sociological; he points to the particularities of the "social organization" of essentially violent modern law.

From out of the tradition of jurisprudence briefly sketched above, however, comes another possibility: that modern law is essentially violent may be reason to reconsider its claim to be "law," rather than reason to think, with Cover in "Violence and the Word," that law essentially occurs in a context of socially organized violence. Some may claim and indeed be correct—as Cover implies—that there exists no justice-seeking law within the state. But this is not necessarily reason to think that law is violence. It suggests equally well, as Cover seems to recognize elsewhere, that one must turn away from state law—whether legal interpretation or institutional mechanisms—for a conception of law as not simply inherently violent. It is not to legal interpretation as instrument of social control or as implement of violence that one must turn to find law—but to aspects of law that confront the *limits* of social control and domination. Only where law and society neither control nor dominate nor trigger behavior, can an actor—whether judge or other—initiate, and thereby be held responsible for, acts. As Cover himself suggests, when social control or domination produces behavior, the acting self is lost.

"Violence and the Word," despite itself, gestures toward a direction in which to go, then. For Cover writes also that the limits of domination lie in language. He finds what little hope exists for "domesticating violence" in speech—in "many voices" as he puts it:

> As long as death and pain are part of our political world, it is essential that they be at the center of the law. The alternative is truly unacceptable—that they be within our polity but outside the discipline of the *collective* decision rules and the individual efforts to achieve outcomes through those rules. The fact that we require many voices is not, then, an accident or peculiarity of our jurisdictional rules. It is intrinsic to whatever achievement is possible in the domesticating of violence.[44]

"Domesticating violence"—taming its excesses, making it presentable and (paradoxically) effective—requires "many voices" for Cover. To do violence "safely and effectively, responsibility for the violence must be shared," he writes. Such shared responsibility is manifest in "secondary rules and principles" that "ensure that no single mind and no single will can generate the violent outcomes that follow from interpretive commitments."[45]

Unfortunately, however, recall that for Cover, a multitude of voices brings with it the probability of incoherence and an absence of unified meaning. Hence the alternatives to the violence of a "single will" seem to be the incoherence of multiple voices—or a silence that leads to further undomesticated violence. In silence, Cover finds the neglect and denial by law and legal scholarship of law's own violence—its violent preconditions, impositions, and projections. "The violent side of law and its connection to interpretation and rhetoric is systematically ignored or underplayed in the work of Dworkin and White," writes Cover.[46]

Simple examination of texts shows, *contra* Cover, however, that the problematic of violence besets the best efforts of judges, legal philosophers, and other commentators to justify and interpret law.[47] Indeed, the problem of violence, as Cover at times acknowledges, serves precisely to motivate attempts to justify and legitimate a law that is undeniably violent and in *need* of justification and legitimation. Dworkin, for instance, says as much when he writes that governments have goals:

> They use the collective force they monopolize to these and other ends. Our discussions about law by and large assume, I suggest, that the most abstract and fundamental point of legal practice is to guide and constrain the power of government in the following way. Law insists that force not be used or withheld, no matter how useful that would be to ends in view, no matter how beneficial or noble these ends, except as licensed or required by individual rights and responsibilities flowing from past political decisions about when collective force is justified.[48]

All the same, Cover claims that the "ideological functions" of law create meanings that "justify" the event of violence to judges while "hiding" the nature of their orders from them.[49] "Violence," he writes, "is so intrinsic . . . that it need not be mentioned."[50] According to Cover, violence lies at the limits of language, as the undeniable yet suppressed context of law.

Cover thus finds violence both in speech—in the "utterances," "words," "language," "mental activity of individuals," and "thoughts" constituting the legal interpretations that authorize violent deeds or events—and in the silence that lies at the limits of legal texts and language. Agreeing with James Boyd White that law is a "system of constitutive rhetoric: a set of resources for claiming, resisting and declaring significance," and arguing also that the domestication of violence involves secondary rules and principles, Cover maintains that law is all those things only in what is *already* a "context of the organized social practice of violence,"[51] a context that precedes speech. "I do not wish us to pretend that we talk our prisoners into jail," writes Cover;[52] legal interpretation is only law when played on a field of pain and death.

THE SILENT SIDE OF LAW

Cover claims that others systematically ignore or underplay the violent side of law and its connection to interpretation. He asserts that a field of pain and death is prior to the rules and rhetoric that others identify as law. But one can acknowledge that we do not talk our prisoners into jail, as Cover puts it, and can even accept the priority of a field of pain and death over the rules and rhetoric of law, without granting violence absolute primacy at law. Indeed, one could say that Cover underplays the silent side of law and its connection to a field of pain and death that is not simply violent but also necessitates a quest for justice.

The field of pain and death, that is, need not simply be identified with violence and its practice. Even granting, as Cover suggests, that pain and death are always experienced "subjectively," violence is not the same as or coextensive with pain and death. Many will suffer pain and all will die. But at least some will do so without simultaneously undergoing the world-destroying, socially organized violence of Cover's law.

Hence the "field of pain and death" without which there is no law is open to a radically different interpretation than that of Cover. Cover writes that as long as death and pain are part of our political world, they must be at the center of a discursively domesticatable violent law. Yet it is at least equally the case that as long as death and pain are part of our so-called subjective experiences, we are *in need of* a common—not simply subjective—world. As long as we are each in some way alone in our pains and deaths, we lack a certain commonality. Language names that lack and, in so naming, establishes a common world. "Law" is the word for this establishing of world—and is the common ordering on the basis of which particular social or normative arrangements are possible. Without law, as creatures who "subjectively" experience our own deaths (and lives and pains and pleasures), we share neither the political world that Cover begins with nor the normative world that he believes law to betray.

Without law in this sense then, common or collective meaning is not simply limited, as Cover would have it, but nonexistent. Rather than arguing that pain and death must be at the center of a violent law as long as they are part of our political world, one can argue that as long as pain and death belong to us, we need law at the center of our world.

The subjectivity of experiences of pain and violence, in other words, does not simply point—as Cover would have it do, following literary scholar Elaine Scarry on torture—to the betrayal of a normative world. It points to the need for normative world, for commonality, for meaning and the sharing of world. As finite beings who will die and who subjectively experience our own deaths and pains, *we* stand precisely in need of the provision of common meaning and a common world. Law is the name of the semblance of order—the assembling, the ordering, the establishing of commonality—that is made of our otherwise "subjective" differences when we take, or interpret, there to be a world that can be judged, rather than mere subjective experiences. This semblance of order, however illusory, that law grants, constitutes the commonality—the "reality of common meaning"—we share, which grounds the particular "normative worlds" about whose betrayal Cover writes. Without this prior semblance of order, without the assembling or gathering that is law, which seeks meaning and gives commonality to world, there would be neither normative world nor betrayal. (To "agree" in this context that "law ought to be interpreted" now seems laughable: the utterance of a law professor playing god. Law is already interpretation. Law—legal interpretation—binds us to the very "ought" of interpretability at issue here.)[53]

In such an account, borrowing as it does from contemporary phenomenology,[54] "law" names something prior to the law of which Cover speaks. It names that on the basis of which Cover's law—or any other law, for that matter—is possible. All "normative activity" (here understood in a prescriptive rather than descriptive sense)—whether one speaks of custom or natural law or morality or legislation, of judicial opinion-writing or Supreme Court holdings or etiquette or other practices that may or may not hold the status of law—presumes something like a commonality or belonging-together of persons in a world that is created and appears in their language. Law is the name of the prior granting of this world to persons-in-common. The fitting-together of persons-in-common and their world is justice, a justice that law strives for and never fully achieves. Further, although justice cannot be accomplished, we need and demand it and we do so in law. Law names our bindingness to a world in which we need justice and the world does not.

Cover's account of a violent law that plays on a field of pain and death provides a possibly accurate sociological understanding of modern law as the social organization of violence. It shares in the predominant legal positivism of an age in which subjects of law, whether citizens or officials, use rules as templates to project imagined futures upon reality; in which social cues trigger the direction and management of social organizations by institutional role players; in which social agents deploy interpretations to claim, resist, and declare significance, no matter how incoherent; in which there is no necessary connection between law and justice, and law manifests itself ultimately and predominantly as social control.

Such an account of law seeks to right the imbalance Cover finds in other scholars' work on interpretation and violence. It does so, however, by putting interpretation in the service of a violence that it can never master and, at best, only renders more effective. Such an account, accurate and acceptable as it may be to those concerned with characterizing modern law, underplays at least one aspect of the tradition of law: its quest for justice—a quest that, one may grant, is both irreducible to the language of law and insufficiently addressed in work on interpretation of law. If Cover finds in the silence of law and legal scholarship a neglect and denial of law's violence, so too one finds in the silences of modern law and of legal scholarship such as Cover's, a neglect and denial of aspirations to justice.

The danger Cover finds in the silence about violence in judicial opinons lies also in the silence about justice in Cover's essay: the danger of forgetting law's aspiration to justice. Aspirations to justice remain to be thought. Somewhere outside of or behind statements of rules and legislation and judicial opinions—the objects of legal interpretation (and of interpretive theories) that serve as implements of violence—they remain. If it pleases Cover to think that those aspirations occur neither in violence nor the word, fine. They remain, however, in the silences of modern law and in the silences of his own text.

How does one hear the aspirations to justice in the silences of modern law? By listening to that which speaks of silence: poetry. Cover writes of literary interpretation what might more properly be said of poetry: that it does not take place in an institutional setting of violence. The poet, unlike the agentic state, may still remind us of our need for justice—a need whose fulfillment our invocation of law used to call for and, who knows?, may yet call for again. If, as Cover puts it, legal interpretation is—or has become—the implement of a violence that destroys both self and common meaning, though, we moderns must look elsewhere than to law to recall the possibilities of justice. We must find the call for justice where we can—in the language of the poets and the silences of law and legal scholarship. Justice lies in silence in the violent law of "Violence and the Word," but this is only to say that there is no justice to speak of, not that there is no justice nor aspiration to it at all.

NOTES

1. Robert Cover, "Violence and the Word," originally published in *Yale Law Journal* 95 (1986): 1601–1629. Reprinted in *Narrative, Violence, and the Law:*

The Essays of Robert Cover, ed. Martha Minow, Michael Ryan, and Austin Saarat (Ann Arbor: University of Michigan Press, 1992), 203–238. Page references used in this chapter refer to the latter volume.

2. Ibid., 206.

3. Ibid., 210, 216.

4. Ibid., 215

5. Ibid., 204, citing James Boyd White, *Heracles' Bow* (Madison: University of Wisconsin Press, 1985), 205.

6. Cover, "Violence and the Word," 204, note 2.

7. Ibid.

8. Ibid., 205.

9. Ibid., 211.

10. Ibid., 210.

11. See Ronald M. Dworkin, *Law's Empire* (Cambridge: Harvard University Press, 1986), 93.

12. H.L.A. Hart, *The Concept of Law* (Oxford: Clarendon Press, 1961), 193.

13. Studies of crime, deviance, and punishment provide obvious examples of sociological scholarship that treats law as social control. But conceiving of law as social control occurs much more broadly and is apparent early in the twentieth century in the writings of such great sociologists of law as Ehrlich, Pound, and Weber. See, too, the essays reprinted in *Law and Control in Society*, ed. Ronald L. Ahers and Richard Hawkins (Englewood Cliffs, N.J.: Prentice-Hall, 1975), especially F. James Davis, "Law as a Type of Social Control," 17–32, and works cited therein.

14. Cover, "Violence and the Word," 224.

15. See, for instance, "The Supreme Court, 1982 Term—Foreword: *Nomos and Narrative*," *Harvard Law Review* 97 (1983): 4; "The Folktales of Justice: Tales of Jurisdiction," *Capital University Law Review* 14 (1985): 170; "Obligation: A Jewish Jurisprudence of the Social Order," *Journal of Law and Religion* 5 (1987): 5. All three are reprinted in Minow et al., eds. *Narrative, Violence and the Law*. Subsequent references to the first work listed will use the shortened title, "*Nomos* and Narrative."

16. In a long footnote (204), Cover refers to a "recent explosion of legal scholarship placing interpretation at the crux of the enterprise of law." He refers to "various articles" in two symposium issues, published in *Texas Law Review* 60 (1983): 373 and *Southern California Law Review* 58 (1985): 1, and singles out Ronald Dworkin and James Boyd White for their eloquence on the issue.

17. Cover, "Violence and the Word," 217

18. Ibid., 236.

19. Ibid., 221.

20. Ibid., 216.

21. Ibid., 235.

22. Michel Foucault, in *Discipline and Punish: The Birth of the Prison*, trans. Alan Sheridan (New York: Pantheon, 1977; paperback, Vintage, 1979), as is now well known, shows how there has been a change in punishment, from the spectacle of torture, which was both public and involved laying direct hold on physical bodies, to the prison, in which punishment is concealed or hidden from the public

and involves only an indirect use of force on the body. Foucault argues that such a shift corresponds to the emergence of a network of social professionals whose evaluations replace the formerly clear juridical powers exercised by judges. He thereby suggests that power is no longer exercised outward from a determinate center (or sovereign) but rather involves a complex of power-knowledge relations of which discipline is but one form (3–31). Foucault then uses the figure of the Benthamite design for a prison named the Panopticon as a model for disciplinary power in which the normalization of subjects occurs through their own participation in strategies of surveillance (195–228).

23. See Michel Foucault, *Power/Knowledge: Selected Interviews and Other Writings, 1972-1977*, ed. Colin Gordon, trans. Colin Gordon et al. (New York: Pantheon, 1980), especially "Two Lectures," 78–108, and "Truth and Power," 109–34. See also Marianne Constable, "Foucault and Walzer: Sovereignty, Strategy, and the State," *Polity* 24 (Winter 1991): 269–93.

24. Some scholars analyze and evaluate speech for the way in which it succeeds in persuading an audience of the claims a speaker intends to make. Foucault would reject this traditional communications approach to discourse. Like J. L. Austin, in *How to Do Things with Words* (Cambridge: Harvard University Press, 1962), Foucault recognizes the "performative" aspect of speech: speech not only says, but also does. He goes further, however, and, in parallel with his critique of the sovereignty of the subject (see note 22 in this chapter), challenges the authoritativeness attributed to the speaker and the meaningfulness of intention and will. See his works cited above, as well as *History of Sexuality, Volume 1: An Introduction*, trans. Robert Hurley (New York: Random House, 1978; paperback, Vintage, 1990); "What Is an Author?" in *Language, Counter-Memory, and Practice*, ed. Donald F. Bouchard, trans. Donald F. Bouchard and Sherry Simon (Ithaca: Cornell University Press, 1977), 113–34; and the appendix to *The Archeology of Knowledge*. The best translation of this appendix is Ian McLeod, "The Order of Discourse" and appears not in *Archeology*, but in *Language and Politics*, ed. Michael Shapiro (New York: New York University Press, 1984), 108–38.

25. Cover, "Violence and the Word," 217.

26. See not only "The Order of Discourse," cited above, but also the great case studies: *Madness and Civilization: A History of Insanity in the Age of Reason*, trans. Richard Howard (New York: Random House, 1965, Vintage, 1973). *The Birth of the Clinic: An Archaeology of Medical Perception*, trans. A. M. Sheridan (London: Tavistock, 1973; New York: Vintage, 1975), *Discipline and Punish* and *History of Sexuality*.

27. Cover, "Violence and the Word," 217–18.

28. Austin Sarat also points out—in another spirit—the sociological character of Cover's analysis. See his "Robert Cover on Law and Violence," in *Narrative, Violence, and the Law*, 255–65.

29. Cover, "Violence and the Word," 223.

30. Ibid., 220.

31. Ibid., 211.

32. See, for example, Elaine Scarry, *The Body in Pain: The Making and Unmaking of the World* (New York: Oxford University Press, 1985).

33. Cover, "Violence and the Word," 236–37.

34. Ibid., 238

35. See Foucault, *Discipline and Punish*, 201:

Hence the major effect of the Panopticon: to induce in the inmate a state of conscious and permanent visibility that assures the automatic functioning of power. So to arrange things that the surveillance is permanent in its effects, even if it is discontinuous in its action; that the perfection of power should tend to render its actual exercise unnecessary; that this architectural apparatus should be a machine for creating and sustaining a power relation independent of the person who exercises it; in short, that the inmates should be caught up in a power situation of which they are themselves the bearers.

36. For one account of the superego as internalized external authority, see Chapter 3 of Sigmund Freud, *The Ego and the Id* (1923), ed. James Strachey, trans. Joan Riviere, vol. 19 of *The Standard Edition of the Complete Psychological Works of Sigmund Freud* (New York: Norton, 1990). For placement in a cultural context, see Chapter 2 of Freud's *The Future of an Illusion* (1927) ed. and trans. James Strachey (New York: Norton, 1961; with introduction by Peter Gay, 1989).

37. See references in note 23 of this chapter.

38. See, generally, Freud, *Standard Edition*. For examples of discussions of the point, see Freud's *The Question of Lay Analysis* ed. and trans. James Strachey (New York: Norton, 1950); and "Analysis Terminable and Interminable," trans. Joan Riviere, and other essays in Freud's *Therapy and Technique*, ed. Philip Rieff (New York: Collier, 1963).

39. The critique of traditional metaphysics invoked here is broadly informed by the works of Nietzsche, Heidegger, and Foucault. In many works, Nietzsche shows how what we believe to be real about the world (the subject matter of metaphysics or of a particular branch of philosophy) grounds itself in a particular understanding of the subject (understood here as subjectivity rather than subject matter). We think (and speak and write) in terms of subjects and objects or, better yet, subjects and predicates, taking on faith and reflecting in our grammar the capacity of subject-nouns to "predicate" or "verb"—to will or cause or produce effects that are somehow in their control. Nietzsche, Freud, and Foucault all explore ways of thinking about a subject who is no longer in control of him- or herself and of his or her deeds.

40. See Marianne Constable, "Genealogy and Jurisprudence: Nietzsche, Nihilism, and the Social Scientification of Law," *Law and Social Inquiry* 19(1994): 551–90 for a more detailed account than what follows of the history of jurisprudence as a Nietzschean unfolding of nihilism, in which in the name of truth, reason turns against each previous formulation about the justice of the law (and the truth of metaphysics).

41. See, for instance, Walter Benjamin, "Critique of Violence," *Reflections* (New York: Schocken Books, 1978), 277–300.

42. In Plato's *Republic*, Book I, Thrasymychus appears at lines 336b ff. Compare the Hobbes of the actual texts of *De Cive* and *Leviathan*.

43. Legal positivism, with its claim of a lack of necessary connection between law and morality, here represents the penultimate moment in the jurisprudential

tradition of contestation over the relation between law and justice. The ultimate moment comes when this claim itself is no longer made. See, for instance, Frederick Schauer, *Playing by the Rules: A Philosophical Examination of Rule-Based Decision-Making in Law and in Life* (Oxford: Oxford University Press, 1991). Schauer provides an account of what he calls "presumptive positivism," in which he describes law as a system of rules. Nothing distinguishes law from other normative social systems for Schauer, beyond the social convention of calling it "law." Schauer epitomizes a further step in the tradition because the claim of an absence (a "lack of necessary connection") still entails the possibility of a relation that forgetting, on the other hand, precludes.

44. Cover, "Violence and the Word," 236.

45. Ibid., 237.

46. Ibid., 204, note 2.

47. The burgeoning literature on the death penalty provides one example; examples need not be limited to contemporary issues, however.

48. Dworkin, *Law's Empire*, 93.

49. Cover, "Violence and the Word," 212

50. Ibid., 214

51. Ibid., 204, note 2, citing James Boyd White, *Heracles' Bow*, 205.

52. Ibid., 211.

53. If language is the naming of world, then law is the establishing of world in the naming—the world comes to be or is established precisely in the interpreting that is the naming. Interpretability is the "ought" or what must be. It is that to which law binds us. Law requires us to have already interpreted the world.

54. See generally the works of Martin Heidegger. The author is indebted to discussions with Philippe Nonet and to Nonet's, "Judgment," *Vanderbilt Law Review* 48 (May 1995): 987–1007.

CHAPTER FIVE

A Judgment Dwelling in Law

VIOLENCE AND THE RELATIONS OF LEGAL THOUGHT

Shaun McVeigh, Peter Rush, and Alison Young

THE WORK of Robert Cover is celebrated for re-sounding one of the major topics of jurisprudential and political thought: how is it possible to reconcile the force of law with the demands of justice? Like many liberal commentators, Cover's response to this question centered on the paradox that to give order to and preserve the law, the law itself must be violent. However, unlike many modern liberal commentators concerned with avoiding oppression, Cover's work is suffused with a sense that such violence is a troubling necessity for which responsibility must be taken. Staying within the general ambit of the resulting jurisprudence, our own reading of Robert Cover's work takes the form of a series of glosses, highlighting the ways in which key motifs of his later work are brought in play in relation to the question of judgment through a jurisprudence of violence.[1]

SHADOWS OF THE FLESH

It is possible to read the jurisprudence of Robert Cover as a resistance to the recurrent hegemony of the philosophy of law in late modernity. The specific objectionable feature of the philosophical trajectory of much of the study of law is that it puts to one side the questioning of the *relations* of legal thought—regarding such questioning as at best an irrelevance and at worst an inconvenience that needs to be kept under house arrest. Legal thought is to be erased and replaced by a submission to that which is exterior to law—reason and its substitutes, social action and moral responsibility.

It is within and against this historical dispensation that Robert Cover reasserted the claims on our attention that jurisprudence makes. Jurisprudence demands that the study of law stay as close as possible to the movement between and the ordering of the elements of legal thought. In a certain manner, the philosophy of law is indicted and held accountable for killing off legal thought. Yet the wager of Cover is that the thought of law remains—albeit in the shadows and on the run. What he invokes under the various headings of commitment and "immediatism,"[2] we will investigate in terms of the *interior wisdom* of law. This interiority is not substantive law but rather the doctrinal body of law as a process—or better, procedure—of representation and action that organizes the relations of the subject to law, of law to the text, and of law to the world.[3] It is within this framing of the discourses of late modern law that the themes of violence and justice are pursued by Cover.

For Cover, the interior wisdom of law is initially figured in relation to acts of violence. The meaning of law is broken on the rack of violent acts. The limit of understanding law as a practice of interpretation would be that, as the English House of Lords remarked, "no one can understand the pain of another."[4] Those of us who are left behind simply rake over and through the scraps and morsels and other remainders that are reminders of a life lived and died as willing or unwilling witnesses to the atrocities and obscenities of the everyday life of law, held in awe and horror at the sacrifices that have been demanded and made.[5] Out of the memories of other and self, out of these memories of pain, blood, and suffering, Austin Sarat and Thomas Kearns take up the provocation of Cover and call for a "jurisprudence of violence": "[I]n our view, any theory of law must locate violence at the center of its concerns."[6] Such a jurisprudence would provide both a normative understanding of law and a thick description of its behaviors and their consequences. The theme of violence renews the jurisprudential concern with the relations of legal thought—here specified as the varied and varying relations among the texts, the justice, and the actions of law.[7] It focuses the attention of the reader on the process by which (in)justice is embodied in the temporal order of law, on the inscription of that body in law as the passion and pain of the subject of law, and on the economy of the scenes through which violence is passed over and passed on as law.

The concern of our response to this call for jurisprudence is with the manner in which the movement between word and deed is to be understood—and, specifically, with how that movement or passage might be understood so as to figure responsibility for, and give meaning to, the pain and suffering of law's violence. As part of our response to the questioning of the relation of violence and justice, we want to investigate some of the ways in which Cover attempted to articulate relations between legal word and deed and the shadow that falls between.[8] The issue is whether the ethical mandate of the "jurisprudence of violence" can be met *without* losing the co-implication of ethics, violence, and law.

Our reading of the interiority of law is engaged through three glosses. The first examines Cover's account of violence; the second examines the messianic and ethical moment of judgment; and the third examines the "middle" ground of legal reason. The first gloss relates to the violence of law. The violence of law, particularly state law, is clearly destructive of much in life. The argument for the irreducible presence of violence in law does not, of itself, make law more jurispathic than jurisgenerative; but it does require a consideration of the varied relations between the two. Violence is also productive of a legal consciousness which is forgetful of its own origins, in violence and justice. What *can* be thought is the relation of jurispathology and jurisgeneration; and, more importantly, *from the inside of law*, this relation can be thought as a question of justice and injustice.

In the second gloss, we examine Cover's positioning of ethics and violence through his accounts of judgment and messianism. Here we draw his thought closer to the noncognitive "ethics of alterity" elaborated by Emmanuel Levinas.[9] The challenge is to develop responses to ethics and justice that respect the vocation of the other as absolute other, an ethics that does not reduce the alterity of the other to the same through the regulative horizon of "our" values.[10] The question for Cover and those concerned with respecting absolute otherness lies in establishing the possibility of a shared horizon of community, or of the good, through which the response to the other can be mediated. At some point the ethical relation must be joined to the reciprocity of legal-political relations.[11] The difficulty is whether this juncture can be enframed without collapsing questions of ethics into questions of either material enforcement or a regulative horizon. By examining how Jacques Derrida has sought to formulate this problem, we direct our reading of Cover's late essays toward the promise of a justice "yet to come" as well as the demands of injustice.

The third gloss turns back from the "ethics of alterity" yet without returning to the broadly empiricist traditions of Anglo-American legal theory. It suggests that the "middle ground" of law has more supple resources available to it than its representation as a "reasoned" system of enforcement. In all his work, Cover struggles to hold and narrate a "middle ground" of law where "commitment" to justice and law meets the institutional practices of law. This task of jurisprudence might be productively considered in terms of reworking the conditions of attachment to law; that is, in terms of the sites and modes of the application of violence (bodily inscription, technological evisceration, governmental ordering, care, etc.), as well as a practice of government. In juridical terminology, this might be considered in the language of jurisdiction. In a more broadly psychoanalytic idiom, law can be seen as a system of affective and libidinal attachment—to the body of the earth, to the body of the king, to the body of the law, to the body of capital, and so on. In a way somewhat analogous to the presumed structures of psychic reality, legal thought can be considered as a material body, as a durable order to which "we" as legal subjects are bound to a greater or lesser extent. Between word and deed, meaning can be read as emerging "between the too warm flesh of the literal event and the cold skin of the concept."[12]

These three glosses retrace, *on the space of law*, the pathway from the questioning of the institution of law to the questioning of the judgment of law in order to reconsider the thinking of judgment. In drawing Cover's work into relation with some of the themes of the "ethics of alterity," his jurisprudence of violence emerges as part of a response to a broader concern that modern jurisprudence lacks or wants judgment.

COMPLICATIONS OF VIOLENCE

The violence of law is news to few and the theme of law's violence can be found throughout positivist jurisprudence and Hobbesian political theory. What Cover's work does capture, however, is one modern variation on the theme. Cover's writing tracks backward and forward between natural law and positivist accounts of violence without ever settling into one position. From a "naturalist" position that presumes an ethical substance to law, he moves toward the acceptance of the necessary violence of law.[13] From a "positivist" position that presumes that the force of (state) law should be analyzed in terms of meaning, Cover seeks to use that force with good conscience for the ends of justice. In this section, we gloss Cover's account of law and violence with that of one presented by Jacques Derrida in his essay "Force of Law: The 'mystical foundation of authority.'"[14] The purpose of doing so is twofold. First, Derrida's essay draws out clearly the difficulties involved in sustaining a position like that developed by Cover. Cover's account of violence and justice requires ever more exorbitant acts of redemption to hold power and meaning in relation and to prevent word and deed from becoming the dead letter of the law. Derrida's account of force and justice is no less exorbitant, but relations are analyzed in terms of a paradoxical relation between justice and force. Second, it is through Derrida's account of the "encryptment" of force in law that we can read the initial positioning of the "interiority of law" developed within Cover's late essays.

Cover's approach to questions of violence can be seen in his "*Nomos* and Narrative" essay, where the "imperial" force of state law is brought into relation with the flourishing of other jurisgenerative nomoi. Law must be able both to establish predictable behavior and to provide meaning.[15] Of interest here are Cover's responses to the tension he finds between these two aspects. In one account, the relationship between force and meaning is phrased in terms of the essential attributes of all normative worlds. In another account, Cover represents the differences between force and meaning-creation in terms of a sociology of ideal-types.[16]

The first account allows him to consider nomic orders in terms of an intrinsic "tension."[17] In this context, the legal order of the United States of America is analyzed in terms of a conflict between the generation of a multiplicity of legal meaning (jurisgeneration) and the maintenance of legal order (jurispathology).[18] The narrative of law, if not of nomic existence, emerges in terms of a series of tensions between jurisgeneration and jurispathology, or between meaning and force.[19]

In the second and ideal-typical account, there are two types of society. On the one hand, there are ideal-typical societies that are paedeic. Members of paedeic societies share, through attachment, a sense of a "revealed, transparent normative order."[20] Such communities have transparent orders of meaning that need no interpretation. Cover finds examples in religious communities. In this account, violence emerges as external to the nomic order. On the other hand, there are imperial (civil) societies where norms are universal and enforced by institutions. These societies maintain themselves not so much through attachment as through separation.[21] The United States of America, for example, is imperial in its precepts, but open as to how those precepts are related to the material world and thus to meaning-creation.[22] In this sociologic of ideal types, the violence of law emerges as a condition of the maintenance of state law.

Both these accounts emerge in the narrative of law as ordering the nomic and social order. The former account is phrased in terms of social existence and the latter in terms of social control (or not infrequently, the narratives of life and death). In this way, the representation of violence takes place in the symbolic order of law, morals, and politics. In terms of the ordering of jurisprudence, this sociologic is distributed between what is, what ought to be, and what might be.

Whereas "*Nomos* and Narrative" thematizes violence as an issue of the violence of state-formation, a different tack is taken in "Violence and the Word." In the latter essay, the concern with violence is related to the violence of judgment. Cover elaborates the antinomy between jurisgeneration and jurispathology by insisting on a structural asymmetry in all legal relations marked by the violence of enforcement. For Cover, the judge and the judged cannot share the same horizon of understanding. In order for a sentence to be legal, it must be enforced or have the potential so to be.[23] It is not simply that law is used coercively to regulate disputes, rather it is that questions of violence are a part of every dispute.[24] In this aspect at least, Cover's account of violence is not far from that offered by Stanley Fish for whom even persuasion must have its force.[25] Where Cover differs from Fish, in his account of violence, is in his insistence on the visceral and physical aspects of interpretation and regulation: violence is about the infliction of physical pain. For Fish, the narrative of the community is the narrative of the community while, for Cover, the narrative of the community is a (traumatic) response to its violent origins. In terms of an older tradition of political philosophy, necessity (politics or fate) imposes limits on the power of narrative constructions of new orders.[26] In "Violence and the Word," Cover accepts the equation of violence with order, but he does so in terms of tragedy. Unlike the Hobbesian sovereign and subject, however, the question of justice and good conscience is still central to the question of law. The tragedy is that good conscience and violence cannot be fully brought together. In a preliminary account, violence for Cover stands as a basis of and a supplement to all narratives of law. As an ontology, violence would be the essence of law; and as a means to a sociologic, violence enacts and exceeds law. For Cover, the phenomenality of violence marks a limit to meaning and justice. It is a point against which shared legal meaning and justice must be invoked, measured, and thought. Hence, the stern reminders that Cover addresses to law and humanities scholars (who fail to acknowledge the relation of law to violence) are reminders that respond to an ethical imperative to do justice to the injustice of law's violence.

Unlike Cover, Jacques Derrida does not phrase the relation between force and meaning in terms of a tragic divorce of pathos and logos. The fault line of violence enables law to be decrypted and legal violence to be (im)properly distinguished from "numb force." What distinguishes "law"s violence' from "numb force" is that the former opens an opportunity to respond to the call of justice. For Derrida, this conclusion is not made solely as part of a pragmatic assessment of the unpleasantness of force outside law, nor is it solely the product of an assessment of the relative efficacy of law in maintaining "the peace." It is a "quasi-transcendental" argument about the way in which force and justice are "brought together" before the law: force and justice are not an optional part of law, they are the impossible condition of possibility of law.[27]

Derrida's account of the force of law shares with that of Cover and Fish the view that violence is tied to the phenomenality and possibility of language. Where Derrida most obviously differs from Fish is in his account of the performative force of law. For Fish, the performance of law is ultimately a question of social fact. Force is not conceptually separable from (social) conflict: interpretive communities do control the conditions of their performance.[28] Derrida, however, worries more about the conditions of possibility (present future) and impossibility (yet to come) of performatives and not simply their efficacy.[29] Three points of distinction can be made briefly here. First, for Derrida, the impulse of the performance of law is itself not purely internal to law; it is a concern for justice. Outside law, this concern for justice is not itself fully distinguishable from violence.[30] Second, the performative force of law is not simply in the service of some prior social order or power.[31] The founding (inaugurating and justifying) moment that institutes law is a *coup de force* that is not itself "inscribed in the homogenous tissue of history, since it is ripped apart in one decision."[32] It is not itself legal but *a*legal. Thirdly, if violence inheres in the possibility of language, language inheres in the possibility of performance.[33] There can be no pure performance of institution (pace Fish). The first point will be taken up in the next section of our essay. Here, the last two points will be pursued further to show how Derrida rephrases the relation between force and justice.

For Derrida, the positing or constituting activity of founding law is never simply a constative act: a constitution performs its constitution, the posited act performs its positioning, legal judgments perform judgment.[34] However, in a move now familiar to "deconstruction," this "bringing together" of constative and performative is in turn not without its effects. The performative and the constative are figured as two different modalities of action. What is performed does not conform necessarily to what is constituted; it always does more or less than what is said of it. The claim of foundation is one that is always met with a complex temporal figuration. For the moderns, law arrives on the scene too early: the issue of violence is always prejudged by law. Violence can only be acknowledged as an irreducible fact of life, once the law has been invoked in its place— that is, once the law has denied, repressed and superseded the question of its own forceful origins and practice. Force comes before the law and is reconstituted as an excess of law.

Of interest here in Derrida's account in "Force of Law" is the consideration of the excess enfolded in law and encrypted as the "mystical foundation of authority." It establishes the dwelling place through which law is instituted and from which law is disseminated.[35] The originary encounter of law (the joining and disjoining of force and violence) does not simply constitute force as the exterior to law; nor does it show violence to be only a fictive inscription of an outside through which the real violence of law is hidden.[36] Finally, it does not repeat (without changing it) the claim that law really is violence, leaving justice and ethics on its outside. The irrelation between the performative force of constitution and the constative act of constitution of law (as a system of right) is not simply cast into a general economy of violence but a differential one of excess. Law is a response to the excess of force of its origins.

The performative meeting of force and justice in law in turn encrypts violence in law—at once threatening law but also making it possible. In "Force of Law," Derrida considers the "violent structure of the founding act" to entomb or "wall up a silence."[37] On the one hand, this silence is an indecipherable ("mystical") rather than unintelligible limit of foundation or its lack thereof.[38] On the other hand, it is this "walled-up silence" that opens the "positivity" of law to questions of normativity and deconstruction. This silence could also be associated with the uncanny and the secret. The encrypting of violence in law is the first positioning of the interiority of law. It creates the spacing and division of legitimate and illegitimate violence. It prevents the simple assertion of the division of inner law (justice) and outer conformity to law (authority). In addition, but in a more familiar way, it opens the law to "what is to come."[39] Where Cover's legal universe is circumscribed by the shadow of violence between word and deed,[40] Derrida's account emphasizes the jurisgenerative aspects of the encrypting of violence in the performance of the word of law. The silence of law could well have walled up the dead body of law, but it could also be an indication of the secret of law—the passion of law that Derrida signs as the openness of law to justice and, we will argue, that Cover testifies as being the immemorial injustice of law.

The encrypting of violence also brings with it the narrative foundation of law—the narrative of what makes these or any laws law, and a tale of their relation to the order of law. In so far as it is a figurative discourse, its object is death. It is a staging of something that does not yet exist, as the U.S. Constitution staged a nation that does not yet exist. It seeks to present the unpresentable in imaginary (phantasmic) or symbolic (legal) form. But, for all the materiality they achieve, such narratives also signal the impermanence of law. The recognition of the work of language at the source of law is a reminder both of the impermanence and contingency of legal form and of its mutability in use and transmission. It is an edifice of law in which, once inside, it is not possible to determine fully the horizon of its foundations.[41]

In following the argument of the "Force of Law," the claim made so far is that, if force and justice "call law into being," it is called into being as a figuration. Yet this figuration neither fully permits originary force to be imagined from the viewpoint of law, nor fully allows law to imagine itself as completely violent. The starting point of our essay was with the problem of words and deeds—words as pure interpretation of law, deeds as forceful enactment. The call for a jurisprudence of violence argued that law is contaminated by violence. In "*Nomos* and Narrative" and in "Violence and the Word," Cover proposes a diremption between force and meaning that can only be acknowledged as tragic. Derrida's formal account of the bringing together of force and justice indicates the way in which law is not sustained as an entity in itself. It is constantly re-created in the form of the crisis of violence—and, specifically, re-created through the meeting of force and justice.[42] In a somewhat different idiom, this formulation draws out the emphasis that Cover gives to law as the bridging moment of the meeting of force and meaning. This meeting Cover gathers into the question of the authority of law.

If there is a point of difference between the formation of force and law presented by Cover and Derrida, it lies with the quality of the recollection or memory of violence. For Cover, the originary violence (force) of law literally inscribes meaning on the body of the victims of law.[43] Sarat and Kearns take this violence as having fully ontological status.[44] This position would seem to commit Cover's protagonists in law to ever more violent attempts to overcome the law.[45] However, reading Cover alongside Derrida's "Force of Law" allows a different role for law to appear, a different place in which to dwell. If it is true for Cover that there is no point, as yet, when law is simply disconnected from violence and capable of passing judgment on it—then it is also the case that even the most contaminated law is never a pure violence, because violence is understood in relation to law as an excess (and law is called into being as a question of justice and force). Cover emphasizes this point in two different registers. On the one hand, there is an obligation to law that is not simply pragmatic;[46] on the other hand, law is defined as the system of "tensions" that bridges a concept of reality and an imagined alternative.[47] Where Cover's argument struggles is not so much with normativity or with an excessive positivism but with the positioning of the normative in relation to violence. The problem lies with the overwhelming phenomenality of violence that Cover finds in law. Here Derrida's "quasi-transcendental" account of the force of law opens the "positivity" of law to normative aspiration in a way that Cover's account does not in any formal manner.[48]

Dwelling in relation to this domain may of course still be no easy business.[49] In "Violence and the Word," dwelling is thought in terms of the utter irreducibility of a pain that gives meaning to the material form of law. The danger of such thinking is that, by setting pain up as a point beyond law through which violence can be understood, pain is rendered unintelligible to law and the limits of law too determinate. Not only does pain make you forget that law is figurative, it renders the figuration of law invisible. Derrida's account of the force of law resists the totalizing impulse of equating law and violence by emphasizing the temporal contortions of the institution of law. The forceful, alegal founding of law does not conform to a uniform temporality of law and life. For all its institutional grounding and historical specificity, the constitution of law must be performed at every moment of enforcement. Again, if we resist the uniform equation of law with the options of total violence or total nonviolence, attention can be given to the range of Cover's figurations of the relation between word and deed. It would also make sense of Cover's pragmatic concern with "the least worst" violence.[50] In the next section, we consider the position of normativity in relation to judgment in Cover's thought and, in the final part of the essay, the question of practical reason is considered through Cover's formulation of jurisdiction.

IMAGES OF JUDGMENT

For many of Cover's critics, once it is acknowledged that there is violence in the law, a threshold has been crossed. It is not just that there is always danger dwelling in the house of the law, although there is, but that there is no value in so dwelling. There is no—or no longer—a proper threshold sustained by law between justice and injustice.[51] What is at issue is the possibility and worth of judgment in such situations. Our gloss of Cover's account of judgment follows the trajectory of the problem of force and justice in law outlined in the previous section. In turning to judgment, we follow the complication of Cover's views of commitment and bonded interpretation through a consideration of the form of judgment and the obligation to law. Departing from the idiom and general topics of Cover's work, Cover's analysis of "the literary turn in interpretation" is turned to the production of an account of justice and judgment.

Against all the odds, the image of the judge sits as the source of all judgment. This image acts as the unifying point of the Anglo-American or common law understanding of law. As opposed to the abstractions of foundations and the problem of distinguishing law from violence and even violence from justice, the judge sitting in judgment is a guarantee both of law's material presence and the possibility of justice. It is judgment that enables justice to be given the force of law and the force of law to be given legitimacy. The authority of the law is sustained by the repeated enforcement of judicial wisdom in the courts, legal thought is maintained by the ceaseless attention to legal doctrine, the force of law is monitored against excess, and so on. In short, the judge holds up a mirror to its subject. It is this image that Cover sets in play to alter the vision of law. In many ways Cover does not depart greatly from this image, although many more than state-appointed judges get to decide in the name of the law. As a good commentator, Cover endlessly complicates what might be taken as good judgment.

To find the work of judgment contaminated by violence—not only interpretive violence but also physical violence—causes a number of problems. Most importantly, it places in question the authority of judgment by deferring the possibility of establishing a point from which to judge the world free from the contamination of violence. Likewise, the possibility of securing a proper transmission of meaning and effect between word and deed is met with the same complication. For Cover, any jurisprudence that marks the criteria of good or bad judgment in terms of conformity to a theory of interpretation fails to give due recognition to the problem. Such theories move from word to deed without hesitation and in so doing leave judgment untouched. It is not an event but a product. The purity of legal judgment and law is saved, but at the cost of denying both the practice and structure of judgment. It is to render judgment beyond any question of justice, beyond the response to a particular event.

Against this, Cover takes two approaches and turns them both toward the violence that inheres in the practice of judgment. First, judgment can be analyzed in relation to the judge who judges. The judge can be judged by their character: the wise judge wisely, the foolish foolishly. This type of analysis pays attention to the persona, dignity, or virtue of the judge. If law was to be related to justice, then to judge wisely would be to judge justly. Until this century, this was the dominant way of justifying common law adjudication.[52] Character in this account marks the central connection between good judgment, justice, and fate. Many would argue that the possibility of evaluating law and justice in these terms was lost long ago and, with it, the view that judgment is a matter of human measurement of and with violence.[53] Second, and more formally, Cover points to those traditions that place questions of judgment in close proximity to those of faith and good conscience. Judgment in this account emerges as the meeting of chance and destiny, of the indeterminacy of judgment subject to the demands of justice—rather than subject to the authoritative presence of a prior law. While this tradition of indeterminate judgment is historically associated with political (and familial) judgment, it also informs the traditions of Aristotelian practical reasoning, and of casuistry and equity. This is the world of "decision with no rule," of the judge as the practical judge of particulars but also of the judge become sovereign or prophet. It is the dominion of the judge who delivers the sentence of the law with conviction.[54]

For Cover, what holds the character and conscience of the judge before the law is the institutional role of the judge. This allows Cover to run the questions of character, conscience, and decision together in considering the meaning of judgment. In Cover's narrative of law, the figure of the martyr or judge does not render an abstract decision but one potentially written in blood. In making the violence of the law visible, the narrative that Cover relates reveals the character of law and, one imagines, renders it open to judgment. In this might be read another version of "immedia-tism" where presence to the law is revealed in its performance.

Form and Obligation

What is gained in Cover's account of the role of the judge is a strong sense that the responsibility of judgment is embodied; it is physical and visceral as well as interpretive. What is more difficult to ascertain in Cover's work is the form of judgment and justice in relating meaning, norm, and vio-lence. In part, this is because Cover was concerned with the production and maintenance of institutional meaning as a practice. For example, in "Nomos and Narrative" Cover addressed the question of instituting meaning through jurisdiction and the question of the transmission of le-gal meaning through the topics of narrative and commitment. However, within this concern, it is not difficult to delimit a space for judgment. In "Nomos and Narrative," Cover offers a brief formulation for the crea-tion of legal meaning:

> [the] [c]reation of legal meaning entails . . . subjective commitment to an objec-tified understanding of a demand. It entails the disengagement of the self from the "object" of law, and at the same time requires an engagement to that object as a faithful "other." The metaphor of separation permits the allegory of dedi-cation.[55]

On its face, Cover's concern with "objectification" is pragmatic. It is a question of how legal meaning is created in practice. The relevant practice is considered in terms of the psychology of commitment necessary to val-idate legal norms. For Cover, this commitment is represented in the form of a narrative that explains how the law came to be and to be one's own.[56] Hence, in a sense, the many narratives that Cover uses to understand the commitment to law.[57] However, the psychology of attachment and sepa-ration need not be analyzed solely in terms of a narrative of object-choice. Cover's formulation of the creation of legal meaning repeats (and mimics) the submission to the Law. The narratives of dedication tell the tale not only of the "objectification of value" but also the tale of how the good comes to be defined *as if* it were subject to the (moral) Law. For our purposes, the act of understanding commitment also opens the ground for judgment *as if* it were lawful. The act of judgment according to law becomes a singular allegory and act of dedication.

For Cover, the narrative of the creation of legal meaning is not com-pleted with the creation of the "object" of law, since the narrative of legal meaning is sealed with an "allegory of dedication." Traditionally we might take this allegory as representing the obligation to law. Yet allegory opens a distance between apparent and ultimate meanings. For example, as an image of obligation, it could be taken as preserving the gap—for action and interpretation—between the unredeemed prosaic world and the possibility of its redemption (through law). Or, and this may not be different, it could represent the irremediable violence of law and justice. Alternatively, in the absence of an authoritive ordering of images, it opens the space of representation and meaning to dispute. In "Nomos and Narrative," the topoi of judgment are elaborated through the narratives of violence found in the assertion of authority and jurisdiction. As allegories, they perform the allegorical structure of legal meaning and judgment.[58]

In "Violence and the Word," Cover's approach to judgment takes a slightly different tack. In that essay, judgment is indeed the central concern. But again no theory of judgment is offered. Instead, Cover moves from a largely psychological account of the violent production of legal interpretation to an administrative account of the possibilities of regulating the violence of institutional legal judgment. In attempting to render the violence of judgment visible, Cover places emphasis on legal judgment being bound to a series of institutional practices and roles, all of which are designed to produce effective physical consequences. The judge is never free in her or his description of the practical activity of enforcing judgment. For Cover, neither the interpreters nor the officials of law (assuming that such a distinction can still be made) can detach what they do from the acts of violence that both set the law in motion (the pathology of jurisgeneration) and follow on from law (the "homicidal potential" of law). "Legal interpretation," Cover writes, "is either played out on the field of pain and death *or it is something less (or more) than law.*"[59] All interpretation is bonded to the social world and it is this bond that distinguishes the practice of legal interpretation from the practice of literary interpretation. Legal interpretation is more directly allied with the practice of political violence and as such is placed on a "different footing" to those (literary) institutions of interpretation whose orthopaedics "bear only a remote or incidental relation to the violence of society."[60] The action of law obtains and retains its meaning from the "ecology of jurisdictional roles," the "field of pain and death" in and on which law and the "practical reasoning" of judges takes place.[61] Violence—as the inscription of pain—is irreducible: "[e]ven the violence of weak judges is utterly real—a naive but immediate reality, in need of no interpretation, no critic to reveal it."[62]

Powerful though Cover's account of the violence of judgment and interpretation is, it dwells uneasily with the account of meaning and power offered in "Nomos and Narrative." In "Violence and the Word," the allegory of dedication emerges as a tragedy. Meaning and good conscience cannot overcome or contain the violence of law. In terms of modern jurisprudential apologetics, this in itself might be taken as a tragedy, as something terrible. But Cover's tragedy is older. It lies, impossibly, in taking responsibility for fate, in being obligated to the law—and here, to the violence of law. Through the bonded nature of the legal sentence, the allegory of dedication appears in ruins. While it might be possible to distinguish analytically between the horizon of meaning and the economy of enforcement, a better reading of Cover renders the dichotomy in terms of differing modalities of legal (nomic) order.[63] In the first section of this essay, we indicated the difficulty of fixing the power of law in a domain separate from its meaning. There, the risk of Cover's analysis appeared both in the refusal to acknowledge the violence (or injustice) of law and in the collapse of law into violence. In pointing to the contamination of questions of force and justice in law, the question of violence was returned to a rather more complex set of relations between law and justice. In this section, we have traced the consequences of this reading into the task of judgment. Cover's insistent call for law (judicial and administrative officials) to take responsibility for the violence of law emerges as an impossible request. The language of justification, redemption, and transformation in law and through law requires that the violence of law be taken into account. Yet, as Cover points out, it needs no interpretation; it remains after all justification. To take violence into account, to justify it through interpretation, is precisely not to respect the violence of law. Rather, it is to subject the violence of law to the language of meaning. The language of justification belongs to the nomos, but between judge and judged there is a limit point to such commonality inscribed in pain and suffering.[64] One temptation is to read the performance of law as violence and so to consider all judgments of law as violent in their form if not entirely in their practice. However, this reading fails to meet the complications of violence that Cover puts to work in his essays. As a narrative place marker, Cover evokes the language of tragedy. It is this language that we will try to follow. Two issues arise: What account of responsibility can be given that can take responsibility for these modalities of law? How are these two modalities of law to be "brought into relation"? The first issue we approach through Derrida's account of justice and the form of the messianic; and the second we approach through a consideration of judgment as decision.

Justice

The language of justice is called up to perform two tasks. One, quite common, is to provide a language of justification for law; and the other is to account for the particular violence of law. This gloss will try to keep these two aspects in relation.

If we turn again to Derrida's "Force of Law," the question of judgment is cast not in terms of meaning and power but in terms of justice and an aporia of judgment. In Derrida's account, the important distinction lies between justice as "infinite, incalculable, rebellious to rule and foreign to symmetry" and law as "calculable, a system of regulated and coded prescriptions."[65] In this formulation, Derrida casts the movement of justice as a movement "beyond law"; beyond the presumed unities of legitimate action, of regulatory ideals of justice (and communication). For Derrida, justice is figured as a movement or gesture in response to the other, the other who precedes me and obligates me. Justice in this sense is quite particular and finite—for example, in response to the pain and suffering of an other. It is being captured by the appeal of the other. Justice here comes "before the law," dealing in particulars, dealing, for example, with the phenomenal violence of law. In the same breath, Derrida also offers a more exalted version of obligation to justice. In "Force of Law," Derrida examines the obligation of justice in terms of the gift, of the gift without return: justice is obligation without debt. "Pure" justice is not owed, it is beyond the economy of circulation and return, beyond the economy of vengeance and restitution. It is more originary than this. Justice is a gift without restraint to the other. Derrida makes no distinction between these two formulations of the obligation to justice. In response you are obligated to the other—it happens. The obligation to the other is extreme; it is without reason and justification.[66]

The concern of justice in Derrida's account is a concern with respect for the other, with the singularity of the other as wholly other. As he points out, this is a necessary and impossible task: justice as responsibility to the other is infinite and "as the experience of absolute alterity [it] is unpresentable."[67] As infinite responsibility beyond calculation, the performance of justice "remains, is yet, to come, à venir, it has an, it is à-venir, the very dimension of events irreducibly to come."[68] Justice is turned to, and proceeds from, not a future that can be realized through calculation in the present, but to and from the impossible, yet to come.

For Derrida responsibility to justice corresponds to a double movement: first, it is a responsibility without limits, hence excessive, incalculable, and before memory; and, second, the responsibility "toward memory is a responsibility before the very concept of responsibility that regulates the justice and appropriateness of our behavior."[69] This is a responsibility for the workings of justice within the (symbolic) order of representation, within the domain of the calculable and the domain of right. For, no matter how singular the demand of justice, no matter how unique the obligation to the other, this demand or these obligations do not arise alone. They are calculated in relation to a third. The judgment of justice in law must respond to both orders.

Initially we suggested that for Cover the limit question of responsibility to law turns on a responsibility for the practice of the phenomenal violence of law. This is so both as a matter of commitment and as a matter of dedication (here understood in terms of representation and address). However, our first gloss of Cover's understanding of violence has pointed out the difficulty that understanding faces when asked to respond to the institutional orderings of violence that might be invoked in relation to law (phenomenal, symbolic, transcendent). By drawing Cover's account of violence closer to the one Derrida extracts from his reading of Walter Benjamin's "Critique of Violence," Cover's account of violence was more closely tied to the varieties of injustice attendant on law and lawful justice. Our reading of judgment suggests a similar gloss to the orthodox interpretation of Cover's account of judgment when that account moves beyond the responsibility for the faceless violence of law and turns to what a commitment to "face-to-face" judgment might entail.

In an institutional context, a better accounting of Cover's concern with the violence of judgment might be phrased in terms of three issues. The first concern is with the proper response to the (imperial) calculability of law. In this context, the limit point of phenomenal violence insists on responsibility for judgment encompassing the face-to-face encounter as a practical reminder (a *memento mori*) that the allegory of dedication is an image inscribed in the flesh. The second concern is with the positioning of the ethical in relation to judgment. Cover considers the first two concerns through the themes of commitment, dedication, and good conscience. Clearly good conscience is more than following the letter of the law. It is through the impossible attempt either to transcend the violence of law or to come to terms with the failure so to transcend, that Cover generates the tragedy of judgment. A final concern is with the phenomenal violence of judgment. Derrida's account of the justice of judgment goes some way toward linking these two aspects of Cover's analysis by offering an account of the singularity of justice that, on its face, neither expels the phenomenality of violence or the demand of justice from the symbolic order of law nor permits the termination of justice in the calculability of law. The attraction and threat here is the proximity of the singularity of violence and the singularity of justice. It is with this disturbing proximity that both Cover and Derrida grapple. They do this through a consideration of the meanings of messianism.

For Cover, the practical question is how to calculate with violence, and the trajectory of his response is toward the figuration of calculation through the elaboration of the typology of legal role and legal actor. Before we follow Cover in the ordering of the bonds of law, it is necessary to complete the relation of Cover's account of meaning to law. So far, our gloss of Cover's account of judgment has turned the gap between word and deed toward the complications of violence. To deepen the gap between word and deed, the account of judgment must be turned to the tension "linking a concept of reality to an imagined alternative."[70] The narratives that Cover offers to outline these links are connected to the possibility of the transformation of law. Of these the most significant, and most considered, are the messianic narratives of redemption. In these narratives, the possibility of meeting the violence of law comes up against one of its limits through the claim of transcendence.

yet to come

One of the most striking features of Cover's later work is his interest in the messianic practices and structures in legal thought, both Judaic and U.S. Constitutional. His concern with the anticipation of "what might be"; with the possibilities of destruction and restoration in what is to come; and with redemption that demands action—all resonate in his formulations of the normativity of law. Likewise, the messianic concern with the disparity between the ideal and the real, faith and its loss in law, and the fulfilled and unfulfilled time of justice all inform his consideration of the commitment to the teleology and jurisdiction of law.[71] Finally, the concern with the possibilities and dangers of the realization of "messianic visions" through law colors Cover's accounts of judgment and the decision-making process. It is through the consideration of the messianic that the links among judgment, normativity, and violence get their fullest treatment.

While the topic of messianism receives specific treatment in "Folktales of Justice" and "Bringing the Messiah Through the Law," it also informs the general structure of normativity he presents in "*Nomos* and Narrative." He writes that a "*nomos* is a present world [of value] constituted by a system of tension between reality and vision";[72] and further, "law is that which holds our reality apart from our visions and rescues us from the eschatology that is the collision in this material social world of the constructions of our minds."[73] In this context, Cover urges, law can be "viewed as a system of tension or a bridge linking a concept of reality to an imagined alternative."[74] Law is both a barrier and passage between the unfulfilled material world and our visions of fulfilment.[75] By holding out a promise of future worlds yet to come, this messianic structure opens up a number of possible relations between the generative and pathological aspects of the world of law.

In "Bringing the Messiah Through the Law," Cover questioned his own presumption that eschatology was always or necessarily antinomian. Instead he considered the case for "legal apocalypticism"[76] or a "Messianic immediatism" that is "powerfully and positively related to religious law."[77] Such a lawful messianism illuminates "the form of commitment that holds to the immediacy of a privileged and strange transformation while insisting on a highly unusual capacity for familiar transformational institutions."[78] This formulation is characteristic of Cover's understanding of judgment and transformation in law. It is this that we will follow here in figuring the interiority of law.

In a powerful consideration of Cover's messianism, Richard Sherwin criticizes Cover for allowing his romantic antistatism to underrate the dangers of "messianic totalitarianism."[79] Sherwin's concern is that messianism undermines the possibility of a nonsectarian liberal state.[80] He identifies three aspects of Cover's work that allow for the overwhelming of the liberal vision of law by (sectarian) violence. In various ways, each aspect repeats the gesture of seeking to transcend or transfigure the order of law and violence by establishing a pure meaning untainted by force and structure.[81] The most profound of these gestures consists in the favoring of a transformation outside of time, the time of messianic irruption that "realizes the world at the end of time."[82] In this time—and in seeking to bring this time about—there is no distinction to be made between acts of law and acts of faith. Eschatology for Sherwin entails a totalization of vision and reality, and of meaning and power. It defeats the possibilities of other visions of law and indeed mortal time.[83] Sherwin also finds a similar totalizing gesture in the idealized division between power (jurispathology) and meaning (jurisgenesis). In this context, redemptive movements must seek freedom from the violent bonds of the existing social order by demonstrating the force of their own commitment to their nomos. Redemptive movements require totalization of force and meaning. And finally, this gesture is repeated in the idealization of narrative that keeps meaning and violence apart and, in so doing, allows for the possibility of untainted meaning.[84] In short the possibility of profane law, politics, and government is lost and, along with it, the possibility of any nonsectarian political and legal order.

The detail of this analysis by Sherwin can be questioned on a number of grounds. Here, however, we give attention to the claim that messianic thought is totalizing and antiliberal (or, more generally, antipolitical).[85] Following the earlier reading of violence and decision, the "system of tensions" that Cover elaborates will be read aporetically to examine the "interiority" of Cover's law.

Our first entry point to the possibility of "a privileged and strange transformation" is with the temporality of the time of justice and the time of law. Like Cover, Derrida utilizes messianism to consider not just the question of transformation but also the possibility of responsibility—responsibility for that which precedes us as that which is to come.[86] In "Force of Law" and *Specters of Marx*, Derrida uses the "messianic" to develop a structure of the promise of a future always yet to come (*à venir*), the structure of "a certain experience of the emancipatory promise."[87] Derrida considers the

> irreducible movement of the historical opening to the future, therefore to experience itself and to its language (expectation, promise, commitment to the event of what is coming, imminence, urgency, demand for salvation and for justice beyond law, pledge given to the other inasmuch as he or she is not present, presently present or living, and so forth).[88]

In this Derrida places emphasis on the general structure of the messianic as the structure of the promise, of a future—justice, democracy, Messiah—always "yet to come." This general structure brings law/justice and decision/undecidable "back to the primary terrain of their opening to the radically heterogeneous"—the impossible that makes responsibility possible.[89] The messianic is the originary opening to the other. It is concerned with the affirmation of what is to come—the wholly or radically other.

What Derrida resists in his account of the "messianic" is the claim to circumscribe a horizon for the future coming—to identify, in the idiom of language and law, the content of the Messiah's message in advance of its arrival. And this is what Cover appears not to resist in his brief comments at the beginning of his essay "Bringing the Messiah Through the Law."[90] However, it is possible to bring Cover close to Derrida in the generality of their use of messianism.

In *Specters of Marx*, the messianic is equated both with the general structure of the promise and with the historical messianisms of the Book.[91] The structure of the promise is not necessarily tied to the specifics of messianic movements. It is turned toward justice. On the one hand, the promise could be the condition of possibility of the emergence of messianisms. Or, and this is in keeping with the more usual formulations of inheritance that Derrida makes, the messianic might be thought of as an ascetic stripped-down version of messianism. Messianic hope removes itself of particular figurations of the Messiah and from particular historical associations of messianism. But it does not thereby become a transcendental structure.[92] This would be a "quasi-transcendent" messianism, a structure that indicates a relation. It would also be a despairing messianism that has given up hope for, or given up counting on, the arrival of the Messiah. If it were possible to count on the arrival of the Messiah, there would be the prospect but no longer the waiting for anyone. It would be law without justice.[93]

This last formulation takes us some distance from the characteristic idioms of Cover's work, but perhaps there is a path to be found. The first commonality is found in the use of messianism as a limit point for considering the possibility of the transformation of law in the name of what is to come. Whatever the specific examinations of messianic, utopian, and redemptive movements, in "*Nomos* and Narrative" Cover employs a general messianic structure of law as being a bridge between and toward possible worlds. For the hope and possibility of transformation of nomic worlds has a general structure that finds expression in particular myths.[94] Where Sherwin finds in Cover's last essay a yearning for complete transformation to the end of time, Cover can be read as attempting to explore the possibilities of a lawful justice—hastening the Messiah, not yet embodying one.[95] In "Folktales of Justice" the specific tasks of practical transformation between unredeemed and redeemed is a general problem of legal judgment.[96] It would also be possible to find a more constrained account of redemption through law. In *Specters of Marx*, the general account of messianism as promise—as the promise of the just performance of the law, yet to come—is used by Derrida to promote an antisectarian politics. It would turn itself into the most universalist critique of existing redemptive legal orders, including the U.S. Constitutional order. Sherwin is right to point to the risk of the messianic moment either falling into sectarianism or withdrawal. But if Derrida and Cover's account is accepted, then this is the risk of all nomic orders: there would be no position from which to judge a nomic order free from the messianic; there would be no jurisgenerative nomic order or possibility of justice at all.

This last point returns us to something like a paradox that Derrida—but not Cover—finds in the messianic. This is the paradox of "sacrifice": the paradox of having to respond, of being obligated to the singularity of the other without reservation, while at the same time having to meet the generality of obligation to all other others.[97] Without the former there can be no obligation; without the latter there can be no ethics or law. In a very different idiom to be sure, Cover comes close to this formulation in the juxtaposition of jurisgeneration and jurispathology.

Judgment/Decision

The messianic promise keeps law open to the yet to come and marks out the impossible justice of law. In Derrida's invocation of force and justice in law, the impossibility of justice in the here and now of present time does not remove any obligation to judge and to decide. The task of judgment is to forge a non-identical bond between justice and law: to let meet the horizon of individual judgment with that universal law *without precisely joining* (spatially, temporally, logically) one to the other.

In "Force of Law," Derrida sketches three moments of the aporetic form of judgment that relate the necessity of the decision to the undecidable.[98] First, the suspension of law: on the one hand, the judge must judge the particularity of the case, judge as if every decision were unique; on the other hand, to be just the judge must follow the law. Without this there can be no "lifting" of repression, no limit to calculation, no relief of law. This is the time of judgment with no rule, the judgment of the practical reasoner (*phronimos*). Second, the undecidability of the decision: no decision can be said to be truly just at the time it was made, precisely because it would have to be both regulated and truly unregulated at the same time. This moment cannot be met or be avoided if a just judgment is to be made: a just decision must pass through the "ordeal of the undecidable."[99] This can be considered the messianic moment of judgment. However, responsibility does not end at this point because, once passed, the decision returns to the order of law.[100] Responsibility must be taken for this return to law as well because a decision that passes through the "undecidable" can be accused of, and identified with, a kind of madness—as a precipitous thoughtlessness, as acting before the invention of the rule.[101] Third and finally, there is the time of the decision itself: although justice precedes knowledge and law and will always be delayed before the law, the demand is that justice be performed at this instant. Calculation must stop, justice must be done.[102] The decision of justice is always mis-timed, not to mention mis-placed and dis-jointed. It is the experience of the impossible.

In all these formulations, the aporia of judgment is an attempt keep open both the singular call to justice as well as the recognition of the necessity of the "third," the necessity of the justice that ranks and orders the claims of other others. In this, there is a continuous falling into law and calculation. Judgment is the impossible task of keeping this falling from producing injustice. However, there is a sense that Derrida's account of justice and judgment is radically different from Cover's. We have already noted that for Cover submission and obligation is to law and not to justice. While Cover is keen to pick up messianic and utopian yearnings for justice, there is a sense that Cover's ear is attuned equally to the soundings of injustice—of the injustice of law and of justice. The distance that Cover keeps from state law and his insistence on the priority of jurisgeneration over jurispathology keep his narratives circulating around the dangers of law.[103] For all the messianic yearnings, it seems to us that Cover takes his question not to be how is it possible to exceed law, but how is it possible to remain with the law.

Cover indicates the absolute singularity of the violence of judgment before the law—and before justice as law. This violence is irremediable in its structure. It is the injustice of law, albeit one quite singular and particular. Like the claim of justice, this violence operates in excess of law, beyond law, both preceding law and yet to come. Yet this matter (of violence) circulates at a level below law as right (law as meaning producing, justifying, etc.). And in this sense Derrida's aporia of justice gives too much to the calculations of law. Judging from within time—in so far as time is not fully, absolutely, disjointed—it is injustice that authorizes the call for justice. Justice as unrepresentable emerges as a limit—in the unauthorized authority of law and in the workings of jurisdiction, in the claim for law to determine its own scope. In our modifying gloss of Cover, the nomos is instituted in pain and suffering. In sum perhaps, in our account of judgment, the strands of Cover's violence offer a stark reminder that left to itself, the incalculable and giving idea of justice is always very close to the bad, even to the worst. For Derrida, this is because it can always be reappropriated by "the most perverse calculation";[104] for Cover, it is because justice is unjust, acts of justice can fail to be just.

In this section we look briefly at two responses to this predicament, neither of them fully authorized nor unauthorized by a direct reading of Cover's essays. In the first instance, we briefly consider Drucilla Cornell's call to reenvision the good. In the second instance, we direct our attention toward a refiguring of the material order of the institution of judgment in terms of the questioning and practice of jurisdiction.

Good Judgment

In the light of this ordering of injustice, should we still be concerned with the Good, with the Law of Law? The writer most closely associated with the ethics of alterity in law is Drucilla Cornell.[105] In *The Philosophy of the Limit*, she takes up the challenge of the yet to come or the beyond and sets it to work in legal thought. For her, the message of deconstruction is the constant mediation and transgression of the limits of law and legal thought. Although law is restricted (by violence, indifference, community, access, and much else besides), these limits are structured by a "beyond" or "yet to come." The ethics of alterity enables these limits to be rethought with justice as a utopian reimagining of legal thought. For Cornell, such a utopian thought is a necessary structure inscribed in law as its exterior. There is no beyond except as the inscription of the exterior as the margin or limit. In this, she criticizes the thought of the other as being outside of Being, of thought. If the thought of alterity is to remain within the bounds of the secular, the other must be located somewhere, and not as pure lack or absence. However, to read ethics in this way is to limit severely the thinking of the other. The thought of the other becomes a trace, a memory, a residue that might make ethics possible. In its place as a direct guide to legal thought, Cornell resurrects the horizon of the Good (or, the Law of the Law) as a way of imagining an ethical criticism of law that would prevent the "madness" of the undecidability of justice falling toward the worst.

What difference could all this make at a level of doctrinal law and courtroom adjudication? The limits within the legal domain become clearer when considering the "double bind" of finding the jurispathic involved in the very construction of the jurisgenerative (paedeic) power of nomos. It is certainly easy enough to find a thematics of the failure to honor the face of the other, of forcing the other to speak in the language of a law that has already defined their condition in advance as being wanting. Cornell elaborates cases of abortion and of sodomy, and to these could be added the cases of "homosexuality in the military."[106] Other examples can be had. The formal structure of substantive criminal law requires the accused brought before the court to reconstruct herself as a typical person—in order to avail herself of the generally available defenses. In broad terms, legal defenses require the other to self-identify according to the formula, "My actions are like any other (ab)normal person's and hence I am excused or justified by law." The brutality of this doctrinal reinscription of personality is evident in the "battered women" cases.[107] Likewise, in rape trials, the complainant's examination by lawyers structured by stereotypical images and myths of women's sexuality, but also, and more fundamentally, the rhetorical form and process of the examination forces the complainant to rub up against, play a role within, and assent to the narrative of the defense.[108] Likewise, the innumerable cases in refugee law that require a return to your country of origin (hence to persecution, and, in some instances, compulsory abortion or death) before the seeker of asylum can claim the status of refugee.[109] While the examples can be multiplied, in the end this does no more than provide examples of injustice. Many suitably phrased ethical principles could do the same.[110]

Within law and faced with the catalogue of its injustice, the interpretation of the suffering of the victim irresistibly shifts from questions of violence to that of the failure of the commonality of the Good. In this way, it defers an immediate imperative[111] to alleviate suffering and defers it to a question of jurisgeneration. Cornell is aware of this deferral but we emphasize here that the structure of the horizon of the Good is just what it says it is: it is a *vision* of the Good; an aesthetics not an ethics. It can never be the first or last word. It is not even clear whether it can say any word of ethics at all.[112]

What such an ethical understanding does bring to law, however, is a better sense of how the time of ethics, justice, and the Good are nonidentical. If the time of law is synchronous (either the no-time of abstract judgment or the rational time of bureaucracy), then the time of justice as ethics in law is never fully present. It is "yet to come," a horizon that can never fully be met in legal judgment—except perhaps as a moment of madness when the time of law and justice coincide. The horizon of the Good is the time of legal imagination. It is present in legal judgment and can be obtained (legal justice), but it cannot be justice. The call of the Good is not necessarily the same as the response to the demand of the other.

If such an ethical theory has summoned a "ground" or established a normative dwelling place against which the undecidability of the justice of judgment can be thought, it would seem that it has been bought at a high cost. To know (and suppress) the alegal foundations of law—that is not yet to discuss the material order of the institution, or the ways in which truth establishes its relationship to the world. In her writings, Cornell offers both a law that performs as if it were principled and a society that functions as if it were connected to the Good. These "as ifs" might help construct imagined communities and move toward the Good. The final difficulty comes in judging whether what has been offered is a theory of responsibility of reading and writing the law, a matter of the endless task of recollection and mourning, or something else, such as, perhaps, a theory of political and legal judgment (as choice). That this question misses the point, the madness of the decision of justice, only indicates the difficulty of placing justice in law. To this extent, then, the violence of law remains as contaminating as it should be, but the different temporalities of legal thought ought to make clearer the ways in which this contamination performs. It suggests also a further complication to the relations between words and deeds. The "shadow" of violence does not simply fall between the two, since words and deeds in law now exist on several horizons and in differing temporalities.

Jurisdiction

As we have suggested, the predicament that faces those of us who wish to dwell in law is how to calculate. Cornell's language of the Good and of law as a system of right is one way of accounting the manner of calculation. Yet, despite elaborating the conditions of a response to violence *in* law, there is a palpable sense of a failure to deal with the violence *of* law. Perhaps she forgets too quickly that the Good is of necessity an aesthetic value (a vision) rather than an ethical value. In her representations of the Good, the law of the land is rapidly transformed into the law of right—by means of a redemptive gesture that seems to be ethically excluded in the analysis of violence. It is precisely with this problem that Cover struggles.[113] With the messianic, the horizon of the Good corresponds too closely to the body of a reformed liberal constitution. The analysis of the limits of law as a philosophy of right aspires to reimagine a society where people can have fully integral bodies—personal, social, and political. Our wager is that, in elaborating the manner of calculation, it is perhaps better to consider obligations or commitments to law and justice as arising in flesh and blood. Where else would we know about injustice?

For Cover, this is a practical question. We consider it here through his formulation of jurisdiction. The jurisdiction of injustice is elaborated in terms of the "field of pain and death" on which the knowledge, representation, and action of legal speech takes place. In order to talk about the manner and manners of calculation, Cover calls in aid an administrative account of the violence of judgment.[114] Here, the law of the land becomes not so much a system of right but rather the field of institutional action within a "posited constitutional order." Calculation is figured as administration and visceral action. Institutional legal judgment is invoked to bind the general and the particular, word and deed, text and context:

> The context of a judicial utterance is institutional behavior in which others, occupying pre-existing roles, can be expected to act, to implement, or otherwise to respond in a specified way to the judge's interpretation. Thus, the institutional context ties the language act of practical understanding to the physical acts of others in a predictable, though not logically necessary, way.[115]

The passage from the contingent to the necessary that practical reasoning represents for Cover is achieved by distributing law into its component institutional parts: courtrooms, prisons, police stations, parliaments, and so on. Judgment—as the genre of calculation—binds through a typology of legal role and legal actor. In the "triple-bonded character" of legal interpretation that Cover narrates (word-deed-role),[116] it is the institutional "role" that organizes the field of legal action and legal understanding. The legal role or "office" enables the generality of violence to be given form and made typical. Judges, jailers, executioners, guards, criminals, protesters, citizens, political officials, the condemned—all appear in Cover's law as so many speaking and acting parts in the institutional "drama" of law. The roles are character-traits (persona or masks through which the individual and the social speak and act), while the given arrangement of roles form a logic of legal life and death—a "system of social cooperation," the social preconditions of effective domination.[117] Thus, the "homicidal quality" of judgment according to law is said by

Cover to dwell in the "office" of the (state-appointed) judge and its connections to other legal roles and legal actors. The judge sits "atop a pyramid of violence."[118] The typical form that relates the subject and object of judgment is the somewhat feudal corporate image of ruler and ruled. It is in relation to these roles that particular judgments are made and articulated. The practical reasoning of the judge restages a role-bound jurisdiction of violence.

However, if Cover lets the government of conduct meet the conduct of government through a "grammar of roles," nevertheless the institutional role does not permit us to calculate solely in terms of an administrative grammar. Calculation is not simply administrative; it is visceral action, a corporeal matter of flesh and blood. The transformation of the interpretation of the word and its understanding of violence into the scarring of flesh, into the spilling of blood, takes place "in the domain of *action*."[119] As we have read, the violence of judgment has become inscribed within and through the violence of foundation (constitution). For Cover, the connection between violence and law "begins at the beginning and never disappears";[120] for Derrida, this drags everything about law into the aporia of the decision (of justice). In addition, judgment requires a knowledge of the actions of law: a knowledge of the procedures, conduct, and manners of law. Such knowledge arises on the viscera of law.

The visceral predicament of institutional legal judgment is that judges do not simply decide.[121] Dwelling in the courtroom, the judge addresses himself or herself to the forms of law and judges whether its topics and promises have been adhered to properly. The question of decision goes to those to whom the letter of the law is destined. Consider the guards and doctors who "jump" to the judge's song in the tableau of the stay of execution in capital cases:

> [T]he almost stylized drama required that the jailers stand ready, visibly ready, to receive intelligence of the judicial act, even if it be only the action of deciding to take future action. The stay of execution . . . was the visible proof of the thread tying the violence of the warden and the executioner to the deliberative act of understanding the judge.[122]

In all Cover's essays, his narratives of blood and flesh are populated by the many who wait upon and witness the spectacle of the word of the law. The address of legal judgment is closed here by jurisdiction (understood as role-bound administration).[123] This closure keeps us circulating among the various speaking and acting parts of the legal institution. Yet at every point judgment needs something else to make calculation possible. For Derrida, this excess is the secret assumption of an interiority of law; for Cover, it is the violence of judgment. Violence installs the wisdom of law at the same time as it keeps law open: it remains as the indelible (if unassimilable) shadows on the "smooth facade"[124] of the constitutional body. The jurisdiction of violence is double-bound: it is distributed among the parts of law and it is the point from which each of the legal parts are put into circulation, related to each other.

Is this opening of the address of law a good thing? For those of us who wish to dwell in law (whether on the margins or elsewhere), it makes possible a number of things. Jurispathology permits us to dwell in law; it allows us to survive, to live on, to endure. To be sure, law kills meaning and it kills people. There is blood on our hands and in our eyes. But this is not yet to say that nothing remains to be said. Administration (as role-bound jurisdiction) does not identify the human (or imaginary) and the legal (or symbolic); human personality is not redeemed by legal personality. Thus, in so dwelling, we are not completely bound into a notion of the subject. Rather, Cover helps us read injustice at the level of the body of law.[125] Rephrasing violence in terms of flesh, the wisdom of Cover's law provides us with direction in the effort to understand the violence of law (and not just the violence in law) without rapidly moving into a language of the subject and its rights and interests. Such a language is spoken in vain when it comes to the violence *of* law. The flesh of law is neither fully legal nor completely nonlegal. Flesh and blood remain as the boundary of law, its permeable limit. It is from this limit or shifting "ground" that the violence of law can be reconstructed.

If a jurisprudence were to be worked from this ground, where would we turn for signposts in the attempt? The opening of justice provides some direction in the effort to reinscribe law. As remarked earlier, this opening cannot produce a theory of interpretation as an alternative ethical code. Even so, this is no bad thing. It suggests that the intervention or interruption of the ethical in law cannot be calculated directly through justice. Furthermore, it has suggested that the question of violence is not irreducible but is itself mediated by questions of justice—when thought from the point of the symbolic order (the legal, conventional world). What themes would flow from these limits? They would be infinite but, in so far as judgment is still concerned with the memory and hearing of law, they can be reconstructed around the questioning and practice of the paths of law. The site of such questioning is not just a concern with the decision of justice and the broken promises of jurisprudence. While the diremption or "chasm" between the aspirations of law and the social actuality they presuppose and reproduce provide some of the content of jurisprudence, there are more compelling resources that remain available to us. The site of the questioning of judgment, as a matter of memory and hearing, would be the material corpus of jurisprudence. This body provides the interior wisdom of law—the "positivity" of law is a fold on the surface and generates the order of human communication that sets in motion the form of human sociality.[126] It is at this level that Cover's thematics of flesh, pain, and blood can be understood as taking hold.

After all, legal thought has carpentered the fundamental elements of the modern body and contributed to the articulation of the modern soul. Law is a strong and durable metaphysics that has given itself a corporeal materiality in the gestures, senses, and affections of the human, technological, and political body. As Yifat Hachamovitch writes,

> [T]here is no human bone that does not also support a dogma, no mouth through which the law does not speak, no kiss that does not also enfeoff. The body is a medieval compilation which we have inherited alongside the *Corpus Juiris* and the barbarian codes. It is a Roman institution hammered together with Christian nails. . . . [I]t is compiled along with the political and juridical concepts of the Justinian compilation, it accumulated a history through the sedimentation of legal signs.[127]

The understanding of the suffering of the body (violence, pain, and blood) is given (force) by law. Bodies, even dead bodies, are not clearly things without law. The spilling of blood has significance beyond the immediate alarm of death. It is the sign of writing against death. In law, it is also the mark of fealty, lineage, association, and possession. Increasingly in evidence and bio-technology, it is the sign of truth, the evidence of presence and departure, the visible trace of our genetic coding and disposition. It is also the mark of Woman—both the fantasy that enables men to believe they possess the Phallus and the site of resistance to the presumption of that same masculine order. For all this contaminated law, violence and blood are a question and judgment of how we live and take responsibility for deathbound subjectivity.

While considerable attempts by the critics of modern and postmodern society have concentrated on reformulating the question of justice, less thought has been given to refiguring judgment. As we have indicated, the refiguring of judgment as ethical practice cannot be done solely by way of justice—if perforce it turns out that the space between the horizon of the Good and that of the real, the symbolic (legal, conventional world) and the imaginary (phantasmic), is one of poorly controlled desires of violent incorporation, sadistic domination, and fear. What understanding of judgment could take account of this? What would it mean for the judicial gaze, the legal eye—beyond the "pretense" of the interpreters (Cover) and the "forgetting" of jurisprudence (Sarat and Kearns)—to recognize pain?

In response, two themes can be reinvoked here. One, if law cannot think without a body, then there is good reason to believe that it thinks with a fragmented, suffering, fleshly body. Two, on the remains of such an anatomy, judgment is articulated in terms of the conditions of attachment to the body-parts of law. On the supposition that judgment is not just a matter of interpretation nor just a matter of consequential enforcement, what is at stake in both these themes is the *techniques of inscription* of nomos, law, and violence. The attachment of law to the world and the text is established through inscription—understood here as the process of naming and marking the body. If judgment is more than the simple separation of words and deeds and the madness of decision, then a jurisprudence would investigate that material. Judgment is a matter of measurement, of relating the eye to the hand that holds the rule, and of handing down the word of the law to those below. Such gestures have a material history of association.[128] It is possible that even the dimmed eyes of judges can be persuaded to jump from the mark of law to the pain of law, their muted voices to stutter, their hands to wander; it is possible that law can be thought around the intimacy of its gestures, the manners of its pains and passions. To examine the combination of gestures that enable, for example, the attachment of an intention (desire) to a dead body, the attachment of consent to a survivor of rape, would be to begin to investigate the ways in which proximate others have dwelt and do dwell in law. Even the body needs to be thought in relation to everything that has been said before.

AT AN END

This essay has questioned the beginnings of the violence of the word of law—and even then only set limits to a particular way of reading. The tendency of many of Cover's protagonists is to identify violence with law, and so to seal violence in law. We have taken a different tack. Here, violence has been distributed among and between the parts of law. In the idiom of jurisdiction, the trajectory of our reading has been to follow the complications that violence installs in the institution, judgment, and address of law—and to do so without losing the process of representation that inscribes the questioning and practices of the paths of law. There is never a moment in which violence is immediate, in which violence arises and takes place as pure interpretation or pure consequential enforcement. To reintroduce and maintain the doctrinal order of law is not, however, to evacuate the questioning of violence: in our reading, the guts of law have been neither eviscerated nor anaestheticized. In all his work, Cover struggled to hold onto and narrate (albeit without theorizing) a "middle ground" of law that would let commitment to law and justice meet the institutional practices of law. Taking our cue from his struggle, we think it is possible to open up for legal thought a space between the aporia of the decision of justice and judgment according to law. Dwelling in and on this space, it becomes possible to reconstruct the *manner and manners* of calculating with violence and hence with the risk of injustice—whether it be the injustice of the law of the land or of the Good.

Here, in our hurry to reconstruct another scene of law, we leave the last words to Robert Cover. For in all our glosses of violence, justice, authority, obligation and the good and administration, there is something in his essays that resists the overarching order of justice, even a justice yet to come. It is not that such reading is unproductive; we think Cover's essays are illuminated—and occasionally corrected—through the work of Derrida. It is more a matter of tone. Cover's narratives consistently catch at the edges of the questions we have addressed. As much as Cover yearns for redemption or justice through law, the essays also resist the affirmative order of messianic justice. For all that there is no essay that does not affirm the obligation to law, his essays also resist the temptation to talk in the name of the law. These questions are brought into the continuing narrative of laws by which we come to live. Against this, Derrida's reading of justice is indeed ascetic, but so too is his account of law. Law is stripped of the agon of authority and of jurisdiction, of the effort of speaking for and before the law. It is stripped, too, of the positioning and attachment of law to the doctrinal body of particular posited law, to the actions of law.

In all this, Robert Cover's narratives may simply be too canny—to find the aporia of institution delayed or spread across the time of law, may only serve to remind us that the possibility of community is already inscribed in legal violence. This inscription in turn brings forth judges, martyrs, scholars, rabbis, rebels, and resistance fighters. To these have been added the figures of the suffering others who inhabit law. Judgment has been pursued to the end and there is still violence dwelling in the house.

NOTES

1. Our reading will take as its point of departure the following texts of Robert Cover as collected and reprinted in Martha Minow, Michael Ryan, and Austin Sarat, eds. *Narrative, Violence, and the Law: The Essays of Robert Cover* (Ann Arbor: University of Michigan Press, 1992): "Violence and the Word" (chapter 5), "*Nomos* and Narrative" (chapter 3), "Obligation: A Jewish Jurisprudence of the Social Order" (chapter 6) and "Folktales of Justice" (chapter 4). In addition, we have relied on these works by Robert Cover: "The Bonds of Constitutional Interpretation: Of the Word, the Deed and the Role," *Georgia Law Review* 20 (1986) 815; "Bringing the Messiah Through the Law: A Case Study," chapter 10 in *Religion, Morality and the Law: Nomos XXX*, ed. J. R. Pennock and J. W. Chapman (New York: New York University Press, 1988), and *Justice Accused: Antislavery and the Judicial Process* (New Haven: Yale University Press, 1975). See also the extended commentaries and responses of Richard K. Sherwin,

"Law, Violence, and Illiberal Belief," *Georgetown Law Journal* 78 (1990): 1785; Austin Sarat and Thomas R. Kearns, "Making Peace with Violence: Robert Cover on Law and Legal Theory," in *Law's Violence*, ed. Austin Sarat and Thomas R. Kearns (Ann Arbor: University of Michigan Press, 1992; paperback, 1995); Austin Sarat and Thomas R. Kearns, "A Journey Through Forgetting: Towards a Jurisprudence of Violence," in *The Fate of Law*, ed. Austin Sarat and Thomas R. Kearns (Ann Arbor: University of Michigan Press, 1991).

2. Consider, for example, the invocations of "a *nomos* completely transparent—built from crystals completely pure" in "*Nomos* and Narrative" (107); the figure of the martyr in "Violence and the Word"; the exemplary judge in the Tiede case in "The Bonds of Constitutional Interpretation" and "Violence and the Word"; and finally those who sought to refound the authority of the semikhah in "Bringing the Messiah Through the Law."

3. What is today called "substantive law" is little more than a philosophy attenuated by disciplinary obligations in the form of the subject matter of law. More generally, on doctrine as a process of representation, see Shaun McVeigh and Peter Rush, "Cutting Our Losses: Criminal Legal Doctrine," in *Criminal Legal Doctrine*, ed. Peter Rush, Shaun McVeigh, and Alison Young (Aldershot: Dartmouth/Ashgate, 1997).

4. *R v. Brown*, 2 All ER 75, 83 (1993).

5. See Sarat and Kearns, "A Journey Through Forgetting," 270: "To speak about law's violence is to speak about its pervasive cultural residue, the way it insinuates itself into consciousness and conditions responses. Every instance of lethal force by law enforcement, every sentence imposed, every execution holds out images of our own fate at the hands of law and coldly reminds us of the way social life is forged and maintained." Compare Michel de Certeau's understanding of the Indian as retaining—in the silence of the "tortured body" and "altered earth"—the memory of what European culture has forgotten in Michel de Certeau, *Heterologies* (Manchester: Manchester University Press, 1986), chapter 16, especially 226–27.

6. Sarat and Kearns, "A Journey Through Forgetting," 212.

7. The work of Cover, and of Sarat and Kearns, sets in play a complex set of relations among the terms of law. In Cover's "Violence and the Word," and the two essays by Sarat and Kearns, there is "law's violence" (without definite articles and operating in generality), "the violence of law" (secular, state-centered, and specific), and "the violence of the word" (both specific to legal judgment and general to the world as imbued with the word of law). To these should be added the violence of the legal sentence (linguistic, juridical, and penal) and the violence of the letter of the law. Rather than treat these as interdisciplinary battlegrounds delimiting the proper scope of study, we are more interested in returning these questions to the elaboration of the many ways of the relation of the law to the world, the body, and the text.

8. Cover concludes "Violence and the Word" with the following Coda: "Between the idea and the reality of common meaning falls the shadow of the violence of law, itself" (238).

9. Among his many publications, Emmanuel Levinas's *Totality and Infinity: An Essay on Exteriority*, trans. Alphonso Lingis (Pittsburgh: Duquesne Univer-

sity Press, 1969) has been the most pertinent for legal theory. The concern in contemporary legal theory to develop an "ethics of alterity" has engaged the work of Levinas either directly or through Derrida's not-infrequent responses to the thinking of Levinas. Among other works, we have in mind Drucilla Cornell, *The Philosophy of the Limit* (New York: Routledge, 1992); Costas Douzinas and Ronnie Warrington, *Justice Miscarried* (London: Harvester Wheatsheaf, 1994); Marinos Diamantides, *Ethical Proximity as a Condition of Law* (doctoral thesis, Department of Law, Birkbeck College, University of London, 1998) and his "Violence of Irresponsibility: Enigmas of Medical Ethics," *New Formations* 35 (1998): 145. In this ethics of alterity, the reading of Levinas by Luce Irigaray has strangely received scant attention: See "Questions à Emmanuel Levinas," *Critique* 36 (1990): 911; and "Fécondité de la Caresse," in *Ethique de la Différence Sexuelle* (Paris: Editions de Minuit, 1984). For an exception, see Alain Pottage, "Recreating Difference," *Law and Critique* 5(2) (1994): 131. Cover's terminology for the otherness of the other is "alternity." "One constitutive element of a *nomos*," he wrote, "is the phenomenon George Steiner has labeled 'alternity': "the 'other than the case' "; the counter-factual propositions, images, shapes of will and evasion with which we charge our mental being and by means of which we build the changing, largely fictive milieu for our somatic and our social existence.'" (*"Nomos* and Narrative," 101, citation omitted).

10. See Douzinas and Warrington, *Justice Miscarried*, 9, chapter 4, especially at 163–71.

11. "The absolutely other [*Autre*] is the other person [*Autrui*]" (Levinas, *Totality and Infinity*, 39).

12. Jacques Derrida, *Writing and Difference*, trans. Alan Bass (London: Routledge and Kegan Paul, 1981), 75.

13. In this, Cover can at times be viewed as a (romantic) heir of revolutionary natural lawyers: see *Justice Accused*, 149–58; see also the figure of the martyr in "Violence and the Word," the antislavery story in *"Nomos* and Narrative," Judge Stern in "The Bonds of Constitutional Interpretation," and so on.

14. Jacques Derrida, "Force of Law: The 'mystical foundation of authority'," *Cardozo Law Review* 11 (1990): 919. Reprinted in *Deconstruction and the Possibility of Justice*, ed. Drucilla Cornell, Michel Rosenfeld, and David Gray Carlson (New York: Routledge, 1992). Subsequent references to this essay will be to that appearing in the edited volume.

15. "Law must be meaningful in the sense that it permits those who live together to express themselves with it and with respect to it. It must both ground predictable behavior and provide meaning for behavior that departs from the ordinary" (Cover, *"Nomos* and Narrative," 107).

16. Ibid., 103–7.

17. This "tension" grounds Cover's ontology of law.

18. Ibid., 155ff.

19. "[T]here is a radical dichotomy between the social organization of law as power and the organization of law as meaning" (ibid., 112).

20. Ibid., 108.

21. Ibid., 110; note further Cover's temptation to associate, via the work of Carol Gilligan, separation with the masculine and attachment with the feminine.

This is part and parcel of Cover's more pervasive concern to think of attachment to law in terms of a narrative of object-choice.

22. Ibid., 110, 112.

23. See Pheng Cheah and Elizabeth Grosz, "The Body of the Law: Notes Towards a Theory of Corporeal Justice," in *Thinking Through the Body of the Law*, ed. Pheng Cheah, David Fraser, and Judith Grbich (Sydney: Allen and Unwin, 1996), chapter 1, 9–10.

24. This is the theme of "Violence and the Word" and of "The Bonds of Constitutional Interpretation."

25. See Stanley Fish, *Doing What Comes Naturally: Change, Rhetoric and the Practice of Theory in Legal and Literary Studies* (Durham: Duke University Press, 1989), chapters 6, 7, and 21, especially 518–20. Our concern here is with Fish's account of violence. Where, of course, Cover differs profoundly with Fish is over the relation between law and morality.

26. Sarat and Kearns, "A Journey Through Forgetting," especially 222–25 [relating the official story of law to the Hobbesian tradition of political and legal thought].

27. In these arguments, as elsewhere, Derrida is arguing about law as right and the law of law as distributed among the many claimants to transcendent authority. As such, there are difficulties of translating these arguments to positivized law, even a positivized law infused with natural right. However, as we suggest later in this essay, it is at least arguable that legal embodiment takes place between these spaces.

28. On this point, compare Fish, *Doing What Comes Naturally*, chapters 2 and 21; and his "The Law Wishes to Have a Formal Existence," in *There's No Such Thing as Free Speech . . . and it's a good thing too* (New York: Oxford University Press, 1994). For Fish, it seems the generality of performance can be stopped by the legal interpretive community. By contrast, as Ernesto Laclau explains and agrees, "the general movement of Derrida's theoretico-political intervention . . . is to direct the historico-political forms back to the primary terrain of their opening to the radically heterogenous. This terrain of a constitutive undecidability, of an experience of the impossible that, paradoxically, makes possible responsibility, the decision, law, and—finally—the messianic itself in its actual and historical forms," "Time Is Out of Joint," *Diacritics* 25, no. 2 (1995): 92.

29. See Derrida, "Force of Law," 16.

30. Ibid., 10: "[I]f justice is not necessarily law [*droit*] or the law, it cannot become justice legitimately or *de jure* except by withholding force or rather by appealing to force from its first moment, from its first word. 'At the beginning of justice there was *logos*, speech or language,' which is not necessarily in contradiction with another incipit, namely, 'In the beginning there will have been force.'" The elaboration of what this might mean emerges as the thematic consideration of Derrida's reading of Walter Benjamin's "Critique of Violence" in the second part of "Force of Law." Other elaborations could be given however. One would be to suggest that archaic justice and violence are connected through injustice. See Stephen David Ross, *Injustice and Restitution: The Ordinance of Time* (Albany: State University of New York Press, 1993), 170–71: discussing narratives that present us with "a violence far beyond what we may find tolerable, revealing the

hidden destructiveness in justice, its injustice . . . [and that] present us with a justice greater than human, divine in its retribution, a justice that would triumph at any cost, however unjust." "In this scheme of things," Ross continues, "archaic injustice reemerges as the violence it bears, marking the destructiveness that belongs to rule. We cannot doubt that even without universality and stability, without repeatability, justice speaks . . . [in these stories]—in an intolerable form. We cannot doubt that justice works intolerably, if silently, in modern prisons." Less phenomenological, even non-phenomenological, would be the argument of John D. Caputo, *The Prayers and Tears of Jacques Derrida: Religion Without Religion* (Bloomington: Indiana University Press, 1997), 208–10. On Derrida's part, in "Force of Law" he leaves as something of an assertion the claim that the concern for justice itself is not fully distinguishable from violence. For further explanation, reference can be made to his reading of Levinas and the metaphysics of violence in Derrida, *Writing and Difference*, chapter 4.

31. See Derrida, "Force of Law," 13.

32. Ibid. Compare Cover's comment on Kenneth Burke in "The Bonds of Constitutional Interpretation," 816–7, "For while one dimension of the agonistic element [in constitutions] of law may be argument; another and more important dimension is violence. While argument may be said to take place within a community, violence frequently marks the failure of community and the metaphors that evoke it [our interpolation]" (817).

33. See Jacques Derrida, "Before the Law," in *Acts of Literature*, ed. Derek Attridge (London: Routledge, 1992), 215–16. For commentary, see Hakan Gustafsson, "As If: Behind Before the Law," *Law and Critique* 7, no. 1 (1996): 99; Panu Minkinnen, "The Radiance of Justice: On the Minor Jurisprudence of Franz Kafka," *Social and Legal Studies* 3 (1994): 349.

34. See Derrida, "Force of Law," 13.

35. See Mark Wigley, *The Architecture of Deconstruction: Derrida's Haunt* (Cambridge: MIT Press, 1993), especially 150–52.

36. See Derrida, "Force of Law," 13. See also Drucilla Cornell's comments on Cover in her *Philosophy of the Limit*, 112.

37. For commentary on this phrase, see Louis Wolcher, "The Man in a Room: Remarks on Derrida's 'Force of Law,'" *Law and Critique* 7, no. 1 (1996): 35.

38. The silence is "mystical" because indecipherable rather than unintelligible. In one sense, the question of authority is quite legible because it is a question internal to law. It is indecipherable because the question of law (legibility) is suspended in the moment of creation. On the one hand, the possibility of evaluation lies before a law "yet to come"; on the other hand, the law is transcendent (violent and nonviolent) because it depends only on who is before it—who authorizes it in an absolute performative whose presence always escapes him (see Derrida, "Force of Law," 35–36).

39. On encrypment, see Jacques Derrida's introductory essay, "Fors," in Nicholas Abraham and Maria Torok, *The Wolf Man's Magic Word: A Cryptonomy* (Minneapolis: University of Minnesota Press, 1986); on the secret, Derrida, "Passions: An Oblique Offering," in *On the Name* (Stanford: Stanford University Press, 1995); on the history of secrecy as the history of responsibility, Derrida, *The Gift of Death*, trans. David Wills (Chicago: Chicago University Press, 1995),

especially 21–27; on silence, Derrida "Before the Law," and, in a Heideggerian idiom, Alexander Carnera Ljungstrom, "The Silent Voice of Law: Legal Philosophy as Legal Thinking," *Law and Critique* 8, no. 1 (1997): 71. For extended discussion of justice as *dike*, see Douzinas and Warrington, *Justice Miscarried*, chapter 1.

40. See Cover, "Violence and the Word," 238. Compare *"Nomos* and Narrative."

41. What is outside the Constitution is defined as outside by it, and either still within the law or subject to sovereign power. Sovereign power is understood by the Constitution as a gap within the order. What the Constitution cannot think or exclude is what comes before it. This paradox is met by Cover in "Violence and the Word" by placing the exemplary figure of the martyr before the law. The martyr is destined to overcome law with the law, to embrace the excess of law in the name of the law. It was this gesture—as much as his feudal tale of corporate legal hierarchy—that sought to guarantee the purity of law. The fatal force of this gesture is that the torture of the martyr becomes necessary for the overcoming of law. We are held to stand in awe of the exemplary nature of the respect for and sacrifice to the law that the martyr makes. At the same time as the torture of the martyr is the most repulsive aspect of organized institutions (108), it is also the most necessary: redemption from the violence of law requires sacrifice; the martyr must be impaled. In Cover, such a gesture is made all the more uncomfortable in that it is placed in the general context of support for the Constitution. The immanent transfiguration of law requires bodies for its sacrifice; the demands of the redemptive transformation of law are fully corporeal. It should also be noted that, in Cover's gesture, the sacrifice of the martyr is an attempt to give material substance to the law, to make it real.

42. Although any reading of "Force of Law" should pay attention to the context of its production. It is not clear whether Derrida is presenting an axiomatic argument or whether the status "quasi-transcendental" indicates something more provisional and occasional.

43. See "Violence and the Word," 207–8. "'Law' is never just a mental or spiritual act," writes Cover. "A legal world is built only to the extent that there are commitments that place bodies on the line. The torture of the martyr is an extreme and repulsive form of the organized violence of institutions. It reminds us that the interpretive commitments of officials are realized, indeed, in the flesh. As long as that is so, the interpretive commitments of a community which resists official law must also be realized in the flesh, even if it be the flesh of its own adherents" (208).

44. Sarat and Kearns, "Making Peace with Violence," 242–43. See also the review article by Nancy Weston, "The Fate, Violence, and Rhetoric of Contemporary Legal Thought: Reflections on the Amherst Series, the Loss of Truth and Law," *Law and Social Inquiry* 22, no. 3 (1997): 733.

45. See Sherwin, "Law, Violence, and Illiberal Belief."

46. Most clearly in Cover's "Obligation: A Jewish Jurisprudence of the Social Order."

47. Cover, *"Nomos* and Narrative," 101; and the autocritique in this respect in his "Bringing the Messiah Through the Law," 202. For a summary paraphrase of the "metaphor" of law as bridge, see Ronald R. Garet, "Meaning and Ending,"

Yale Law Journal 96 (1987): 1801, 1808–15, concluding that "[i]f law is a bridge, then, it is clearly a strange sort of bridge: one that does not simply remove an obstacle to movement, or permit us to move freely from one shore to another, but instead serves precisely to hold the shores apart, and to preserve 'tension' between them" (1810).

48. Instead, it is the narrative of law that carries the burden of Cover's argument.

49. For commentary on this point in terms of Hannah Arendt and Michel Foucault, see Thomas Dumm, "The Fear of Law," *Studies in Law, Politics and Society* 10 (1990): 29–57.

50. See Austin Sarat, "Robert Cover on Law and Violence," in *Narrative, Violence, and the Law: The Essays of Robert Cover* , ed. Martha Minow, Michael Ryan, and Austin Sarat (Ann Arbor: University of Michigan Press, 1992), 255–66, especially 264.

51. See Edmund Jabès, *The Book of Margins* (Chicago: Chicago University Press, 1993), 43; Sherwin, "Law, Vilence, and Illiberal Belief"; Sarat and Kearns, "Making Peace with Violence"; Cheah and Grosz, "The Body of the Law"; Weston, "The Fate, Violence, and Rhetoric of Contemporary Legal Thought"; Cornell, *The Philosophy of the Limit*; Drucilla Cornell, "From the Lighthouse: The Promise of Redemption and the Possibility of Legal Interpretation," *Cardozo Law Review* 11 (1990), 1687.

52. This is the image of common law adjudication as a matter of experience, breeding, and technique. Such an approach would still be instructive if there were any agreement as to the proper qualities of judicial character that did not automatically announce the arrival of the judge in heaven or in the drawing room (either corporate or domestic). For the historical detail, see Allen D. Boyer, "Sir Edward Coke, *Ciceronius*: Classical Rhetoric and the Common Law Tradition," *International Journal for the Semiotics of Law* 10, no. 8 (1997), commenting on the character required by the oratorical tradition (11–12) and concluding (36): "the idealized figure of the classical orator bears a striking resemblance to the idealized figure of the common law judge."

53. This is, of course, not to say that the practice of courtroom law is not completely dominated by such assessments, both as a concern of forensic rhetoric and hermeneutic pre-judice. It is to say that judges are invisible men under their judicial robes, to the extent that the judicial office still comes draped with the consolations of such virtuous raiments. A detailed reconstruction of the history and theory of the differential shift from traditionary models of adjudication to a governmental model of adjudication can be had in W. Tim Murphy, *The Oldest Social Science? Configurations of Law and Modernity* (Oxford: Oxford University Press, 1997), especially 59–101. In a less historical vein, see generally on this loss, Alistair MacIntyre, *After Virtue* (London: Duckworth, 1985); MacIntyre, *Whose Justice? Which Rationality?* (South Bend, Ind.: University of Notre Dame Press, 1988); Nigel E. Simmonds, *The Decline of Juridical Reason* (Manchester: Manchester University Press, 1984); and James Boyd White, *Heracles' Bow* (Madison: University of Wisconsin Press, 1985), chapter 9.

54. See Douzinas and Warrington, *Justice Miscarried*, chapter 3.

55. Cover, "*Nomos* and Narrative," 145.

56. Ibid., 145.

57. Cover considers narrative to be "the literary genre for the objectification of value" (ibid., 145), to which should be added that the narrative could just as well be termed a narrative that fills an abyss: see Jean-François Lyotard, *The Differend: Phrases in Dispute*, trans. Georges Van Den Abbeele (Manchester: Manchester University Press, 1988), 147–50. Alongside this, the allegory of dedication is found in the image of law.

58. The symbol is the flash of totality, whereas allegory is a matter of profane time. In this respect, compare Cover's symbol of the perfect law of the paedeia with the allegory of dedication to law found in the analysis of texts. The distinction is a familiar one and is pertinent to Cover's consideration of messianism discussed later in this essay. For brief commentary, but elaborated within a distinct context of messianism by Benjamin and Scholem, see Susan A. Handelman, *Fragments of Redemption: Jewish Thought and Literary Theory in Benjamin, Scholem and Levinas* (Bloomington: Indiana University Press, 1991), chapter 4.

59. Cover, "Violence and the Word," 210.

60. Ibid., 210, note 15, displacing Fish on legal interpretation. For a more sustained and aporetic reading of Fish on literary interpretation, see Samuel Weber, *Institution and Interpretation* (Minneapolis: University of Minnesota Press, 1987), especially chapters 1, 3, and 4.

61. See especially Cover's "Violence and the Word," 223–24, for example, and his "Bonds of Constitutional Interpretation," 820–21, for example.

62. Cover, "Violence and the Word," 213; see also his "Bonds of Constitutional Interpretation," 818.

63. See Cover, "*Nomos* and Narrative," 107–9; Douzinas and Warrington, *Justice Miscarried*, 213.

64. See Cover, "Violence and the Word." He concludes, "[A]s long as legal interpretation is constitutive of violent behavior as well as meaning, as long as people are committed to using or resisting the social organization of violence in making their interpretations real, there will always be a tragic limit to the common meaning that can be achieved" (238). Compare Levinas's "equitable honoring of faces" as cited in Derrida, "Force of Law," 22.

65. Derrida, "Force of Law," 22.

66. See Derrida, *The Gift of Death*, chapter 3, 66–74.

67. Derrida, "Force of Law," 27.

68. Ibid., 27.

69. Ibid., 19–20.

70. Cover, "*Nomos* and Narrative," 101.

71. See Cover, "Bringing the Messiah Through the Law," 202.

72. Cover, "*Nomos* and Narrative," 101 (our interpolation).

73. Ibid., 102.

74. Ibid., 101.

75. See also Cover's discussion of "redemptive constitutionalism," which is phrased in specifically eschatological terms, in "*Nomos* and Narrative," 131–32; and in "The Bonds of Constitutional Interpretation," 832. In the latter, Cover suggests that the right-to-life movement—in the Unites States of America, at least—is a species of redemptive constitutionalism.

76. See Cover, "Bringing the Messiah Through the Laws," 203 (which relates his case study of legal apocalypticism—the attempt in Safed in 1538 to create a court that would bring the Messiah to the Holy Land—to his broader concerns developed primarily in "*Nomos* and Narrative"). On the renewal of the semikhah at Safed, see also his "Folktales of Justice," 188–95.

77. Cover, "Bringing the Messiah Through the Law," 202.

78. Ibid., 204

79. Sherwin, "Law, Violence, and Illiberal Belief," 1800–1. He summarizes one of his arguments as being that "by curbing Cover's tendency to romanticize narrative, the existential strains within his pre-messianic writing can be used to rescue his understanding of interpretive commitment from the danger of messianic totalitarianism."

80. Ibid., 1819.

81. Ibid., 1809.

82. Cover, "Bringing the Messiah Through the Law," 203.

83. See Sherwin, "Law, Violence, and Illiberal Belief," 1804.

84. As Sherwin puts it (ibid., at 1806), "Narrative truth thus obtains a kind of crystalline purity, while imperial principles of order provide structure from without."

85. Aside from our attention to this claim, most obviously Sherwin simply ignores the style and tone of Cover's analysis. Where Sherwin seeks a central ground of normality, Cover examines the limits of law. Sherwin writes of "constraining legal violence" through constitutionalism, and of "avoiding the need . . . of violence" (ibid., 1828) through persuasive reasoning and reasonable commitments. Neither of these approaches to a discourse ideal seems to register the extent to which Cover finds violence in the law. It is as if the analysis of legal judgment in "Violence and the Word" has not taken place. Again Sherwin notes that "[n]o community can be expected to defer to power when the coherence of its world is threatened with extinction" (ibid., 1830), without then connecting that claim to the analysis of religious communities that Cover makes. In like manner, Sherwin converts "limit points" and the whole analysis of "tension" into determinate positions. In so doing, Sherwin wishes to mark a strong divide between transcendent and immanent readings of the U.S. Constitution. Our own analysis tends in the opposite direction.

86. See Cover, "*Nomos* and Narrative," 101; "Folktales of Justice," 175–76.

87. Jacques Derrida, *Specters of Marx: The State of the Debt, the Work of Mourning, and the New International*, trans. Peggy Kamuf (New York: Routledge, 1994), 59.

88. Ibid., 167.

89. See Ernesto Laclau, *Emancipation(s)* (London: Verso, 1996) 75. See also Laclau, "Time Is Out of Joint."

90. It is necessary to be a little circumspect about this claim since this essay is unfinished. See also the concluding paragraph of "Folktales of Justice," 201: "The caution which the Utopian jurist exercises in this regard is parallel to the caution that the state's judge exercises before the King. Both thereby maintain the connection between law and reality. Both risk losing law to the overpowering

force of what is and what is dominant. Integrity in both kinds of judges is the act of maintaining the vision that it is only that which redeems which is law."

91. Derrida, *Specters of Marx*, 168–69. Our analysis of Derrida's comments here closely follows that of John Caputo in his *Prayers and Tears of Jacques Derrida*, 118–25.

92. See Derrida, *Specters of Marx*, 168.

93. Ibid., 169.

94. Cover's contrast between and use of history and myth in "Folktales of Justice" comes close to the use of "quasi-axiomatics" made by Derrida in "Force of Law" and *Specters of Marx*. The major distinction is to be found in Derrida's method of formalization in terms of "quasi-" and Cover's use of narrative genres of types.

95. Did Cover want the Messiah to come? Of course but not yet. . . . Joseph Karo—both a legalist and a man of faith—could be said to have an exemplary understanding of messianism by following two laws or by understanding law in two orders of time: one secular and profane and the other religious. See Cover's discussion of Joseph Karo in "Folktales of Justice," 188–95 and in "Bringing the Messiah Through the Law," especially at 208–9

96. Cover, "Folktales of Justice," 194.

97. See Derrida, *The Gift of Death*, 68: "I cannot respond to the call, to the request, to the obligation, or even the love of another without sacrificing the other other, the other others. *Every other (one) is every (bit) other [tout autre est tout autre]*, every one else is completely or wholly other. As a result, the concepts of responsibility, of decision or of duty, are condemned a priori to paradox, scandal and aporia. . . . As soon as I enter into relation with the other, with the gaze, look, . . . request, love, command, or call of the other, I know that I can respond only by sacrificing ethics, that is, by sacrificing whatever obliges me also to respond, in the same way, in the same instant, to all others." For a similar point, see "Force of Law," 17.

98. For a more detailed discussion of the decision and the undecidable, see Jari Kauppinen, "Law without Place: Topology and Decision. Questions of Line and Literature," *Law and Critique* 9 no. 2 (1998): 225.

99. Derrida, "Force of Law," 24–25.

100. Ibid., 24.

101. Ibid., 26.

102. Ibid., 24–26.

103. Derrida's reading of Walter Benjamin's "Critique of Violence" is concerned with the relation of divine and mythic force and justice. On the other hand, Cover is more concerned with the injustice of law and justice. To this extent, there is a sense that all Derrida's talk of justice is simply beside the point for Cover.

104. Derrida, "Force of Law," 28.

105. See Cornell, *The Philosophy of the Limit*; "From the Lighthouse"; and, for her subsequent elaboration of a vision of the good in specific contexts, see Drucilla Cornell, *The Imaginary Domain: Abortion, Pornography and Sexual Harassment* (New York: Routledge, 1995). For her explicit engagement with Robert Cover, see *The Philosophy of the Limit*, chapter 4, 103–115.

106. The former examples are briefly set out in terms of regulation and judgment in Cornell, *The Philosophy of the Limit*, 159–63 (discussing *Bowers v. Hardwick* and the violence in law), and 147–54 (discussing *Roe v. Wade* and the role of the judge). For more extended discussions, see her *Imaginary Domain*. The example of "homosexuals in the military" is analyzed in terms of a "politics of the performative" by Judith Butler, *Excitable Speech* (New York: Routledge, 1997), chapter 3.

107. For broadly comparable discussions of such doctrinal reinscription and judicial responsibility, see Alison Young, "Femininity as Marginalia: Conjugal Homicide and the Conjugation of Sexual Difference," in *Criminal Legal Doctrine*, ed. Peter Rush, Shaun McVeigh, and Alison Young, chapter 6; Danielle Tyson, "'Asking For It': An Anatomy of Provocation," *Australian Feminist Law Journal* 13 (1999): 66; and for the range of defenses discussed in terms of their structure of identification, see Peter Rush, *Criminal Law* (Sydney: Butterworths, 1997), chapters 11–13.

108. For the detail and exemplification of this point, see Alison Young, "The Wasteland of the Law, the Wordless Song of the Rape Victim," *Melbourne University Law Review* 22, no. 2 (1998): 442.

109. For extensive discussion of refugee law relevant to our concerns here, see Douzinas and Warrington, *Justice Miscarried*, chapter 6.

110. Of course, this is not to diminish the continuing need to catalogue the injustices of law in society. It is, however, to suggest the horizon of the good against which such a cataloguing often proceeds.

111. The first word is an "imperative": see Levinas, *Totality and Infinity*, 199.

112. In this respect, consider Cornell's discussion of Adorno and the priority of aesthetics over ethics in *The Philosophy of the Limit*, chapter 1.

113. In this respect, Cornell's reading of Cover is inaccurate: she misses the tension that violence installs in the Good.

114. This account is primarily set out in Cover's, "The Bonds of Constitutional Interpretation" and "Violence and the Word." Much is repeated between these two essays, with "legal interpretation" being assimilated to "constitutional interpretation." Our attention devolves upon "Bonds of Constitutional Interpretation," and subsequent unacknowledged quotations are from this essay and distributed throughout it.

115. Cover, "Violence and the Word," 216. Appending footnote: "One might say that institutions create the context for changing the contingent into the necessary" [citations omitted].

116. Cover, "The Bonds of Constitutional Interpretation," 821. Summarizing in a lapidary formula, Cover elaborates: "Constitutional interpretation is a form of bonded interpretation, bound at once to practical application, to the deeds it implies, and to the ecology of jurisdictional roles, the conditions of effective domination." (820–21). This is repeated as "legal interpretation" in "Violence and the Word," 223–24.

117. Cover, "The Bonds of Constitutional Interpretation," 820, 822, and throughout.

118. Ibid., 819 [homicidal quality], 818 [pyramid], and 824: "The deed is connected to the judicial word by the social cooperation of many others through

their roles—as lawyers, police, jailers, wardens, magistrates." For commentary disputing the empirical limits of this pyramidal image, see Douglas Hay, "Time, Inequality, and Law's Violence," in *Law's Violence*, ed. Austin Sarat and Thomas R. Kearns (Ann Arbor: University of Michigan Press, 1992; paperback 1995), chapter 5.

119. "The Bonds of Constitutional Interpretation," 817.

120. Ibid.

121. And nor do legal actors in other social movements: ibid., 832.

122. Ibid., 826–27.

123. For Cover, the address of law is closed either by a messianic claim (see previous section of our essay) or by an administrative type of jurisdiction.

124. Ibid., 821.

125. In contrast to the Christian tradition which places justice and injustice at the level of the soul (or, in more contemporary terms, at the level of the self), Cover's concern with the body is part of the Judaic impetus of his work.

126. We have elaborated this in terms of the doctrinal order of modern criminal law in McVeigh and Rush, "Cutting our Losses." On the fold more generally, see Gilles Deleuze, *Foucault*, trans. Sean Hand (Minneapolis: University of Minnesota, 1988), 94–123, and *The Fold: Leibniz and the Baroque*, trans. Tom Conley (Minneapolis: University of Minnesota, 1993).

127. Yifat Hachamovitch, "One Law on the Other," *International Journal for the Semiotics of Law* 3, no. 8 (1990): 187. The suggestion is exemplified over the *longue durée* of the law of murder in Yifat Hachamovitch, "The Dummy: An Essay on Malice Prepensed," in *Criminal Legal Doctrine*, ed. Peter Rush et al., chapter 2.

128. See Alphonso Lingis, "The Society of Dismembered Body Parts," *Pli* 4, nos. 1 and 2 (1992): 1–21. In brief terms, Lingis elaborates three productive couplings that are of relevance: voice with hearing, hand with surface inscription, eye with pain. For Lingis (if not for Nietzsche), it is writing that breaks the connection between the eye and pain. The question is whether law has been irretrievably occupied by the modern textuality.

CHAPTER SIX

Why the Law Is Also Nonviolent

Peter Fitzpatrick

IT WOULD BE as well to insist on the accuracy for Cover of the famous and histrionic sentence that opens "Violence and the Word:" "Legal interpretation takes place in a field of pain and death."[1] Or, put in terms of his title, "the word" necessarily operates in a milieu, in a field of "violence" but it is not itself violent. This may seem a not entirely propitious beginning for a piece that is to convince us of the violence of law, a work that is to show us—and such is the message for which it is so well known—that judges cannot avoid the charge of doing violence simply by saying that they are interpreters of the law and that law's violence is done by others—by the police, warders, executioners.

Again and again, Cover draws a distinction. "There is a radical dichotomy between the social organization of law as power [as a violence] and the organization of law as meaning,"[2] and he would "insist" that law as the word becomes violent only "in the context of the organized social practice of violence."[3] Cover wants to prevent law from being suffused in its violent context. Why? Clearly, or consistently, this would not be to protect any element of law from its implication with violence. His whole essay is oriented against the kind of claim for law being set against violence. But in making his supposedly radical case that law is imbued with violence, Cover seems driven to confirming conservatively that law is distinct from violence.

We could begin to unravel that mystery by asking why, even in the dim dark ages of 1986, Cover's linking of law and violence should be so revelatory and remarkable. He does give the exercise critical edge by setting it against a then fashionable interpretive approach to law. While agreeing with such an approach, that law can be understood as interpretation, Cover would want to sully the purity of the pacific word by showing that it had a dark, contrary connection to violence. As much as this initial conjunction and disjunction of violence and the word shapes Cover's whole argument, his engagement with the interpretive approach as such is almost wholly confined to a ground-clearing footnote.[4] It seems to have contributed little to the *frisson* that his article caused. The reaction probably had more to do with his central and stark claim that the word is destroyed in violence.

After sniping at interpretation as sedate orthodoxy in his first paragraph, Cover proceeds to offer us a trio of excitations on violence destroying the word which relate basically to the rest of the article, even if he does not make the relation very explicit. This trio concerns torture, martyrdom, and revolutionary violence. I will eventually touch on all three, but the most apt for now is the first, on torture. This is derived from what Cover sees as "Elaine Scarry's brilliant analysis of pain."[5] Scarry provides Cover with the foundations of his whole argument, if still rather inexplicitly. For a start, pain, whether inflicted by torture or otherwise, is divorced intrinsically from language. Pain, for Scarry, "actively destroys" or "negates" language thereby "bringing about an immediate reversion to a state anterior to language, to the sounds and cries a human being makes before language is learned."[6] Scarry also makes the obverse point that language destroys pain: "[E]ach depends on its separation from the other. To bring them together is to destroy one of them."[7] For Cover likewise, interpretation as the language of judges is somehow opposed to the very pain or violence that it brings about—but, for the sake of accuracy, it should be added that Cover does not make the point by way of an immediate reference to Scarry. Nor does he make much specifically of another generous endowment that seems to shape his whole argument, Scarry's naturalist assumption about pain. This is pain as "a primary physical act," as "a pure physical experience of negation, an immediate sensory rendering of 'against.'"[8] On Scarry's final contribution Cover is a little more forthcoming. He cites Scarry to the effect that the pain of torture is "world-destroying" or, in Cover's terms, it destroys "the victim's normative world."[9] More expansively, for Scarry the destruction of shared language by pain and torture is the destruction of civilization.[10] There is, as Scarry puts it, a "simple and absolute incompatibility of pain and the world."[11]

We could begin to see that this incompatibility is nothing too simple and rather less than absolute by looking in a preliminary way at the varieties of violence. For Cover, it is Scarry's notion of pain and torture that provides the exemplar of violence. This, as a general conception of violence, is quite literally conservative. What is being conserved is the irenic and, as Scarry has it, the civilized condition that violence destroys from without. That condition is one of a given "world" of shared language, the restful domain of reason and pacific order, ever complete in itself. With this numbed normality, violence can only be justified in the maintenance or restoration of the concordant world. And in occidental myth, this justified violence is the preserve of law. Law, thence, as it is so often put, has the monopoly on violence and, along with that endowment, violence outside of law becomes transgressive and illegitimate. In this view, law is not simply confined to some extraneous or supporting role, however. It has, somehow, to be not only violent but also intrinsically associated with the nonviolent norm. It is pervasively placed in the ordered world and operatively integral to it. More specifically, law provides "an immanent principle that unites the parts into a whole, that makes this whole the object of a general knowledge and will whose sanctions are merely derivative of a judgment and an application directed at the rebellious parts."[12] Law's violence is coextensive and more than coextensive with this primary ordering position. The violence and the incipient violence of law must constantly support the ordered world in and beyond its full range, support it against the violent and disintegrating forces of disorder within or hovering ever beyond that range. In its quality of expectant and responsive violence, law must extend further than and encompass the world it sustains. Law, in its turn, must forever chase and mark itself against a transgressive violence beyond—"the outside into which . . . [law] is always receding."[13] Yet this transgressive violence in *its* turn, in its being transgressive, emanates from and is in thrall to that determined norm that is the law.

There is, then, *in* the violence of law a contrary combination of determining force and responsive expectancy. How may this dichotomy be overcome? Put another way, how may the dissipation of responsiveness be contained so as to secure the palpably determinant? The usual occidental approach would be to compromise each of these two elements by cross-cutting them in a delimiting generalization about violence and its contained determinant being. The standard expedient, and it is the one used by Cover, is the rendering of violence as the painful infliction of physical force.[14] Where may this marking-apart, this cutting classification, of violence come from, if not itself from an arbitrary violence? Cover, as I have indicated, derives his answer from Scarry and her naturalist assumption about pain—its being observable as "a primary physical act" and so on—supplemented presumably by the "naturally" easy observation of physical force being inflicted. The assured adequacy of this natural language will be rejected later.

Such simple meaning now has its rival conceptions of violence. A standard story of the West connects a decline in "physical" violence with the progress of its civilization, but revisionist histories would typify such civilization as itself a tentacular violence, not just in its suppression and exclusion of others who do not accord with its norms, but also in the deeply disciplinary application of those norms to those who do conform.[15] Violence, in this refinement, is often given content by another variety of naturalist assumption, no longer now an ascription positively corresponding to the violence but, rather, the assumption of a primal entity negatively opposing it. Foucault's occasional espousing of "the body" and "the pleb" would provide instances.[16]

Another, and more thoroughly radical departure from the conventional view of violence would reject a putative resolution in naturalist terms and accommodate the dichotomy between responsiveness and determination that I have located in the violence of law. This entails "a more embracing structure of violence which refuses the logic of opposition" between violence and nonviolence.[17] Much of the present chapter will now be an engagement with this "more embracing structure." It could be introduced here in a stark contrast with Cover's own point of departure, his adoption via Scarry of torture as the paradigm of language-destroying or word-destroying violence, and that stark contrast could come from Blanchot's disturbing *aperçu* on torture:

> Torture is the recourse to violence—always in the form of a technique—with a view to making speak. This violence, perfected or camouflaged by technique, wants one to speak, wants speech. Which speech? Not the speech of violence—unspeaking, false through and through, logically the only one it can hope to obtain—but a true speech, free and pure of all violence. This contradiction offends us, but also unsettles us. Because in the equality it establishes, and in the contact it reestablishes between violence and speech, it revives and provokes the terrible violence that is the silent intimacy of all speaking words.[18]

The relation between torture and language will also be taken up more expansively later but it has been used here to intimate a seemingly more extensive assertion: an assertion that there can be no placid normality apart from violence, such as the normality of the contained word. There cannot, that is, be an "expelling of the violence of Being."[19] There is always something, something "other," infinitely disrupting what is, as it were, within—what is seemingly known and what is held to. This "within," in turn, comes "for the time being" from the violent expulsion or delimiting of that alterity. Violence, therefore, cannot be denied a priori and excluded from some detached and placid domain.

Somewhat more pointedly for the engagement with Cover, "the word" cannot rest secure in some *soi disant* completeness, cannot be "fully self-present . . . immediate and transparent."[20] It cannot subsist in an "impossible purity" whence a violence from without "would come to pounce upon it as a fatal accident."[21] Or, rather, in its operative assertion as complete, the word cannot be just that. It can only endure in a continuing relation to what is necessarily and constantly rejected, suppressed, or adapted to *make* it complete. Put in another perspective, the word cannot exist and endure in a solitary stasis. The distinctive affirmations of its putative integrity, of its seeming stillness, are themselves indistinguishable from the myriad of decisions needed "to deal with" whatever would impinge upon it. This "dealing with" involves and invokes, in the very violence of its exclusions and assimilations, a responsiveness to whatever would impinge, a responsiveness that is quite other to the violence of decisive assertion, a responsiveness that is nonviolent. This responsiveness, in turn, cannot effectively *be* without the violent assertion of position, a position from which it may depart and a position to which it may return. So, violence and nonviolence are each necessary for the operative existence of the other. To be so, each must also be different from the other—there is something, after all, to the logic of "opposition."[22] More precisely, the relation between them is one of apposition. These will be my central contentions and they will return when we are looking at the judicial word. But before leaving this introductory foray, the resort by Cover, via Scarry, to naturalist assumption should be placed in this alternative setting of violence. This assumption, by referring violence to a primordium of pain physically inflicted, gave it a basis apart from its involving and ever unresolved relation to nonviolence. As such, this assumption joins a very long list of stratagems that have come and gone and that have sought to enclose or deny the dynamic of responsive and unsettling relation to the nonviolent—stratagems that would include other varieties of the natural, the assertion of finalities and Utopias such as the end of history and the transcendence or objectivity of the law.

To conclude this overlong introduction, it could be said that Cover does capture something of the violence of the word. For Cover, the word is preserved whole. It must then be inherently a violent assertion of self-presence, even if for Cover it is nonviolent. This same enduring word is necessarily dependent on a nonviolent responsiveness to what is beyond it, a responsiveness that, without more, would dissipate and destroy the word. For Cover also, the word is destroyed in its going beyond, even if it is destroyed in its connection with violence. So a precise reversal of Cover's attribution of violence and nonviolence produces the dichotomy of violence that I have just outlined in a preliminary way—a dichotomy that the detail of Cover's analysis unwittingly and abundantly supports, as we shall now see. What I have also tried to outline, again in a preliminary way, is how the dichotomy imports a dynamic of violence, one that avoids the utter duality of Cover's scheme, a scheme in which the word of the law has to be nonviolently extant even while destroyed by violence. This is a dynamic which, as I hope we will also see, "allows the possibility of a different relation to law and violence to emerge," a relation bringing with it the possibility of an always and evident "lesser violence."[23]

Dividing the Indivisible

To return to the beginning: "Legal interpretation takes place in a field of pain and death."[24] The word operates through violence but is not in itself violent. There is between them a "radical dichotomy."[25] What Cover variously describes as interpretation, meaning, judicial utterance, word, or language act becomes effective or operative only when, as he puts it, joined, bonded, cooperating with, or embedded in, variously, violence, practice and practical application, deed, context, institutional modes of action, or physical act.[26] The "link between judicial utterance and violent deed" is "virtually certain" but not inexorable.[27] In all, "interpretations which occasion violence are distinct from the violent acts they occasion."[28] This division is intimated, probably founded—who knows?—in Cover's naturalist notion of pain, a notion that seems to connect with his invocation of Scarry. This is "physical pain," effected "in the flesh" or "in blood," through "actual deeds" or action; the violence of its infliction is "utterly real" when compared to a "figurative violence" that writers inflict on "literary parents."[29]

We could begin to join together what has thus been put asunder by trying to locate the moment when interpretation becomes operatively linked to action, or to locate the point at which legal interpretation becomes, so Cover must claim, "capable of transforming itself into action," or, more dramatically, to locate the rupture, yet necessary connection, between the pristine word and its destruction in violence.[30] Concretely, if by now a little repetitively,

> these two—judicial word and punitive deed—are connected only by the social cooperation of many others, who in their roles as lawyers, police, jailers, wardens and magistrates perform the deeds which judicial words authorize.[31]

What, then, do we find if we look, with Cover's help, for this site of connection, for this transformative point. Precisely, nothing. Paralleling Scarry's dictate that pain obviates language, Cover finds that there can be no common interpretation as between the judge who causes pain to be administered and the defendant on whom pain is inflicted. He also finds that there can be no common interpretation among all the different actors involved in the legal process with their many different perspectives. There is not a shared interpretive experience. There is no site of common meaning at which an interpretation can finally form in order to be automatically trans-formed. Even the judges, who are arbitrarily endowed by Cover with some common commitment to interpretation, never produce a simply transformable interpretation:

> For here in the United States there is no set of secondary rules and principles more fundamental than those which make it impossible for any single judge, however Herculean her understanding of the law, ever to have the last word on legal meaning as it affects real cases.[32]

And in that diversity, a distinct uniformity of interpretation becomes impossible.

It should follow that the judicial decision cannot simply provoke some automatically corresponding action by the police, the warder, the executioner, and such, but Cover insistently wants this to happen and he does so, it would seem, for a reason central to his pivotal contention. This contention has it that judges in enunciating the (legal) word cannot hide behind it and thus avoid being implicated in violence. That is not because the enunciated word is violent in itself, but rather because it connects almost inexorably with the infliction of violence by others. And, in turn, this connection comes about because officials inflicting violence are hierarchically subordinate to judicial authority, and because the assertion of that authority establishes in the officials a "shift" from the norm of "autonomous behavior to agentic behavior cybernetically required to make hierarchies work."[33] This abstruse formulation begins to make sense with the realization that it truncates and echoes Cover's foremost source on automatic effectiveness of the judicial word, the source being Milgram's famous, or infamous, study of obedience to authority, which Cover summarizes this way:

> In the Milgram experiments, subjects administered what they thought were actually painful electric shocks to persons who they thought were the experimental subjects. This was done under the direction or orders of supposed experimenters. The true experimental subjects—those who administered the shocks—showed a disturbingly high level of compliance with authority figures despite the apparent pain evinced by the false experimental subjects.[34]

Judges, as seen by Cover, provide interpretations that "trigger agentic behavior"; "they are engaging a violent mechanism through which a substantial part of their audience loses its capacity to think and act autonomously."[35] This is the explanatory connection Cover provides between the inviolate word and its execution.

Cover's reading of Milgram is conveniently superficial even if what he is claiming is fully in accord with some of what Milgram says. But Milgram says many things, and these are often inconsistent. Indeed, his "analysis" of the experiments—and it is from this analysis that Cover derives his formulation—is profoundly and revealingly confused, and nowhere more so than in its treatment of the very "agentic shift" on which Cover so foundationally relies. Broadly, and in Milgram's terms, "the agentic shift" involves a sharp change when the human individual is confronted by authority, a change from normally "autonomous" behavior to something like an automatic response.[36] Our engagement with this agentic shift should not be rushed, however. It is just as central for Milgram as it is for Cover: "[I]t is the keystone of our analysis."[37] Its significance cannot be gauged without placing it at least briefly in the unfolding of Milgram's elaborately constructed tale. This engagement will also help overcome a difficulty in analyzing Cover's "Violence and the Word" from within, as it were; and that difficulty involves the diverse and fleeting quality of Cover's own perceptible points of engagement. Milgram is at least consistently focused in his concerns and in criticizing him we can extract something of a position from which to engage with Cover.

It may help simplify Milgram's complex account, entailing as it does many different experiments and an enormously wide-ranging analysis, to describe more precisely at the outset what is being derived from it here. My interest is not immediately in its scientific validity or cogency. Perhaps Cover should have been a touch cautious about whether the behavior in various laboratories of a small number of people in and around New Haven between 1960 and 1963 would correspond to the behavior of all officials in, it would seem, the United States who had at any time been or ever would be the recipients of judicial direction. Certainly such punctilios would have meant little to Milgram who was, as we shall see, usually ready to expand the range of his claims.[38] The object here, rather, will be to contest the viability of observing the behavior of Milgram's subjects as automatic, or as autonomous for that matter. The purpose is not just to displace Cover's reliance on such observation, but also to indicate what can be observed and to bring out the integral quality of its implication with violence.

The horror felt at the behavior of Milgram's subjects has heightened the force of the standard view of it. These subjects willingly or, as Milgram so often claims, without coercion inflicted what appeared to be severe, often unbearable and even life-threatening pain on a stranger, all at the behest of a remote authority figure, "the experimenter." The presence of such authority triggers this behavior in a quasi-automatic way. Authority secures an obedience that overrides the subjects' normal autonomous condition. That is the message that emerges, albeit confusedly, from Milgram's analysis, as we shall see. In contrast to this straightforward conclusion, however, the experiments themselves are both more and less alarming. The experiments do not, for a start, make up the simple scene, so often and so readily depicted, of the subject made to believe that he or she is participating in a "study . . . concerned with the effects of punishment on learning," who then administers progressively more intense electric shocks to an incompetent "learner" at the behest of the experimenter.[39] There were no less than eighteen different experiments varying and changing the elements involved. The experiments were, understandably enough, oriented toward establishing the comprehensive impact of authority on the subjects. So, even when the supposed learner responded in ways that convincingly indicated his or her health or even life to be at risk because of the increasing level of the shocks, the subject continued to administer them at the behest of the experimenter. Or when this authority figure was replaced by an "ordinary" person, compliance fell away. And so on through many permutations. But these numerous experiments were sufficiently nuanced to provide indications quite contrary to authority's pervasive effect.

This is not to deny that Cover's empathetic reading of "the agentic shift" is not amply justified. Milgram wants "agentic" to be an adjectival form of "agent" but he prepares the ground carefully for a perverse meaning. True, an agent acts for or at the behest of another, but the agent is not an automaton. The automaton is merely an extension or tool, whereas agency imports a certain independent effectiveness of the agent. For Milgram, however, authority impels an agentic shift in which the agent is authority's extension or tool. There is a shift to "a different state," "a transition from the autonomous to the systemic mode."[40] It is clear that Milgram wants "systemic" to be taken literally as indicating a transformation within the entity as a whole. He derives the systemic element from two cumulative sources. One is the supposed evolution of society into an organized form in which hierarchic leadership becomes particularly suited to effectiveness and survival.[41] This process is then overlaid on a cybernetic model, and that must be what Cover's invocation of "agentic behavior cybernetically required" refers to. The cybernetic model reveals that self-regulating elements can only become part of a hierarchical organization if there are "internal modifications" in them.[42]

Milgram often ponders what such an alternative modification may amount to in "specifically human terms." "Where in a human being," he asks, "shall we find the switch that controls the transition from an autonomous to a systemic mode?" Despite having "no doubt" that it is a matter ultimately of "shifts in patterns of neural functioning" and related chemical effects, "it is totally beyond our technical skill" to locate such things. The elusiveness of the physiological is compounded because "psychological matter" is also "difficult to get at." The absence of any ascertainable palpability to "the agentic state" does not inhibit Milgram's making it central to his whole project and endowing it with a distinct and forceful existence. So, we are told that it entails a "restructuring of internal mental processes," or that it involves "an alteration in the internal operations of the process" in which "the decisive factor is the response to authority." Thence "individuals become thoughtless agents of action"; or, "a new creature replaces autonomous man, unhindered by the limitations of individual morality, freed of humane inhibition, mindful only of the sanctions of authority." There is "a *real* [his emphasis] alteration in the state of the person . . . precisely equivalent" to the cybernetically induced "major alterations in . . . automata." In all, the individual is not "the source of his own behavior" and action is not something the individual has "*decided* [his emphasis] to do."[43]

Matters seem, however, to be considerably more mixed than this systemic effect, this completeness of internal determination, would indicate. "No action of itself," Milgram tells us, "has an unchangeable psychological quality. Its meaning can be altered by placing it in particular contexts." "The act of shocking the victim," stems "from the fact that subjects have become integrated into a social structure." And indeed, changes in the "social conditions of experimentation" produced a great diversity of results. It would seem, furthermore, that context may quite counter the erstwhile exclusive "internal mental processes." Soon after revealing the "degree of parallel between obedience in the laboratory and in Nazi Germany"—to the effect that there "must be . . . a common psychological process" at work—Milgram goes on to conclude that "in the final analysis, what happened in Germany from 1933 to 1945 can only be fully understood as the expression of a unique historical development."[44]

The quality of the subject's relation to context proves to be decidedly less than Pavlovian. The subject "defines himself" as responsive to a "social situation" of authority, "gives himself over to authority," has "a sense of commitment and obligation" and still has the capacity of "evaluation" and the facility "to recapture control of his own regnant processes." Putting the contrast in another way, "the ego-ideal," although "wholly absent" and utterly "given up" in the agentic state, can somehow subsist in the ability to maintain a positive "self-image." Within authority's once total domain, there remains the subject's "moral choice." In much the same vein, when he later rebuts attacks on the "ethics" of his research, Milgram produces a panegyric of its enabling resistance to the felt assertions of authority. In that same defense of his research, Milgram rejects the charge that subjects were forced to administer the shocks and proceeds to do so by declaring that "between the command and the outcome there is a paramount force, the acting person who may obey or disobey"; to which he adds that "many subjects did, indeed, choose to reject the experimenter's commands, providing a powerful affirmation of human ideals." When he had previously been analyzing and reporting on the experiments, Milgram was less forthright on this score, and understandably so, since disobedience negates the innate switch into the agentic state. Still, on the rare occasions where Milgram confronts disobedience in his analysis, he has to concede that "the agentic state created in the laboratory is vulnerable to disturbance." Disobedience is "the ultimate means" for the subject to bring the "strain" induced by the experiment "to an end," even if this "is not an act equally available to all." This very diversity negates the monadic completeness of the systemic force.[45]

There were other reactions less than disobedience but just as significant. Contrary to Milgram's repeated claims that the involvement of subjects in the experiments was voluntary throughout and that they were never constrained, large and devious pressures were brought to bear on them.[46] Given these, it is almost as "powerful [an] affirmation of human ideals" to find not only that subjects disobeyed but also that "many" constantly protested, "frequently" felt considerable "tension," or "often expressed disapproval." As Milgram helpfully puts it, "if the individual's submergence in the authority system were total, he would feel no tension as he followed commands:" "every sign of tension, therefore, is evidence of the failure of authority to transform the person to an unalloyed state of agency"—remembering that for Milgram, agency imports the complete opposite of autonomy. He offers something of a resolution in the finding that "transformation to the agentic state is, for some subjects, only partial," but this belies the unitary quality of his "agency" as does the variety of conditions and outcomes of the numerous experiments. When exposed to the diversity of influences brought to bear in the experiments—the degree of propinquity to the victim, the presence of group support, and so on—subjects do not robotically flip into a uniform agentic state but respond in a variety of ways to the variety of conditions.[47]

Why does Milgram cling so contrarily and persistently to an agentic shift overriding all else? Precisely, I would now argue, because it provides a primordium that stills the irresolution between a determination of behavior by factors beyond the subject's range and the subject's voluntary control of his behavior. The agentic shift can be seen performing this function not just in the obsessively repeated assertions of ultimacy but also in the increasing desperation of the assertions as the analysis proceeds. By the time we reach the study's final appendix, this desperation has gone to the extent of rejecting other work in psychology that would support his claim about the effect of authority, simply because that work detracts from the sole force of the agentic shift. This other work is made up of the well-known identification of the authoritarian personality—a personality that, among other things, is inclined to obey authority—and the less-well known identification of an innate "moral judgment" correlated with obedience.[48] These are, in the end, dismissed, as "oversimplified": the basis of personality is "complex" and yet to be "discovered."[49] Were Milgram to admit these other explanations of obedience, they would, of course, subsist along with, or even against, the agentic shift and displace its primal completeness and force.

Milgram, in all, identifies two extremes in discerning human behavior, neither of which can be sustained by itself. One extreme is the automatic determination of behavior in the agentic shift. Here Milgram understandably adopts the characteristic stance of the psychological sciences in purporting to derive an internal state of the subject from the observation of external conditions. The other extreme has Milgram asserting just as strongly, if not as frequently, that it is the individual's volition and choice that is effective. But in neither extreme can there be some position apart, a position from which the subject can know itself or be known in itself in its assured completeness. As far as we "can tell," there is no site from which a totality of determination may be comprehended to the effect that behavior is observed as automatic, even if it were, and the possibility of volitional behavior thence dismissed. For the same reason, the subject also cannot be entirely "in the know" and assuredly perceive its behavior to be the result only of its own volition. Where then do we "stand"? As Milgram obliquely recognizes, in between the two extremes of determined and volitional behavior. This is evident not just in Milgram's alternation from one extreme of behavior's origin to the other, but also in his repeated intimations of the unresolved nature of being in between them. Thus, as we saw, subjects were anxiety-ridden, full of "tension," oriented toward compliance with commands in one moment and questioning or rejecting them in another. In short, and as Milgram again helpfully puts it, subjects "are implicated in a deep and genuinely felt predicament."[50]

Milgram provides no enduring resolution to this predicament. Even within the supposedly contained bounds of the laboratory, the subject has constantly to change and respond to the varied and contrary demands of the experimenter and the learner, all in complex combination with the immense diversity of sedimented influence affecting individual choice. And as the inducing ignorance of the subject dramatically illustrates, no decision can ever "furnish itself with infinite information and the unlimited knowledge of conditions, rules, or hypothetical imperatives that could justify it."[51] There is, then, "an ordeal of the undecidable" that is not only anterior to but also inhabits and persists in and beyond the decision: "the undecidable remains caught, lodged, at least as a ghost—but an essential ghost—in every decision, in every event of decision"; and "each case is other, each decision is different and requires an absolutely unique interpretation, which no existing coded rule can or ought to guarantee absolutely."[52] There is an ever uncontainable element in the decision, a "secret," a mystery, a "madness."[53] Furthermore, and again as far as we can "tell," in the experiment there was no automatic correspondence of stimulus and response in the subject without the mediation of the decision. The very existence of Milgram's primal matter, obedience to authority, depends upon the possibility of disobedience and a deciding between them. But neither the response nor the responsibility involved in a decision is ever complete. The decision can never give effect to all that may conceivably be relevant to its making. The decision is always inherently inadequate.

The violence of the decision, and of the word of the decision, lies in this productive inadequacy, in the necessity that "cuts" into and fails to "do justice" to all the factors that could innumerably pertain to it.[54] This decisive violence may indeed be accompanied and given force by "physical violence," but the actuality of the physical is not essential to it.

Writing of the "terrifying . . . violence that founds," the violence of revolutionary origin, Derrida remarks that it "appears savage" in its unrestrained illegality. He makes the point, however, so as to show that this is a violence indistinguishable from the ordinary operation of the law: "[V]iolence is not exterior to the order of *droit*. It threatens it from within"; and so we must "recognize meaning in a violence that is not an accident arriving from outside law."[55] The "meaning" of this violence subsists in what is ever "undecidable" in law and in the legal decision itself. So, this violence "threatens the entire judicial order itself," yet "that which threatens law already belongs to it."[56] It can thus be readily granted that there is point to both the standard story of law's intrinsic opposition to violence as well as to those mildly revisionist claims that law itself is violent. As the guarantor and exemplar of the stable and determined norm, law is and must be against any violence that would disrupt such a condition, yet law's determinate state itself results from the violent, decisional "cutting" into all that insistently comes from beyond it.

The constituent inadequacy of the decision does not merely afflict its initial making but must extend to its continued assertion. There is a constant remaking of the decision as it encounters situations that are inevitably new. To stay "the same," the decision must alter in its relation to what is ever different. In its sustained existence, then, the decision cannot endure as a settled stasis but must enable what is other to it to enter repeatedly the neither complete nor enclosed and always fungible boundary marked out by its own determinative assertion. The seeming paradox, then, is that the decision is continually "conserved" *and* "destroyed"; it has to be "regulated and without regulation."[57]

So, in the violence of its making and of its sustained remaking, the decision must also and inextricably be nonviolently responsive. It must, that is, accommodate, give way to, and give a way to, what comes from beyond it. At the same time, that which demands accommodation, the active alterity beyond, cannot simply be placid and expectant. It must have some bearing on, some complicitious connection with, the specific violence of decision bringing it into determination. No more than the violence of decision can the decision's nonviolence be in itself. Such nonviolence must be prehensively oriented toward the violence of decision that, for its own efficacy, nonviolence must submit to and yet insistently challenge. In sum, the violence and the nonviolence are each necessary for the efficacy of the other, yet, in this, each is necessarily distinct from the other. There is a relation of "difference and . . . co-implication" between them.[58]

In a summary way, we can now agree with Cover that the word of the judicial decision is destroyed by violence. It is destroyed in each fresh act of decision required to effectuate it but, contrary to Cover now, for that very purpose it has also to be conserved in the ensuing decision. Cover advances only one connecting and disconnecting dynamic, miraculously allowing the word to go forth and become effective yet be destroyed, and that dynamic is the agentic shift. Although it is saddling Cover with too much coherence, I will take this sole explanatory dynamic and use it to initiate an analysis of each of the three sets of recipients of the judicial word which Cover considers: first officials who execute the word, then defendants, and finally other judges. But before doing that, I will return to Cover's initial trio of excitations and move on from torture to another of them, "our own" Declaration of Independence, in order to provide a compact illustration of the violence which I have just attempted to delineate and to contrast this with Cover's notion.[59]

Declaring the Word

The Declaration will prove to be the first of several telling instances of how Cover, very much against the grain, cannot help but show how the word is violent, and how it is yet in this also nonviolent. After quoting the part of the Declaration that performatively declares independence, Cover goes on to typify it as one of those "great issues of constitutional interpretation that . . . clearly carry the seeds of violence."[60] Here Cover is at one with that tradition which sees transitions to modernity in terms of a violent and popular revolutionary rupture—"the blood that has dried on the codes of the law." [61] But the specific violence that Cover adduces here is strangely oblique. The violence he associates with the Declaration is that the signatories could have been gruesomely executed for treason by the British. It is, he then goes on, "precisely this embedding of an understanding of political text in institutional modes of action that distinguishes *legal* [his emphasis] interpretation from the interpretation of literature."[62] This serves to confirm that, while the word and violence are in themselves separate, they are actively and exceptionally connected through law. Yet when Cover comes to summarize the situation, he is more equivocal: "Revolutionary constitutional understandings are *commonly* [emphasis added] staked in blood. In them, the violence of the law takes its *most blatant* [emphasis added] form."[63] What this seems now to be saying is that revolutionary rupture and the initiation of its resulting law can be effected without bloody violence. But this is all strangely disjointed. The violent action that Cover advances here is that which attends punishment for treason. The Declaration did not take its "great" force as "constitutional interpretation" because, or merely because, it was connected to the possibility that the founding fathers could have been hanged and quartered. The Declaration was sustained for a complexity of reasons, but a necessary prelude to them all was that the revolutionary rupture had *been* already in the Declaration itself. It was the word(s) of the Declaration that focused and gave force to and *were* the ruptural violence, even if this act of revolutionary decision was attended by the prospect of another violence that could have been inflicted on its begetters should their asseveration be adjudged illegitimate. But this element of illegitimate violence, as we saw in the last section, is not something apart from an otherwise wholly legitimate law. Along with Derrida, it could be said that this illegitimate violence is not just the violence of a singular origin "back then," but an incessant violence that inevitably follows from there not being a pure and enduring origin, or that inevitably follows from law having to originate in each act of legal decision. That is, the violence, the irreducible "madness," of the act of decision is inextricably and repetitively *in* law. And this violence is in a way illegitimate because it cannot simply and already follow from and be fully justified by what comes before it. It is always something of a self-transgression. There is, as we have just seen, always in every legal decision an element of "fresh judgment" coming from beyond any existing, "present" law or other legitimating source.[64] It is the very assertion of the present and putative solidity of the law, and of the Declaration itself, that requires and is this "decisive" violence.

Yet, as we also saw, this very violence of assertion was only possible in an integral relation to a quality of responsive nonviolence. The remarkable thing about a declaration, for Žižek, is that its utterance brings about a new "state of things as already accomplished."[65] Wondrous as this may be, the same could be said for any declaration of what the law "is." Law can only be as it is declared if it adequately and newly draws into its protean self whatever is beyond it—whatever precedes and what follows it. Although usually seen as a solid origin from which laws then flow, the Declaration itself exhibits this protean quality of law. As Cover recognizes elsewhere, law is enfolded by its own narative.[66] And the Declaration does tell a story of long oppressions and forebearance tested to a limit. This is a story saturated with existent legality. There issues from it a constitution in embryo drawing on legal material from Europe, from the English revolutionary constitution, from the "American" colonies, and from the Continental Congresses. Indeed the signatories to the Declaration could be seen "as defenders of a history accomplished" rather than producers of a "sudden" or "extraordinary birth outside the processes of time."[67] In the Declaration itself, Jefferson's draft proclaiming the necessity for the colonies "to expunge their former systems of government" became instead the moderated necessity "to alter their former systems of government."[68]

What is determinedly declared does not respond only to that which precedes it. The Declaration did not become a hermetic origin but remained integrally responsive to what followed it, and such it is sometimes observed to be.[69] For example, the Declaration is made "in the name & by the authority of the good people of these colonies." In the process, lineaments of such a people are invoked. Governments derive "their just powers from the consent of the governed." The inhabitants of the colonies are already hailed as "citizens," and the monarchical British excluded. They are also hailed as civilized and distinguished from "the merciless Indian." But this violent proclamation is not sufficient. A people cannot confer authority or do anything else that the Declaration commits them to until they are constituted in a continually responsive relation to it, constituted as a people and endowed with the means to do, and to continue to do, such things. The "people" of the United States in this capacity comes into existence only through and after the Declaration, with the ensuing constitution, with various laws made pursuant to it, and with laws made by the member states of the federation. The people is a great posterior complexity—one created and continually re-created by the law that is supposed to have come from it. Law, then, is created by that which it creates. There is in such a scheme no resolving reference for law apart from itself—no reference either separate from or other than law. And in this circularity law can neither resort to nor itself be an encompassing assurance. There is nothing here before the law or, reversing the perspective, what is before the law is nothing. It is in this "original" nothingness that law is needful of and impelled to the violence of determining decision.

Returning to Cover, the thing about the Declaration, and about declaring or interpreting any law, is that it fuses what Cover wants to hold separate. As we have seen, he repeatedly distinguishes the word not violent in itself from the violence needed to give it enforceable effect.[70] It is the addition of this violence that renders the word or the interpretation legal. "Meaning" created by judges needs exterior "violence" in order to "enforce" it, to give it inescapable effect.[71] But I will now show that these two stages mark different decisions each involving a necessary violence, and it is precisely in order to effect and sustain the violence of these determining decisions that they must reach responsively and nonviolently beyond themselves.

EXECUTING THE WORD

The argument in the present section has already been covered at a remove in the analysis of Milgram. In this setting, the argument relates to those officials whom Cover advances as carriers of the spurious agentic shift—those who, as we have already seen, supposedly destroy the word by inflicting physical violence in its execution. Hopefully, the contrary contention need not be labored. The voice of judicial authority may well be driven deep, but it should by now be clear that the jailer, the executioner, and so on cannot move automatically in conformity with some externally set determination, or at least cannot be known to do so. Executive action ever entails the decision, new interpretation, fresh judgment. Cover obliquely recognizes as much when looking in rather more detail at what can happen in cases of capital punishment. He notes that different courts can hand down different judgments in the same case. One court may order execution and another a stay, for example. When this happens, "someone else—the warden, for simplicity's sake—is expected to determine which of these two pieces of paper [containing the contrary directions] to act upon according to some highly arbitrary, hierarchical principles."[72] Given such principles, which would elevate the authority of one piece of paper over another, what the warden should be doing is "paying relatively automatic heed to the pieces of paper which flow from the judges."[73] The paradox of being relatively automatic concentrates the argument against the agentic shift. How this, or any other, "automatic" can become relative is left unspecified. Equally ethereal is how, in what is supposed to be an automatic response to authority, a choice can nonetheless be made between two authorities. Yet the dissolution of the agentic shift goes further. Judicial hierarchy is found to be not so clear-cut in its assertion of authority. It is only "relatively inflexible."[74] With this pliancy, it can and does happen that the warden is faced with a difficult decision between competing judicial directions when there is no rigid guide as to which should be preferred. So, occasionally the warden will be faced with something like a pure choice, even if the great bulk of the warden's decisions will be "relatively" routine—much like the life of most judges.

Taking the argument a little way apart from Cover's text, we could question what would happen to the agentic shift if the authority-charged judicial word were to be executed by officials for whom judges and academics may have more regard. A supinely automatic reaction to the judicial word would hardly be attributed to the psychiatrist at the state asylum to which the judge had committed the defendant, because, borrowing the old succinct verdict, he or she is guilty but insane.

This general situation, the executing of the word, can be seen very differently and more accurately by adopting the terms of Cover's other famous essay "*Nomos* and Narrative."[75] At first, Cover seems to erect here a type of duality as sharp as that which would drive distinction between the word and violence. In a rendition of what nomos can signify,

Cover sees law in terms of "a normative universe . . . held together by the force of interpretive commitments. . . . These commitments—of officials and of others—do determine what law means and what law shall be."[76] Immediately he goes on to illustrate the hermetic "force" of such commitment by adding that,

> If there existed two legal orders with identical legal precepts and identical, predictable patterns of public force, they would nonetheless differ essentially in meaning if, in one of the orders, the precepts were universally venerated while in the other they were regarded by many as fundamentally unjust.[77]

So, the manifest word of the law may be exactly the same in two instances while the law itself would in each be entirely different. So nomos would signify not only the contained word of the law but also its integral responsiveness to what is beyond.[78] That is, there can be different universes, or worlds, or locations where the word of the law is the same but the law in each is different because of the varying "interpretive commitments" to what the word of the law may be. Returning to "Violence and the Word," we could now say that the word of the judge will be different from the seemingly same word of the warder, the psychiatrist, and others, including other judges who interpret the word in different, sometimes radically different, perspectives. For the reign of a singular law, this cannot be merely a matter of difference, however. There is a recognized element of commonality between these different locations. And as Cover himself has it, "Legal precepts and principles are not only demands made upon us by society, the people, the sovereign or God. They are also signs by which each of us communicates with others."[79] Cover obliges us further when he puts much the same point in the setting of his central argument: "[T]hese two—judicial word and punitive deed—are connected only by the social cooperation of many others, who in their roles as lawyers, police, jailers, wardens and magistrates perform the deeds which judicial words authorize."[80] So, Cover's key connection is brought about now *only* by social cooperation, no longer by the automatic transmission that is the agentic shift. There is a milieu in which "social cooperation" characteristically occurs and it is called community. When we are to be with each other in community, we cannot be all the same as each other in a complete and impossible commonality, but neither can we be entirely different to one another, each completely isolated and unrelated. With community we are, rather and in a way, in between sameness and difference, in between commonality and distinctness. In this always intermediate domain, connection is made not in agentic shifts but through modes that in themselves match this in-between quality of community—through, among other things, the word. It should follow, then, that the word can neither be uniformly the same in its varying locations nor may it deliquesce into the differences of these same locations. The word in community, returning to the terms borrowed in my opening analysis, is always being conserved and destroyed.[81]

RECEIVING THE WORD

If we take various members of the little community Cover presents to us, then we might expect that the judicial word would remain most intact in its being received by the defendant. It is, after all, the defendant who would seem to have the least capacity to destroy the word. Yet Cover's central contention is that the word is quite destroyed in the violence of its being brought to bear on the defendant. It is not clear exactly how this comes about in the defendant's own reaction to the word. Cover here abstains from explanation in terms of the agentic shift. The conditions for it do seem to be in place, however. The judge does have authority over the defendant and the defendant does have to respond to the sentencing word. But what the defendant is doing here in relation to the word is deciding, and continually deciding, just how far the leeways, no matter how narrow, for resisting or conforming to the word will be followed. Perhaps obviously, given the notorious range of reactions that defendants can have to the judicial word, not just to its first utterance but also to its constant application thereafter, it would be rather difficult for Cover to sustain an application of the agentic shift here, to present the picture of a docile and "relatively automatic" response to this assertion of authority. So how is the word destroyed yet still effective in this setting? Cover does not say how it is still effective, and he cannot because in his scenarios the word is simply destroyed in the word and violence being totally incompatible. What becomes effective is a violence unaccompanied by the word. Cover makes these claims in the terms of Scarry's argument that pain destroys language—terms that are insupportable, as I now hope to show.

There is, for Scarry, a radical uncertainty to pain: "[P]ain comes unshareably into our midst as at once that which cannot be denied and that which cannot be confirmed."[82] Hence elemental pain destroys or negates language as something we share. To repeat from the section introducing my chapter, pain impels "an immediate reversion to a state anterior to language, to the sounds and cries a human being makes before language is learned."[83] Amplifying her case now beyond Cover's citations, we find Scarry claiming that for pain to survive and for language to survive "each depends on its separation from the other. To bring them together is to destroy one of them."[84] The "unshareability" of pain pits it essentially against a language embodied in community and "civilization"—in a "making" or "creation" that is the opposite of torture as "destruction."[85] Pain is "world destroying"; there is, to repeat further, a "simple and absolute incompatibility of pain and the world."[86]

Philosophical obsession with the question, if nothing else, would suggest there are problems with how we know the pain of an-other. Pain can indeed occasion, as Scarry says, a "split between one's sense of one's own reality and the reality of other persons."[87] But for Scarry this split is "absolute." To begin seeing the situation as otherwise, we could evoke the earlier analysis of Milgram and the limits of what we can know of ourselves. If the division were absolute, if pain and language quite negate each other, if pain is incompatible with the creatively knowing world, how in the world are we ever to know that? How can we know that pain is not, or perhaps even is, transformable into language? How can that be rendered in communicable knowledge? And how, if pain and language are so chasmically separate, can pain be brought into any relation with language at all? How could we ever begin to speak or write of pain?

Scarry proceeds not only to write a book on the subject but to devote much of it to torture as the paradigm of pain-destroying language. Torture, however, in its paradigm mode, could be said to be a situation in which pain and language are closest to each other, are most related and compatible, because it is a situation in which pain generates speech (in the confession) and speech is integrally coordinated with pain (in the interrogation). Scarry herself not only renders pain in language but makes that language encompass the pain incomparably, incommensurably felt by the other. She writes of what the prisoner under torture specifically "experiences" and she affirms that in the confession "the torturers compel the prisoner to record and objectify the fact that intense pain is world destroying"—that is, destroying of the prisoner's subjective (for want of a better word) world.[88] Scarry is now somehow able to determine the content and existence of that which cannot be known.

Silently caught in these contradictions, Scarry becomes rather less absolute. To take a few of a great many instances: "Physical pain has no voice, but when it at last finds a voice, it begins to tell a story."[89] Or, the tortured prisoner "has almost no voice—his confession is a halfway point in the disintegration of language."[90] There seem to be other halfway points. We are supposed to be able "to witness the moment when pain causes a reversion to the pre-language of cries and groans"; this is an "immediate reversion" as befits the witnessable moment, yet it is to come about non specifically—as a result of a pain which is "prolonged."[91] Likewise, it is only "intense" pain that is said to be "world destroying."[92] So, the sharp and immediate moment of absolute change becomes blunted and graduated, and rather difficult to see as absolute. Just how much pain, how prolonged, how intense, is needed to destroy language or the world?

My contrary argument, as must be obvious by now, is that the pain which we can know as between ourselves is *in* language. This is not to deny an unknowable dimension to pain—the pain that is "unshareable" between us, the pain that occasions a "split between one's sense of one's own reality and the reality of other persons."[93] But it is to say that "we signify . . . when the present cannot be presented."[94] To elaborate: we cannot fully know the pain of the other—or at least know whether we fully know it. This particular pain is symptomatic of our existence. There is something of the other always beyond what is determinedly known. We can never relate to an-other in fully cognizable, eternally set terms. And to delimit that relation in language is not just to recognize but also to deny the other, to deny the other's uncontainable "fullness" and specificity. Yet this is a necessary denial if there is to be any relation at all. The infinity of our possible relation to the other has, in Derrida's terms, to be violently cut into so as to make determinate relation possible.[95] The resulting language of relation cannot be that placid sharing, that civilized commonality that for Scarry typifies language in its supposed opposition to the unknowable singularity of pain. Language is how we live "in" pain, not in some fantasy of community divorced from it. Language always seeks, and always fails, to fill the painful divide, the "split between one's sense of one's own reality and the reality of other persons," but it cannot encompass the divide and resolve it in common, set terms. Language is imbued with this split and driven by it.

We can call on Cover to confirm all this. Right at the outset he extracts from Scarry the lesson that, in destroying language, torture as pain brings about "the end of the bonds that constitute the community in which the values [of the victim] are grounded."[96] There can be no common meaning between people divided by pain. But immediately, and much like Scarry's equivocations, we are presented with a painful world of common meaning: "[T]he torturer and the victim do end up creating their own terrible 'world.'" And then, more expansively, Cover hails it as "literally miraculous . . . whenever the normative world of community survives fear, pain, and death in their most extreme forms." This *aperçu* becomes his entrée for talking about martyrdom, something discussed in the next section.[97]

JUDGING THE WORD

Cover comes closest to recognizing this insistence of language, and to contradicting the basis of his argument, in the ways he describes the transmission of the word within the judiciary. He sees the word here as changing in its differing judicial adoptions yet staying recognizably the same within something like a community of meaning. This is a sentient, intelligent process. There is no blanking agentic shift as the word issues from a higher judicial authority to a lower, much less a painful destruction of the word. But neither can the word, as Cover recognizes, voyage in a perduring sameness, although he does make an uneasy concluding claim for some ultimate fixity of the word.

The significance of Cover's reversal and of the pull toward fixity could be set by returning to martyrdom, the remaining member of Cover's trio of initial excitations—torture and revolutionary violence having already been accommodated. This, in the context of Cover's argument, may be the most obscure of the trio but it is the most pellucid for the purposes of mine. It concerns the community of martyrs as they instance a "normative world," together with its constituent word, miraculously surviving "fear, pain, and death in their most extreme forms."[98] I will return to the persistence of the word as a miracle but will for now refine the matter of the extremes, drawing initially on Cover's depiction of martyrdom:

> Martyrdom, for all its strangeness to the secular world of contemporary American law, is a proper starting place for understanding the nature of legal interpretation. Precisely because it is so extreme a phenomenon, martyrdom helps us see what is present in lesser degree whenever interpretation is joined with the practice of violent domination. Martyrs insist in the face of overwhelming force that if there is to be continuing life, it will not be on the terms of the tyrant's law. . . . Martyrs require that any future they possess will be on the terms of the law to which they are committed (God's law).[99]

There is an exquisite mutuality between the law of the tyrant and the law of the martyr. The tyrant's law in its complete and autonomous assertion cannot respond to what is other to it. The martyr explicitly instances this alterity. Autonomous and unresponsive law kills the martyr, just as it kills all that is other to it. The martyr's law is diametrically opposite. Being entirely other to the determined law, the martyr cleaves to a law that can accommodate otherness, and that law can only be the law of God, or of some equivalent encompassing entity placed beyond a profane finitude with its necessary, and necessarily limiting, determination. Either outcome is hardly auspicious for the word of the profane law. Either it kills and is left with no one to rule over or it dissipates in its complete response to the other. I will now filter Cover's analysis of the judicial word through this divide.

We have seen how this divide, or something like it, figures in Cover's text, how he wants the word to stand by itself yet take responsive account of those to whom it is addressed, at least of those who must "violently" enforce it. Although the word must be able to stand apart from this applied violence, it is, as we also saw, that same violence that has destroyed the word and deprived it of "common meaning" as between those who prescribe and those who suffer legal violence. Not only does this assertion and dissipation of the word attend the violence of its execution, but Cover, as we saw, cannot help but locate both these things within the judicial decision itself.

In a sense, however, Cover's conception of the judicial word is entirely conventional. He wants to hold the word inviolate in a way that would seem to accord with its being objective, whole and apart, uncontaminated by its relation to anything else, and "as not itself participating in the events under scrutiny."[100] This mode of perception can be extended to any "positing" of an autonomous law—as in legal positivism for example—that is then brought to bear on what is apart from it. This, if the oxymoron can be tolerated, is the normal extreme. It is the law, the word of the tyrant. But Cover's conception of the judicial word is also more rigorous than the standard fudging that would see it as complete yet engaged with what it would effect. For Cover the nonviolent completeness of the word and its very existence dissipate in the violence necessary for the word to have effect. This stark division between the word's utterance and its destruction is what I have suggested propels Cover's article and gives it critical impact. While judges may (perhaps a large "may") want to see their discourse as civil and distinct, it is, at bottom, implicated in and reliant on violence to give it effect. The orientation of this critical dynamic is from an insulated word and an insulated judiciary toward a wider world that is forced to do their bidding. Yet for this purpose, the word, along with the import of what it wants to happen, has to be conserved. The resulting mystery of how the word is thus destroyed *and* conserved has, I hope, been accommodated in my argument.

A muted recognition of this dichotomy of the word within judicial decision can be extracted from the difficulty that, in Cover's scenarios, the word encounters in moving beyond its initially insulated judicial assertion to a place where it becomes effective, yet does so in what would, in his terms, be a nonviolent way. The word is effective, for example, in activating the executors of violence, even though violence is not being brought to bear on them—the warder, the executioner, and so on. Cover deals with this as a matter of automatic effect in the agentic shift, but this shift, as we have seen, is a nonsense. The issue can be put more starkly, however, by enquiring of situations where the word goes forth and has effect unattended by any violence at all or by the threat of any violence if it is disregarded—using violence here in Cover's sense of physically inflicted pain. Judges, for example, direct words at each other, either to "fellow judges" at the same level or up and down the judicial hierarchy. In one way, Cover remains consistent here since he emphasizes that a dissipation, if not outright destruction, of meaning is involved. It is "fundamental" in the United States that no single judge can "ever . . . have the last word on legal meaning as it affects real cases": either that word would be subject to appellate review or if it were uttered in a final appeal court the singular judicial word would be one among many contributing to the decision.[101] Nonetheless, there must be some effective cohering of the word. Cover does reassure us that "a central task of the legal interpreter is to attend to the problematic aspects of the integration of role, deed and word,"[102] and thereby generate applicable meaning for the imposition of violence. Even so, this can only entail, for Cover, not a singular, perfectible meaning but a "collective," "compromise" meaning.[103] There remains nonetheless a hankering for something more monadically assured. In concluding his article, Cover resurrects the solitary word by noting that "a common and coherent meaning" can be achieved to an "extent," and that "a convergence of understandings on the part of all relevant legal actors is not necessarily impossible."[104] More on that shortly.

In its judicial voyages, then, Cover does provide a setting, albeit piecemeal, in which the word dissipates yet is affirmed, is destroyed yet conserved. To contain dissipation or destruction and to reconcile these with the finality of decision, Cover advances compromise as the operative solution. Compromise can indeed be part of what happens in adjudication but it is usually and indicatively *sub rosa*. It is neither exactly nor entirely what happens. As we saw early in this present chapter, and as the martyr served to recall, neither the extreme of comprehensive determination nor that of a responsiveness beyond determination is sustainable in itself. There has doubtless to be a compromise in the sense of finding some effective resolution in between the extremes. But to equate the outcome compendiously with compromise, as Cover does, is to deny the force and valency of the extremes. True, neither extreme can existently endure by itself, but in combination they constitute and impel the decision, and in so combining each must still remain distinct rather than be lost in the soup of compromise.

All of which is to do no more than abruptly summarize my introductory argument, but that argument could now be illustrated by looking at how Cover deals with the dissipation of meaning in another setting. Immediately after dealing with judicial compromise, he shifts the focus to "all relevant legal actors" who have to interpret and execute the word, and here he finds an enduring "multiplicity of minds and voices": "a convergence of understandings . . . is very unlikely" even if it "is not necessarily impossible."[105] Here Cover reverts to being too sharp in his separations. Such a convergence of understandings is necessarily both impossible and possible. Each decision in the overall process is, as we saw, unique, inevitably partial, and never completely presentable. It is not, therefore, capable of converging with anything. But neither is it ever simply alone. The decision must relate, and continue to relate, to the other decisions in the process. It is always different yet when in relation it must also be the same. The word then endures as the nexus and the commonality in between decisions for so long as it remains adequate in this. And it was this combining of difference and sameness, of singularity and commonality, that was identified earlier as community.

There is one final attempt touched on by Cover to resolve the exigent irresolution of community in law, and that is by resort to the ideal:

> There is a worthy tradition that would have us hear the judge as a voice of reason; see her as the embodiment of principle. The current academic interest in interpretation, the attention to community of meaning and commitment, is apologetic neither in its intent or effect. The trend is, by and large, an attempt to hold a worthy ideal before what all would agree is an unredeemed reality. I would not quarrel with the impulse that leads us to this form of criticism.[106]

Cover goes on to express some scepticism about "the extent" to which there may be a realization of common understanding and hence, presumably, a realization of the ideal, but he still allows for its feasibility.[107] What may give the ideal force and where it may come from are left unstated. Such matters would seem to partake of Cover's initial invocation of the miraculous—the miraculous survival of community in the face of that "fear, pain and death" that should destroy it—since the ideal can triumph over and redeem "reality."[108] What we seem to have here is the modern notion of the ideal that justifies our giving operative weight to something which our intelligence doubts or denies.

Conclusion

Cover's account, then, shares with my contrary analysis a concern about the word and what is beyond it as separate yet connected. Cover would hold apart the nonviolent word and the violence of its execution by demarcating violence as the painful infliction of physical force. This separation thence becomes partly a matter of things being necessarily so, since contact with violence destroys the nonviolent word, but it is also a matter of critical revelation and impetus, of showing how the judicial word is implicated in the very violence it must stand apart from. Like so much critique, however, Cover's could not leave the shadow of what it would dissent from. It served, rather, to affirm the supposed distinctness and completeness of the judicial word. Far from being disturbed, the integrity of the judicial word was confirmed by its dependent relation on an exterior violence, since contact with violence would not reveal the partiality of the word but simply destroy it. It was a matter of all or nothing. Less explicitly, and on the other side of the divide, violent punishment was thereby presented as distinct and *sui generis*, a point I will return to shortly.

In stark contrast, my analysis held violence and nonviolence joined and integral to each other; but, in sympathy with Cover now, that very connectedness required that they also be apart. This entailed a different conception of violence—not one confined to the painful infliction of physical force, and not one that destroyed the word, but instead one constituent of the word itself. Such a violence also provided force and sustained focus as the word moved, as it always had to move, beyond the confines of its determined "completeness." This movement meant that the word had to be not just violently determining but also nonviolently responsive to what lay beyond it "for the time being," and that nonviolent responsiveness in its turn could not have effect except in the violence of determination. On these voyages, the word is neither simply destroyed nor simply conserved but is ever being destroyed and conserved—destroyed in its responsiveness and conserved in its being repeatedly determined. This was not a matter of "compromise" or of any other encompassing combining of these two imperatives. They were instead distinctly coexistent, existing in apposition, yet integral to each other—"neither one nor two."[109]

All of which does not amount merely to some little rearrangement of thought. What the analysis here makes pivotal is the decisive choice in-between the violence of determination and the nonviolence of responsiveness. There was no assured and reassuring point at which that choice could be made. There could never be a full knowledge or accommodation of all that pertained to it.[110] Its "grounds" could never be settled or complete. There always is and always would be something more that it has failed or will fail to take account of. The unknowing not only makes for the "madness" of the decision, something we have considered; it also entails the sacrifice of those upon whom the decision is brought to bear, something not considered but that could now serve to indicate the concentrated quality of the decisive choice. Perhaps that quality can be conveyed most readily when the partiality of the decision is explicit, or close to it. For example, in jurisdictions still accepting the M'Naghten Rules, it must by now be conspicuously discriminatory for cognitive and not volitional incapacity to relieve the accused of criminal responsibility. And in some jurisdictions, defenses based on mental incapacity do not extend beyond cases of unlawful killing.

The most telling instance, however, is provided by the death penalty. Cover makes much of it. It is his paradigm punishment, and as such both exceptional and the same. It is the same in being another form of punishment, another form of a reified violence somehow following on the word of judgment. Cover concentrates on sameness. Yet death, as it is said, does make a difference. All too often after the execution, factors emerge that seriously question or contradict the attribution of responsibility for the criminal act. By then it is, rather obviously, too late. All of which should make us uneasy about the price paid, and not solely in cases of capital punishment, for the putative finality and assurance of the legal word. And it should also make us uneasy about attitudes to and the treatment of those inevitably sacrificed. Cover would, however, faintly retrieve capital punishment for the cause of sameness and the entirely effective determination of responsibility by adopting the standard and erroneous line that cases of capital punishment are the most carefully handled—but he also footnotes literature referring to "the inevitability of caprice and mistake."[111] Inevitability indeed.

NOTES

1. Robert Cover, "Violence and the Word," *Yale Law Journal* 95 (1986): 1601. The engagement with this piece was provoked by Austin Sarat. I am grateful to him also for his searching comments on a prior draft.

2. Cover, "The Supreme Court, 1982 Term—Foreword: *Nomos* and Narrative," *Harvard Law Review* 97 (1983): 4, 18. All subsequent notes will refer to this work by its shortened title, "*Nomos* and Narrative."

3. Cover, "Violence and the Word," 1602, note 2.

4. Ibid.

5. Elaine Scarry, *The Body in Pain: The Making and Unmaking of the World* (Oxford: Oxford University Press, 1985), 4. Scarry's argument is "brilliantly" disposed of in Colin Perrin, "Breath from Nowhere: Justice and Community in the Event of Human Rights" (Ph.D. thesis, University of Kent, 1996), 196–211. Here and in the later analysis of Scarry, I rely considerably on Perrin's work. Compare generally to Rolando Gaete, "The Torturer's Tale," *International Journal for the Semiotics of Law*, 9 (1996): 306.

6. Scarry, *The Body in Pain*, 4.

7. Ibid., 145.

8. Ibid., 28, 52. Cover does cite Scarry in a footnote where she mentions another naturalist assumption, "the sheer and simple fact of human agency": ibid., 29, and Cover, "Violence and the Word," 1603; note 5.

9. Cover, "Violence and the Word," 1603; and Scarry, *The Body in Pain*, 29.

10. This resonates reassuringly with the common view that civilization advances in the decline of violence. In more robust terms, as Fitzjames Stephen had it, violence, and particularly the violence of law, "played the leading part in the creation of civilization" (see Eric Stokes, *The English Utilitarians and India* [Oxford: Clarendon Press, 1959], 294). And for Kipling violence was the motor-force

of an implacable progress (see Ashis Nandy, *The Intimate Enemy: Loss and Recovery of Self Under Colonialism* [Delhi: Oxford University Press, 1983], 69).

11. Scarry, *The Body in Pain*, 50.

12. Gilles Deleuze and Félix Guattari, *Anti-Oedipus: Capitalism and Schizophrenia*, trans. Robert Hurley et al. (Minneapolis: University of Minnesota Press, 1983), 212.

13. Michel Foucault, "Maurice Blanchot: The Thought from Outside," trans. Brian Massumi, in Michel Foucault and Maurice Blanchot, *Foucault/Blanchot* (New York: Zone Books, 1987), 34.

14. Cover does attribute a violence to interpretation but only to distinguish it as "figurative" in opposition to the "real" violence that would "deal pain and death" ("Violence and the Word," 1609, note 20). This point will soon be set in my text: see the first paragraph in the next section, "Dividing the Indivisible." Cover does describe judges as "jurispathic" in that their interpretations "kill the diverse traditions that compete with the State" (ibid., 1610). Perhaps this point is made figuratively.

15. See, for example, Michel Foucault, *Discipline and Punish: The Birth of the Prison*, trans. Alan Sheridan (1977; paperback, Harmondsworth: Penguin, 1979). And see note 10 of this chapter.

16. See, for example, Michel Foucault, *The History of Sexuality, Volume One: An Introduction*, trans. Robert Hurley (Harmondsworth: Penguin, 1981), 96. This opposition is for Foucault complex and implicated with the violence: there are "no spaces of primal liberty" (Foucault, *Power/Knowledge: Selected Interviews and Other Writings 1972–1977*, ed. Graham Burchell et al., trans. Colin Gordon et al. [Brighton: The Harvester Press, 1980], 142).

17. Richard Beardsworth, *Derrida and the Political* (London: Routledge, 1996), 21.

18. Maurice Blanchot, *The Infinite Conversation*, trans. Susan Hanson (Minneapolis: University of Minnesota Press, 1993), 42–43. More starkly, "[E]very word is violence" (Blanchot as quoted in Steven Shaviro, *Passion and Excess: Blanchot, Bataille and Literary Theory* [Tallahassee: Florida State University Press, 1990]), 17.

19. Emmanuel Levinas, "Transcendence and Height," in his *Basic Philosophical Writings*, trans. Simon Critchley (Bloomington and Indianapolis: Indiana University Press, 1996). 11. Perhaps these borrowed points could themselves be seen as violent, a violence asserting violence, truly an "originary violence" (Jacques Derrida, *Of Grammatology*, trans. Gayatri Chakravorty Spivak [Baltimore: The Johns Hopkins University Press, 1976], 106, 110). I do not consider this seeming circularity here. What my argument will implicitly place "before" it, and before any claim to completeness for a primal assertion of violence, will be an intractable and constituent relation of violence and nonviolence.

20. Derrida, *Of Grammatology*, 119.

21. Ibid., 110, 135. Violence is "not an accident arriving from outside law" (Jacques Derrida, "Force of Law: The 'Mystical Foundation of Authority,'" trans. Mary Quaintance, in *Deconstruction and the Possibility of Justice*, ed. Drucilla Cornell et al. [New York: Routledge, 1992], 35).

22. See Beardsworth, *Derrida and the Political*, 21.

23. Ibid., 11–12, 19–20. Such a perspective also enables distinctions to be made between different kinds of violence, something denied in the false solidity of violence as the painful infliction of physical force thence contrasted en bloc to nonviolence.

24. Cover, "Violence and the Word," 1601.

25. Ibid., 1602, note 2.

26. Ibid., throughout.

27. Ibid., 1624.

28. Ibid., 1613.

29. Ibid., 1609, note 20.

30. Ibid., 1617.

31. Ibid., 1620.

32. Ibid., 1625.

33. Ibid., 1615.

34. Ibid., 1614. The rendition of Milgram used here is Stanley Milgram, *Obedience to Authority* (London: Pinter & Martin, 1997). In line with Cover's acceptant attitude toward Milgram's interpretation of the "experiments," my analysis is of Milgram's text. It does not extend to the quality or purport of Milgram's "experimental" observation, as to which see Ian Parker, "Obedience," *Granta* 71 (2000): 99.

35. Cover, "Violence and the Word," 1615.

36. Milgram, *Obedience to Authority*, 150–52.

37. Ibid., 151. Should this and what follows on the autonomous or determinant nature of "the agentic shift" not be read to the sound of dead horses being flogged? Would that it could. Quite apart from the centrality of this shift to Cover's argument, and quite apart from the completely acceptant way in which Milgram's study is usually referred to, the world is more and more awash with assured claims to the locus of determination of human thought and action—geneticism and evolutionary psychology being two in vogue. My argument is not that such claims are wrong but that we cannot know them to be right.

38. Although Milgram describes his subjects as "people," the advertized call for "persons needed for a study of memory" opens with the offer to "pay five hundred New Haven men" (ibid., 31–2). There was one experiment on forty women concerned with the "specifically female" (ibid., 80). For sensitivity to the specifically "native," see ibid., 155. Milgram's experiments have been replicated at different times and places with broadly similar outcomes.

39. See Milgram, *Obedience to Authority*, 21, 35.

40. Ibid., 150–51.

41. The key points in Milgram's analysis are always contradicted, usually sooner rather than later. Here, for example, what was evolutionary adaptation ensuring survival becomes "a fatal flaw nature has designed into us, and which in the long run gives our species only a modest chance of survival" (ibid., 205). Since my engagement is not with Milgram's text as such, these numerous contradictions are ignored except for the main one that I am about to uncover.

42. Ibid., 149. To avoid excessive footnoting, references to quotations from

Milgram's book in the next four paragraphs will be gathered in order at each paragraph's end.

43. Ibid., 150–1, 30, 191, 150, 192, 205, 152, 48.

44. Ibid., 27, 184, 192, 193.

45. Ibid., 151, 12, 13, 164, 149, 174 and 177, 11 (and on moral choice compare 26 and 163), 219–20, 216, 173, 175.

46. Obviously effective pressures included the clinical austerity and the seeming technological sophistication of the testing environment, the effect of the payment to take part, and the quality of the experimenter's monotonously insistent commands to continue administering the electric shocks. The last was probably very significant. What comes across in transcripts of experiments is the sinister menace in the experimenter's commands combined with the strongest of suggestions that incalculable but dire consequences will ensue if the subject did not proceed with the shocks (e.g., ibid., 90–94). Milgram seeks to minimize such pressures or he ignores them. An example of minimizing: an experiment sought to neutralize the effect of the other experiments being conducted in the intimidating setting of Yale University. To do this, the process was shifted to another, nondescript laboratory in the nearby city of Bridgeport. Milgram takes up the story: "[A]s it turned out, the level of obedience in Bridgeport, although somewhat reduced, was not significantly lower than that obtained at Yale. A large proportion of the Bridgeport subjects were fully obedient to the experimenter's commands (48 percent of the Bridgeport subjects delivered the maximum shock versus 65 percent in the corresponding condition at Yale)" (ibid., 87). A very generous test for lack of significance. On the pressure of obligation and for a jurisprudential engagement with Milgram, see Bernard Jackson, *Making Sense in Jurisprudence* (Liverpool: Deborah Charles Publications, 1996), 56.

47. Milgram, *Obedience to Authority*, 23, 28, 50, 58, 172–3.

48. Ibid., 223–26.

49. Ibid., 226.

50. Ibid., 60.

51. Derrida, "Force of Law," 26.

52. Ibid., 23, 24.

53. Ibid., 26; see also Jacques Derrida, *The Gift of Death*, trans. David Wills (Chicago: University of Chicago Press, 1995), 65.

54. On cutting and doing justice, see Derrida, "Force of Law," 24.

55. Ibid., 34–5, 40.

56. Ibid., 33, 35.

57. Ibid., 23.

58. Borrowing the phrase from Jacques Derrida, *Specters of Marx: The State of the Debt, the Work of Mourning, and the New International*, trans. Peggy Kamuf (New York: Routledge, 1994), 177, note 4.

59. See Cover, "Violence and the Word," 1605.

60. Ibid., 1606.

61. Foucault, quoted in James Miller, *The Passion of Michel Foucault* (London: Harper Collins, 1993), 289.

62. Cover, "Violence and the Word," 1606.

63. Ibid., 1607.

64. Derrida, "Force of Law," 26.

65. Slavoj Žižek, *Enjoy Your Symptom! Jacques Lacan in Hollywood and Out* (New York and London: Routledge, 1992), 97.

66. Cover, "*Nomos* and Narrative." In what follows I am referring to the full text of the U.S. Declaration, not just the culminating declaration itself.

67. Garry Wills, *Inventing America: Jefferson's Declaration of Independence* (London: The Athlone Press, 1978), xvii, xix, xxxviii.

68. Ibid., 375.

69. Ibid., generally. The very declaring of a position can be seen as a promise that has to be effected and repeatedly sustained: see Derrida, "Force of Law," 38.

70. I do not return here to Cover's equivocation where he recognizes some "figurative violence" in the word as against the "utterly real" violence that judges can put in train. See Cover, "Violence and the Word," 1609, including note 20.

71. Ibid., 1619.

72. Ibid., 1626.

73. Ibid.

74. Ibid., 1627.

75. Cover, "*Nomos* and Narrative."

76. Ibid., 7.

77. Ibid.

78. Compare to Dudley Young, *Origins of the Sacred: The Ecstasies of Love and War* (London: Little Brown, 1992), 317–18. Something of this responsiveness may be caught by Cover in his seeing law as going beyond the concern "to achieve social control" and embracing "the attempt to build future worlds" (Cover, "*Nomos* and Narrative," 18).

79. Cover, "*Nomos* and Narrative," 8.

80. Cover, "Violence and the Word," 1620.

81. Derrida, "Force of Law," 23.

82. Scarry, *The Body in Pain*, 4.

83. Ibid. To be exact, in this particular rendition of the point, Scarry says "prolonged" pain has this immediate impact. More on this shortly.

84. Ibid., 145.

85. Ibid., 4, 21.

86. Ibid., 29, 50.

87. Ibid., 4.

88. Ibid., 29. My analysis does not deny that something like this is not, at times, an aim of torture, but even here "making speak" is a mode of attempting to destroy the prisoner's world (see Gaete, "The Torturer's Tale," 309). Nor does the analysis deny that, at times, this aim is pursued when the person tortured no longer speaks to it.

89. Scarry, *The Body in Pain*, 3.

90. Ibid., 36.

91. Ibid., 4, 6.

92. Ibid., 29.

93. Ibid., 4.

94. Jacques Derrida, *Margins of Philosophy*, trans. Alan Bass (Chicago: Uni-

versity of Chicago Press, 1982), 9. Blanchot again, writing of another "insurmountable abyss: "[I]f, in fact, there is infinite separation, it falls to speech to make it the place of understanding" (Blanchot, *Infinite Conversation*, 128).

95. Derrida, "Force of Law," 24.

96. Cover, "Violence and the Word," 1603.

97. Ibid.

98. Ibid., 1603.

99. Ibid., 1604. The picture of the martyr that now follows is somewhat overdrawn by its setting. The martyr in my account is not meant to be taken as purely otherworldly, as acting "only for the salvation of his soul" (compare to Carl Schmitt, *The Crisis of Parliamentary Democracy*, trans. Ellen Kennedy [London: MIT Press, 1988], 48). Martyrdom, in agreement with Cover now, can be oriented toward a "political" avowal of this world, "the affirmation of value, up against the boundary of death" (John Bowker, *The Meanings of Death* [Cambridge: Cambridge University Press, 1991], 39).

100. Marilyn Strathern, "Discovering 'Social Control,'" *Journal of Law and Society*, 12, no. 2 (1985): 128.

101. Cover, "Violence and the Word," 1625.

102. Ibid., 1619.

103. Ibid., 1628. The involvement of "many voices" somehow puts the word in a position where in Cover's own account it seems to overcome the very violence that is supposed to destroy it. This multiplicity of the word "is intrinsic to whatever achievement is possible in the domesticating of violence" (ibid.). To domesticate violence then, presumably the word must endure in the face of violence and be more effectively extensive than it.

104. Ibid.

105. Ibid., 1628–29.

106. Ibid., 1628.

107. Ibid.

108. Ibid., 1603, 1628. Here I use "miraculous" not only in the general sense of wonderous but also more specifically as emanating from God and thus able to override reality—the god of Cover's martyr encompassing all that is other to reality. Only such a god can override the natural order in which community would be destroyed by "fear, pain and death."

109. Compare to Jacques Derrida, "The Law of Genre," in Jacques Derrida, *Acts of Literature*, trans. Avital Ronell (New York and London: Routledge, 1992), 231.

110. Here and throughout I have emphasized the effect of unknowing, but "accommodation" leaves space, as it were, for ethical demands beyond knowledge (see, for example, Emmanuel Levinas, "Is Ontology Fundamental?" and "Transcendence and Height," in Levinas, *Basic Philosophical Writing*, 7 and 17).

111. Cover, "Violence and the Word," 1622, including note 50.

The Contributors

MARIANNE CONSTABLE is Professor of Rhetoric at the University of California, Berkeley.

PETER FITZPATRICK is Anniversary Professor of Law at Birkbeck College, University of London.

THOMAS R. KEARNS is William H. Hastie Professor of Philosophy and Professor of Law, Jurisprudence & Social Thought at Amherst College.

SHAUN MCVEIGH teaches law at Griffith University, Australia.

PETER RUSH is on the Faculty of Law, University of Melbourne.

AUSTIN SARAT is William Nelson Cromwell Professor of Jurisprudence and Political Science and Professor of Law, Jurisprudence and Social Thought at Amherst College.

JONATHAN SIMON is Professor of Law at the University of Miami.

ALISON YOUNG is Professor of Criminology at the University of Melbourne.

Index